✿✿Forbes

TRAVEL GUIDE

Formerly Mobil Travel Guide

SOUTHERN
CALIFORNIA

2011

R05011 97805

ACKNOWLEDGMENTS

We gratefully acknowledge the help of our representatives for their efficient and perceptive inspections of the lodgings listed. Forbes Travel Guide is also grateful to the talented writers who contributed to this book.

Front Cover image: ©iStockphoto.com
All maps: Mapping Specialists

ISBN: 9781936010936
Manufactured in the USA
10 9 8 7 6 5 4 3 2 1

CONTENTS

SOUTHERN CALIFORNIA

Acknowledgments	2
Star Attractions	4
Star Ratings	5-7

WELCOME TO SOUTHERN CALIFORNIA | 8

Southern California's Best Attractions	10
Top Hotels, Restaurants and Spas	11
Your Questions Answered	12

SAN DIEGO

Welcome to San Diego	15
What to See	15
Where to Stay	26
Where to Eat	33
Spas	37
Where to Shop	37
Side Trips	39

PALM SPRINGS AND THE DESERT

Welcome to Palm Springs and the Desert	50
What to See	51
Where to Stay	54
Where to Eat	57
Spas	59
Joshua Tree National Park	60
Death Valley National Park	61

ORANGE COUNTY

Welcome to Orange County	63
Aneheim	63
Catalina Island	67
Irvine	69
San Juan Capistrano	69
Coastal Towns	70

LOS ANGELES

Welcome to Los Angeles	82
Highlights	84
Side Trips	166

CENTRAL COAST

Welcome to the Central Coast	34
Ojai	171
Santa Barbara	174
Pismo Beach	184
San Luis Obispo	185
Morro Bay	187
Cambria	188
Paso Robles	189

INDEX | 192

MAPS | 216

STAR ATTRACTIONS

If you've been a reader of Mobil Travel Guide, you will have heard that this historic brand partnered in 2009 with another storied media name, Forbes, to create a new entity, Forbes Travel Guide. For more than 50 years, Mobil Travel Guide assisted travelers in making smart decisions about where to stay and dine when traveling. With this new partnership, our mission has not changed: We're committed to the same rigorous inspections of hotels, restaurants and spas—the most comprehensive in the industry with more than 500 standards tested at each property we visit—to help you cut through the clutter and make easy and informed decisions on where to spend your time and travel budget. Our team of anonymous inspectors are constantly on the road, sleeping in hotels, eating in restaurants and making spa appointments, evaluating those exacting standards to determine a property's rating.

What kinds of standards are we looking for when we visit a property? We're looking for more than just high-thread count sheets, pristine spa treatment rooms and white linen-topped tables. We look for service that's attentive, individualized and unforgettable. We note how long it takes to be greeted when you sit down at your table, or to be served when you order room service, or whether the hotel staff can confidently help you when you've forgotten that one essential item that will make or break your trip. Unlike any other travel ratings entity, we visit each place we rate, testing hundreds of attributes to compile our ratings, and our ratings cannot be bought or influenced. The Forbes Five Star rating is the most prestigious achievement in hospitality—while we rate more than 5,000 properties in the U.S., Canada, Hong Kong, Macau and Beijing, for 2011, we have awarded Five Star designations to only 54 hotels, 23 restaurants and 20 spas. When you travel with Forbes, you can travel with confidence, knowing that you'll get the very best experience, no matter who you are.

We understand the importance of making the most of your time. That's why the most trusted name in travel is now Forbes Travel Guide.

STAR RATED HOTELS

Whether you're looking for the ultimate in luxury or the best value for your travel budget, we have a hotel recommendation for you. To help you pinpoint properties that meet your needs, Forbes Travel Guide classifies each lodging by type according to the following characteristics:

★★★★★These exceptional properties provide a memorable experience through virtually flawless service and the finest of amenities. Staff are intuitive, engaging and passionate, and eagerly deliver service above and beyond the guests' expectations. The hotel was designed with the guest's comfort in mind, with particular attention paid to craftsmanship and quality of product. A Five-Star property is a destination unto itself.

★★★★These properties provide a distinctive setting, and a guest will find many interesting and inviting elements to enjoy throughout the property. Attention to detail is prominent throughout the property, from design concept to quality of products provided. Staff are accommodating and take pride in catering to the guest's specific needs throughout their stay.

★★★These well-appointed establishments have enhanced amenities that provide travelers with a strong sense of location, whether for style or function. They may have a distinguishing style and ambience in both the public spaces and guest rooms; or they may be more focused on functionality, providing guests with easy access to local events, meetings or tourism highlights.

Recommended: These hotels are considered clean, comfortable and reliable establishments that have expanded amenities, such as full-service restaurants.

For every property, we also provide pricing information. All prices quoted are accurate at the time of publication; however, prices cannot be guaranteed. Because rates can fluctuate, we list a pricing range rather than specific prices.

STAR RATED RESTAURANTS

Every restaurant in this book has been visited by Forbes Travel Guide's team of experts and comes highly recommended as an outstanding dining experience.

★★★★★Forbes Five-Star restaurants deliver a truly unique and distinctive dining experience. A Five-Star restaurant consistently provides exceptional food, superlative service and elegant décor. An emphasis is placed on originality and personalized, attentive and discreet service. Every detail that surrounds the experience is attended to by a warm and gracious dining room team.

★★★★These are exciting restaurants with often well-known chefs that feature creative and complex foods and emphasize various culinary techniques and a focus on seasonality. A highly-trained dining room staff provides refined personal service and attention.

★★★Three Star restaurants offer skillfully prepared food with a focus on a specific style or cuisine. The dining room staff provides warm and professional service in a comfortable atmosphere. The décor is well-coordinated with quality fixtures and decorative items, and promotes a comfortable ambience.

Recommended: These restaurants serve fresh food in a clean setting with efficient service. Value is considered in this category, as is family friendliness.

Because menu prices can fluctuate, we list a pricing range rather than specific prices. The pricing ranges are per diner, and assume that you order an appetizer or dessert, an entrée and one drink.

STAR RATED SPAS

Forbes Travel Guide's spa ratings are based on objective evalua-tions of more than 450 attributes. About half of these criteria assess basic expectations, such as staff courtesy, the technical proficien-cy and skill of the employees and whether the facility is clean and maintained properly. Several standards address issues that impact a guest's physical comfort and convenience, as well as the staff's ability to impart a sense of personalized service. Additional criteria measure the spa's ability to create a completely calming ambience.

★★★★★Stepping foot in a Five Star Spa will result in an exceptional experience with no detail overlooked. These properties wow their guests with extraordinary design and facilities, and uncompro-mising service. Expert staff cater to your every whim and pam-per you with the most advanced treatments and skin care lines available. These spas often offer exclusive treatments and may emphasize local elements.

★★★★Four Star spas provide a wonderful experience in an invit-ing and serene environment. A sense of personalized service is evident from the moment you check in and receive your robe and slippers. The guest's comfort is always of utmost concern to the well-trained staff.

★★★These spas offer well-appointed facilities with a full com-plement of staff to ensure that guests' needs are met. The spa facil ties include clean and appealing treatment rooms, changing areas and a welcoming reception desk.

WELCOME TO SOUTHERN CALIFORNIA

THE BEACHES, THE MOVIE STARS, THE endless sunny days. That's life in Southern California. From dining and shopping in Los Angeles to the numerous attractions in San Diego to the lively beach communities, Southern California—or SoCal—is teeming with diversions. Hit the surf, explore the many wilderness areas or get away from it all in the deserts.

Few places offer such a breadth of cultural and natural landscapes. The Pacific Ocean forms the western border while the arid east is home to the Mojave and Colorado deserts. The southern border separates California from Mexico while the Tehachapi Mountains, a range rising about 70 miles north of Los Angeles, separates SoCal from the rest of the nation's most populous state.

Many of the area's towns blossomed around Spanish missions built in the late 18th century after Spain seized colonial rule of the area from its original Portuguese explorers. California changed hands twice more—flying the Mexican flag starting in 1822, after Mexico won independence from Spain. A short-lived California republic followed before Commodore John D. Sloat raised the United States flag over Monterey in July 1846. Two years later, California officially became part of the U.S. That year, 1848, marked another enormous event in California history: the discovery of gold. The California Gold Rush set off a mass migration that transformed the sleepy, placid countryside into bustling towns. The 49ers who came for gold ultimately found greater riches in the fertile soil of the valleys.

Today, California has the largest population of any state in the Union—24 million people live in Southern California (making it the second-most populated region in the country behind the Northeast corridor). Spend some time here and you'll see why.

YOUR QUESTIONS ANSWERED

IS IT POSSIBLE TO DRIVE TO BIG SUR FROM LOS ANGELES IN ONE DAY?

Big Sur is about 700 miles from Los Angeles. Without traffic, it's about a six-hour drive. But this is a trip you don't want to rush. From L.A., you'll take the 101 North to Big Sur—one of the most beautiful drives in the entire country. The coastal road offers some of the most spectacular scenery and it's a drive you must do at least once. We also recommend a stop right outside Cambria at the Hearst Castle. This is right on the way and the magnificent home is one of the best sights in the state. The spectacular home took of William Randolph Hearst took 30 years to build and it includes all of the original furnishings. Tours take place every two hours and you'll want to devote at least three hours for this visit. The bus ride to the top of the house takes about 15 minutes, and there's an interesting film you can view before starting the tour. If you leave Los Angeles very early, you can do all this and still get to Big Sur before sunset. However, we don't recommend trying the drive at night as the roads are curvy and visibility is poor. If you don't have at least three hours to sunset while you're at Hearst, it's best to stay overnight in Cambria or Saint Luis Obispo before making the trek to Big Sur.

HOW FAR IS DISNEYLAND FROM LOS ANGELES?

The trip from Los Angeles to Anaheim is easy. Just take the southbound I-5 freeway toward Orange County for about 40 minutes and you're there. Finding parking is easy, too; spots are abundant and organized according by Disney characters (an aid to help you navigate the massive lot). Trams with friendly voiceovers shuttle you to and from the lots and the park. You will need an entire day—if not two or three—to see everything. The park is divided into various "lands," including Fantasy Land, Tomorrow Land, Adventure Land and Frontier Land. The candy-colored Fantasy Land gives you the classic Disney experience with Sleeping Beauty's Castle, the Mad Hatter's Tea Cups and the pleasant Dumbo ride, which flies gently in the air.

Frontier Land includes the Mark Twain Riverboat and Big Thunder Mountain Railroad. Join India Jones on a thrilling adventure in Adventure Land or zoom through space mountain in Tomorrow Land. If you have time, you can also hop over to Disney's California Adventure, a theme park that specializes in more

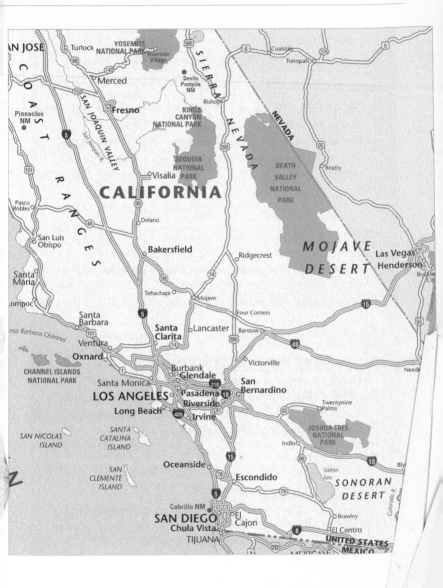

intense rides and is the new host to Disney's Electrical Parade, a nighttime event that showcases light-bulb-encrusted Disney floats. Or, just stick around Disney after dark, when the theme park glitters. The "Main Street, U.S.A." portion of the park is particularly wondrous when the white lights turn on, and the Castle glows in pink and blue lights.

WHAT IS THE BEST AREA TO STAY IN LOS ANGELES?

Los Angeles has often been described as 40 suburbs without a city. Another way to think of it is as 40 small cities that don't have much in common, and therefore little need to interact. The residents of Beverly Hills, Burbank and Bell Gardens do come together on occasion, but as soon as the Lakers game is over, they all get back in their cars and return to their separate incarnations of Southern California. Visitors usually stick to four distinct areas. If it's sun and sand you seek, make a beeline for the beach communities of Malibu, Venice and Santa Monica. Malibu is full of surfers and million-dollar homes right on the water; Venice is funky as ever, especially on the honky-tonk boardwalk; Santa Monica is a cross between the two, with a popular amusement park on the pier and an outdoor shopping plaza anchoring the city's downtown. If you've come to shop, you might never leave Beverly Hills. The super-glitzy stores of Rodeo Drive are here, as are some of L.A.'s most fabulously expensive homes. For shopping on a mere mortal's budget, try the Beverly Center or The Grove, L.A.'s premier malls-cum-entertainment centers, and home to retailers ranging from Gucci to trendy H&M. L.A. does have an actual downtown, which includes Frank Gehry's Walt Disney Concert Hall, several top-flight museums, Chinatown, Little Tokyo and Mexican marketplace Olvera Street. While downtown L.A. is supposedly undergoing a renaissance, the sidewalks still roll up at night, so hotels here cater primarily to business travelers. West Hollywood is (ironically) the most centrally located part of Los Angeles, and home to the hippest restaurants and nightspots of the moment along Melrose Avenue and the Sunset Strip. And unlike Hollywood proper, which is somewhat seedy, you might see movie stars here. Just don't expect to find parking.

HIGHLIGHT

WHAT ARE THE TOP THINGS TO DO IN SAN DIEGO?

VISIT THE GASLAMP QUARTER

This once downtrodden 16-block downtown neighborhood has been revitalized, and is now a hot spot for fine dining, bars and shops. The area is also home to boutique hotels including The Ivy and the W.

STROLL ALONG THE EMBARCADERO

The two-mile stretch of downtown waterfront is the best way to get a feel for the city. See the Midway aircraft carrier, visit the Fish Market and relax in Tuna Harbor Park.

SPEND THE DAY IN BALBOA PARK

No visit to San Diego is complete without a visit to this spectacular patch of green in the city. The 1,200-acre park offers days of fun— it's home to 15 major museums, the Old Globe Theater, and a giant outdoor pipe organ. Take a stroll along the main throughfare and take in the Spanish Baroque buildings and then enjoy a picnic lunch underneath the more than 90-year-old Moreton Bay fig tree.

HIT THE BEACH

San Diego is home to dozens of beaches. Which ones you visit depends on what you're in the mood for. Surfers head to Ocean Beach which looks like it came straight out of a 1970's movie. The sidewalk along Newport Avenue includes inscribed sidewalk tiles with messages on them which anyone can purchase.

GO TO THE ZOO

What's a visit to San Diego without visiting the world famous zoo. Located within Balboa Park, the zoo is home to more than 4,000 rare and exotic animals representing 800 species, many of which are displayed in natural habitats. Kids will enjoy the petting paddock and animal shows.

SAN DIEGO

Can't decide between the city and the beach? You don't have to. In San Diego, there is plenty of culture, great shopping and wonderful restaurants—plus beaches with top-notch surfing, snorkeling and sea lions that crawl to the shore to sun themselves. Weathermen here have it easy: every day is 70 degrees and sunny.

It wasn't too long ago that San Diego was a sleepy little town, a place where movie stars came to get away from it all. In the past 10 to 15 years, however, the city has grown by leaps and bounds. It now has a population of 1.3 million (2.8 million countywide) and is the seventh-largest city in the United States. Much of the growth has come from people who want to shop in shorts all year. Other growth has come from companies that have relocated here because of the ease of recruiting workers. The area is also filled with Navy and Marine personnel from bases nearby.

San Diego is where California began. In 1542, explorer Juan Rodriguez Cabrillo was commissioned by the governor of Guatemala to take a voyage up the California coast under the flag of Spain. He reached "a very good enclosed port," now known as San Diego Bay (a Cabrillo statue stands at the edge of Cabrillo Park on the spot where he is believed to have anchored). In the mid-18th century, when it was feared that Russian interest in Alaska was a prelude to Southern expansion, Spanish missionaries came to California, and Father Junipera Serra built the first of his 31 famous California missions in San Diego.

San Diego is a city in which the arts flourish. Balboa Park, the largest urban cultural park in the country, features 15 museums, numerous art galleries, free outdoor concerts, the Tony Award-winning Old Globe theater and the world-famous San Diego Zoo. (The upscale community of La Jolla, a few miles up the coast, is the site of the La Jolla Playhouse, another Tony Award-winning theater.) There are quirky museums, like the Museum of Making Music. And kids won't know what to do first: swim in the ocean, visit SeaWorld, pan for gold in an old hard-rock gold mine, go to Legoland, explore the tide pools or visit the Aerospace Museum and Hall of Fame, where they can go on a motion-simulator ride that takes them on different planes throughout time.

The greater San Diego area also offers much to see and do, as well as luxurious resorts. Base your stay on your interest—city or beach—and then plan day trips to see the outlying areas.

WHAT TO SEE

AEROSPACE MUSEUM AND HALL OF FAME
2001 Pan American Plaza, San Diego, 619-234-8291; www.aerospacemuseum.org

Learn about the extraordinary accomplishments of the world's leading aviation pioneers, including the Wright brothers, Amelia Earhart, Neil Armstrong and others at this popular museum. The museum houses rare aircraft including a Navy F6F Hellcat and a model of the Montgolfier brothers' hot air balloon of 1783, the first to lift humans into the air. Kids will love the aviation hangar where they can experience a flight simulator in a real wind tunnel and "walk" the moon's surface in a space suit. Other exhibits range from examining alien life to the interesting history of the Ford building which now houses the

museum. There's also a 3D/4D theater.

Admission: Adults $16.50, seniors $13.50, children 3-11 $16, children under 2 free. Daily 10 a.m.-5:30 p.m.

BALBOA PARK

1549 El Prado, San Diego, 619-239-0512; www.balboapark.org

Located in the heart of the city, this 1,200-acre park includes galleries, museums, theaters, restaurants, miles of garden walks, a huge outdoor pipe organ and countless activities, from concerts to plays (be sure to check the website for a calendar of events). Ride the 1910 carousel and take a trip on the miniature railroad. Of course, the park is also the site of the world-famous zoo.

Admission for some museums; varies. Day passes are available through the website.

BELMONT PARK

3146 Mission Blvd., San Diego, 858-488-1549; www.belmontpark.com

Get ready for a day of old-fashioned fun at Belmont Park. The seaside amusement park has a vintage wooden roller coaster and other rides, as well as the largest indoor swimming pool in Southern California.

Hours vary by season.

CABRILLO NATIONAL MONUMENT

1800 Cabrillo Memorial Drive, San Diego, 619-557-5450; www.nps.gov/cabr

In late autumn of 1542, explorer Juan Rodriguez Cabrillo and his crew arrived at what he called a very good enclosed port, the San Diego Harbor. Today, his statue looks out over one of the most beautiful views in all of San Diego. The grounds of this national park include a historic lighthouse. From late December to mid-March, natives come to this site to watch the annual migration of Pacific gray whales. Don't miss the coastal tide pools, particularly exciting during winter's low tides, when the sea pushes back to reveal a unique world of marine plants and animals in little pockets of the earth.

CORONADO ISLAND

619-435-8788, 866-599-7242; www.coronadovisitorcenter.com

Coronado is a place for walkers. Once across the bridge, park your car and stroll past homes with gardens of flowers native only to this part of the country, and through the quaint stores of Orange Street, which includes San Diego's largest independent bookstore (Bay Books). Hop the ferry to Ferry Landing Marketplace, a center of fine dining, specialty shops, art galleries and bike rentals. There's also a waterfront park, fishing pier, beach, bike path, family amusement center and farmers' market every Tuesday from 2:30-6 p.m.

THE EMBARCADERO

1300 N. Harbor Drive, San Diego

The city's eastern waterfront is a hub of shopping, restaurants and attractions. Visit the Maritime Museum to see the *Star of India*, the world's oldest merchant ship still afloat—it was built in 1863. While you are here, you can also go aboard the *USS Midway*, now a naval museum to get an idea of ship life. In addition, the area is home to the Museum of Contemporary Art San Diego, Tuna Harbor (where commercial fishing boats dock) and Seafood Village—just look for the carousel. You'll find a variety of shops and restaurants there. From here you can

also take a harbor cruise of hop aboard the Coronado Ferry (Broadway Pier), which makes hourly trips between San Diego and Coronado.

GASLAMP QUARTER
Downtown San Diego; www.gaslamp.org

This 16½-block national historic districts bordered by Broadway on the north, Sixth Avenue on the east, Harbor Drive on the south and Fourth Avenue on the west, formed the city's business center at the turn of the century and includes many Victorian buildings. It fell into disrepair over the years but has now been revitalized and is a hot spot for fine dining, bars and shops.

HORTON PLAZA
324 Horton Plaza, San Diego, 619-239-8180;
www.westfield.com

Horton Plaza has reinvigorated downtown San Diego, and it's not difficult to see why. Sixteen years of research went into the design of this whimsical, multi-level shopping mall with more than 140 specialty shops, department stores and restaurants. The black concrete and narrow walkways were patterned after those found in European marketplaces, and many merchants display their goods on carts.
Monday-Friday 10 a.m.-9 p.m., Saturday 10 a.m.-8 p.m., Sunday 11 a.m.-6 p.m.

HUMPHREY'S CONCERTS BY THE BAY
2241 Shelter Island Drive, San Diego, 619-220-8497;
www.humphreysconcerts.com

The 1,295-seat venue, with palm tress on one side and the harbor on the other, has staged such recent acts as Ringo Star, Chris Bott and the Gypsy Kings.

KEN CINEMA
4061 Adams Ave., San Diego, 619-819-0236;
www.landmarktheatres.com

Seeing a film at the Ken means hard seats and subtitles. But for movie buffs, that's an invitation, not a deterrent. This San Diego landmark has long been the local place for art films, foreign cinema and revivals.

KOBEY'S SWAP MEET
3500 Sports Arena Blvd., San Diego, 619-226-0650;
www.kobeyswap.com

This is San Diego's largest and most popular open-air market, featuring furniture, fashion, electronics and

---

WHAT ARE THE CITY'S TOP MUSEUMS?

San Diego Air & Space Museum:
This engaging museum features rare aircraft, a kids' hangar, a 3D/4D theater and lots more.

Museum of Man:
Learn all about ancient Egypt, the Maya culture (and how they used to record time) and human evolution at this museum, which also features an excellent children's discovery center where kids can learn about ancient Egypt by bartering in a market and dressing up in royal costumes.

The New Children's Museum:
This beautiful museum encourages kids—and adults—to be more creative. It's a great place to gain an appreciate for art and spend the day just being a kid, no matter what your age.

WHAT ARE THE BEST PLACES FOR FAMILY FUN?

Balboa Park:
This 1,200-acre park offers plenty of fun for the entire family, including galleries, museums, theaters, restaurants, recreational facilities and the world-famous zoo.

The New Children's Museum:
Built in 2008, this super-creative children's museum puts a playful spin on contemporary art with pieces that kids can touch, climb or move. There's also plenty of messy, hands-on art making opportunities.

San Diego Junior Theatre at the Casa Del Prado Theater:
This San Diego institution (Raquel Welch is an alum), founded in 1947, has adapted kids' literature like *Nancy Drew* and *James and the Giant Peach*. Children not only perform but also work on costumes and lighting, serve as the stage crew and even staff the ticket windows.

SeaWorld San Diego:
You didn't think you could come to San Diego and not visit Sea World did you? Open since 1964, SeaWorld has continued to add attractions and animals. The park has ten different shows, eight rides and more than 20 exhibits and attractions. Don't miss Cirque de la Mer, an on-the-water acrobatic performance.

fresh produce. The faithful come frequently and ar usually in place when the doors open at 7 a.m. Th back section, with its secondhand goods, is a bargai hunter's delight. Vendors sell food and beverages, an live entertainment gets shoppers ready to spend.
Friday-Sunday 7 a.m.-3 p.m.

MARITIME MUSEUM SAN DIEGO

1492 N. Harbor Drive, San Diego, 619-234-9153; www.sdmaritime.com

The Maritime Museum of San Diego has one of th finest collections of historic ships, including the world oldest active ship, *Star of India*, which hosts movies i the summer on its deck. The maritime museum uses state-of-the art digital projector to display the films o a special sail rigged to the main mast. Fridays are dat nights, while Saturdays are family nights with popula children's movies.
Admission: adults $14, seniors $11, children 6-17 $8, childre under 6 free. Daily 9 a.m.-8 p.m.; movies start after sundown.

MINGEI INTERNATIONAL MUSEUM OF WORLD FOLK ART

1439 El Prado, San Diego, 619-239-0003; www.mingei.org

Six galleries here contain art exhibits of people from cultures around world. Many art forms—such a: costumes, jewelry, dolls, utensils, painting and sculpture— are shown in different collections and changing exhibi tions. Also residing at the museum are a theater, a library, a research center and educational facilities.
Admission: adults $7, seniors $5, children 6-17 $4, childrer under 7 free. Tuesday-Sunday 10 a.m.-4 p.m.

MISSION BAY PARK

2688 E. Mission Bay Drive, San Diego, 619-276-8200; www.sandiego.gov

This aquatic park on 4,235 acres is more than 50 percent water, and is a popular place (more than 15 million people visit every year) for swimming and water sports, picnics, volleyball games and more. It is also the home of SeaWorld San Diego.

MISSION SAN DIEGO DE ALCALA

10818 San Diego Mission Road, San Diego, 619-281-8449; www.missionsandiego.com

San Diego de Alcala marks the birthplace of Christianity in the Far West. It was California's first church and the first of the 21 great California missions. This remarkable shrine, still an active Catholic parish, provides an interesting look into San Diego's Spanish

heritage, as well as an understanding of the beginning of Catholicism in this corner of the world. The San Diego Trolley makes a stop just half a block from the mission, which is a National Historic Landmark. There is also a gift shop and a visitors' center.

Daily 9 a.m.-4:45 p.m.

MOUNT WOODSON ROCK CLIMBING
Highway 67, between towns of Poway and Ramona

Mount Woodson may be the best place for rock climbing in Southern California. There are super-thin cracks, super-wide ones, mantles, edging, low-angle climbs and friction climbing. You can bring your own equipment and practice leading cracks or climb walls with problems ranging in difficulty levels. For simpler climbs, bring a chalk bag and you're off. To explore, make sure you're with someone who knows these routes. To get here, park about three miles north of the Highway 67/Poway Road junction in the vicinity of the state forestry fire station. A short dirt trail passes through the trees until it hits a paved road, which winds all the way to the top of Mount Woodson.

MUSEUM OF CONTEMPORARY ART SAN DIEGO
1100 & 1001 Kettner Blvd., San Diego; 700 Prospect St., La Jolla, 858-454-3541; www.mcasd.org

Permanent and changing exhibits featuring contemporary painting, sculpture, design, photography and architecture are on display in two locations: one downtown in the historic Jacobs building (the former Santa Fe Depot), and the other in La Jolla, where you also get pretty ocean views and a great museum store offering contemporary art books and statment-making design objects. The collection includes more than 4,000 workds created after 1950, including a collection of pop art from the 1960's and 1970's, art from Latin America and installation art. The museum is known for promoting emerging and under-recognized artists.

Both locations: Admission $10, seniors $5. Free third Thursday of the month from 5-7 p.m. Monday-Thursday 11 a.m.-5 p.m., until 7 p.m. third Thursday of the month. Closed Wednesday.

MUSEUM OF MAN
1350 El Prado, San Diego, 619-239-2001; www.museumofman.org

Get to know your ancestors at this comprehensive anthropological museum. Permanent exhibits include an exploration of human evolution, as well as a display of Maya monuments and one of best collections on ancient Egypt. The former covers four million years of human evolution and includes more than 100 touchable replicas of early humans. The Children's Discovery Center allows kids to experience aspects of royal and ordinary Egyptian life in the 18th Dynasty by bartering in an Egyptian market, navigating a small boat on the Nile and dressing in costume. They can also learn more about the role of anthropologists and archaeologists—they just might discover what they want to be when they grow up.

Admission: Adults $10.00, seniors $7.50, children 13-17 $7.50, children 3-12 $5, children under 3 free.

MUSEUM OF PHOTOGRAPHIC ARTS
1649 El Prado, San Diego, 619-238-7559; www.mopa.org

Changing exhibitions spotlight works by world-renowned photographers from the early 19th century to today. The collection includes more than 9,000 images from 850 photographers. Temporary exhibits have featured everything from rock and roll snapshots to photographs exploring the aesthetic of beauty.

Admission: Adults $8 adults, seniors $6 seniors, children $5. Free guided tours Sunday. Tuesday-Sunday 10 a.m.-5 p.m.

THE NEW CHILDREN'S MUSEUM

200 West Island Avenue, San Diego, 619-233-8792; www.thinkplaycreate.org

Opened in 2008, The New Children's Museum is a playful space for kids to think and create. The museum features contemporary art exhibits that kids can touch, climb or move; studios where they can create art themselves with recycled materials; and a lovely outdoor park that the entire family can enjoy. Encourage your kids to get messy in one of the art-making studios and then head across the street for a picnic while watching the trolley and trains go by. There's also an organic café on site.

Admission: $10, seniors $5, children under one free. Free second Sunday of the month. Monday-Tuesday, Friday-Saturday 10 a.m.-4 p.m., Thursday 10 a.m.-6 p.m., Sunday noon-4 p.m. Closed Wednesday.

OCEAN BEACH FARMERS' MARKET

1868 Bacon St., San Diego, 619-224-4906; www.oceanbeachsandiego.com

Sample delicious treats at this farmers' market in Ocean Beach, which takes place every Wednesday. In addition to fresh local produce, you can munch on homemade baked goods, crepes, kabobs, olives, hummus and lots more. You can also look at jewelry and hear local musicians play, while kids can enjoy llama rides—yes, llama rides.

November-March, Wednesday 4-7 p.m.; April-October, Wednesday 4-8 p.m.

OLD GLOBE

1363 Old Globe Way, San Diego, 619-231-1941; www.theoldglobe.org

The Old Globe is one of three associated theaters on a grassy complex in Balboa Park, the other two being the Cassius Carter Center, an intimate, 225-seat theater, and the 612-seat Lowell Davies Festival Theater, used in the summer primarily for Shakespeare. This 581-seat venue, a replica of Shakespeare's theater in London, is frequently used for pre-Broadway tryouts. Many new works are also produced here.

Tours: Saturday-Sunday 10:30 a.m.

OLD TOWN

Mason St. and San Diego Ave., San Diego

The historic section of the city has many restored or reconstructed buildings, including old adobe structures. On the northern end is Old Town San Diego State Historical Park, which has several historic sites that operate as museums. These include the Wells Fargo Museum, where you can see an original stage coach; Casa de Estudillo, an adobe hacienda from 1825; Presidio Park, the site of the first mission in California; and much more (there's even a cematary for 500 19th century residents). Don't miss The Whaley House. In the mid-19th century, New Yorker Thomas Whaley came to San Diego via San Francisco, where gold beckoned. This home, which was constructed for him in 1856, was the first brick building in San Diego County. The bricks were made in his own kiln, while the walls were finished with plaster made from ground seashells. The inside of the house has an illustrious heritage as well. Not only have five generations of the Whaley family lived here, but apparently so have a few spirits. This is one of two authenticated haunted houses in California. To see it all, sign up for a walking tour led by a costumed volunteer or hop on a trolley tour. Specialty shops and restaurants also abound in Old Town.

Admission: Free. Daily 10 a.m.-5 p.m.

REUBEN H. FLEET SCIENCE CENTER
1875 El Prado, San Diego, 619-238-1233; www.rhfleet.org

This science museum offers the latest in interactive and virtual reality exhibits that will test your knowledge and engage your senses. The newest Block Busters exhibit gives you a chance to build your own free-form structures with thousands of wooden KEVA (Knowledge-Exploration-Visual Arts) planks which require any glue or connectors. See what you'll look like at 70 in the Aging for all Ages exhibit, and learn about the ways we generate energy in the SO Watt! gallery. The Do-Undo exhibit records your every move and then instantly replays them forward (as executed) and backwards (in time reversal). The Virtual Zone features games and experiments. Be sure to catch an IMAX film in the Dome Theater.

Monday-Thursday 9:30 a.m.-5 p.m., Friday 9:30 a.m.-9 p.m., Saturday 9:30 a.m.-8 p.m., Sunday 9:30 a.m.-6 p.m.

SAN DIEGO EARLY MUSIC SOCIETY
3510 Dove Court, San Diego, 619-291-8246; www.sdems.org

The San Diego Early Music Society, a group dedicated to preserving European medieval, Renaissance and baroque music, brings musicians from all over the world to play six times a year at the lovely St. James by-the-Sea Church. Performers frequently play on authentic instruments such as a harpsichord or a baroque guitar. The group also holds concerts featuring local musicians six Sundays each year at the San Diego Museum of Art in Balboa Park.

SAN DIEGO HALL OF CHAMPIONS SPORTS MUSEUM
2131 Pan American Plaza, San Diego, 619-234-2544; www.sdhoc.com

Sports fans will appreciate the exhibits on more than 40 sports in the area at this museum located in Balboa Park. Check out the exhibit on legends (and San Diegans) Tony Hawk, Andy MacDonald and Bike Sherlock, all the *Sports Illustrated* covers featuring San Diego natives, the Breitbard Hall of Fame and more.

Admission: adults $8, seniors $6, children 7–17 $4, children under 7 free. Daily 10 a.m.-4:30 p.m.

SAN DIEGO HARBOR EXCURSION
1050 N. Harbor Drive, San Diego, 619-234-4111, 800-442-7847; www.sdhe.com

A one-hour (12-mile) narrated tour highlights Harbor Island, Coronado and the Navy terminals at North Island and 32nd Street. The two-hour (25-mile) narrated tour also includes Shelter Island, Ballast Point (where Cabrillo is believed to have first landed in 1542), the harbor entrance, the ship yards and the Navy's submarine base.

Daily.

SAN DIEGO JUNIOR THEATRE AT THE CASA DEL PRADO THEATER
1650 El Prado, San Diego, 619-239-1311; www.juniortheatre.com

Few children's theater groups have entertained one million people or boast alums like Raquel Welch. This San Diego institution, founded in 1947, has put on Broadway standards like *Guys and Dolls* and *Oliver!* The company has also adapted kids' literature such as Nancy Drew and *James and the Giant Peach.* Children not only perform but also work on costumes and lighting, serve as the stage crew and even staff the ticket windows.

Days and times vary.

SAN DIEGO MUSEUM OF ART
1450 El Prado, San Diego, 619-232-7931; www.sdmart.org

The region's oldest, biggest and more visited art museum houses a renowned permanent exhibit which includes a broad collection of European, American Latin American and Asian art. The museum is perhaps best known for Spanish old master paintings; it also has a strong collection of European paintings ranging from the Renaissance and Baroque eras to Impressionism and Post-Impressionism. The Asian art collection features South Asian paintings, sculptures and ceramics.

Admission: adults $12, seniors $9, children 6-17 $4.50, children 5 and under free. Tuesday-Saturday 10 a.m.-5 p.m., Sunday noon-5 p.m.

SAN DIEGO NATURAL HISTORY MUSEUM
1788 El Prado, San Diego, 619-232-3821; www.sdnhm.org

See dinosaur fossils (or the "real" things in the 3D theater), view rare gems, go whale watching (the museum has partnered with a cruise line to take people out on the water) and more. The Kid's Habitat includes a dinosaur dig and shark school. Plan a visit as part of your day in Balboa Park—the museum is located behind the giant Moreon Bay fig tree.

Admission: adults $13, seniors $11, children 13-17 $8, children 3-12, $7, children 2 and under free. Sunday-Thursday 10 a.m.-7 p.m., Friday-Saturday 10 a.m.-9:30 p.m.

SAN DIEGO OPERA
Civic Center Plaza, 1200 Third Ave., San Diego, 619-533-7000; www.sdopera.com

The San Diego Opera Company was born in 1965 and has grown to become one of the most respected opera companies in America. Between January and May, the company presents five productions and several concerts. Brief English translations of the opera lyrics are projected onto the stage.

SAN DIEGO SCENIC TOURS
2255 Garnet Ave., San Diego, 858-273-8687; www.sandiegoscenictours.com

Take a narrated bus and harbor tour of the city. One of the tours explores nearby Tijuana, Mexico.

Daily.

SAN DIEGO TROLLEY
707 F St., San Diego, 619-233-3004; www.sdcommute.com

The 47-mile light rail system goes east to Santee and north through Old Town from downtown, serving many major shopping centers in Mission Valley and

Qualcomm Stadium for easy access to Chargers games. A day pass is only $5 and available at vending ticket machines.
Daily.

SAN DIEGO ZOO

2920 Zoo Drive, San Diego, 619-231-1515; www.sandiegozoo.org

Widely considered the nation's top zoo, this complex located in Balboa Park houses more than 4,200 rare and exotic animals representing 800 species, many of which are displayed in natural habitats. The children's zoo features a petting paddock and an animal nursery. There are also walk-through aviaries. Check out the animal shows that take place daily. Take a 40-minute guided tour aboard double-deck bus or go on the aerial tramway for a nice view of the zoo.
Admission: Adults one-day pass $37, children 3-11 $27. Daily; hours vary.

SEAPORT VILLAGE

849 W. Harbor Drive, San Diego, 619-235-4014; www.spvillage.com

Designed to look like a 100-year-old fishing village, this area provides a place to sit at the water's edge and sip a glass of wine or wander through the 75 specialty stores. Four restaurants are on the premises. Don't miss the Broadway Flying Horses Carousel, originally built at Coney Island in 1890.
Daily 10 a.m.-10 p.m.

SEAWORLD SAN DIEGO

500 SeaWorld Drive, San Diego, 800-257-4268; www.seaworld.com

Check out the more than 400 penguins or sit and watch in amazement as orca whales Shamu, Baby Shamu and Namu entertain. Open since 1964, SeaWorld has continued to add attractions, making it one of the most popular San Diego activities. The park has ten different shows, eight rides and more than 20 exhibits and attractions. The Shark Encounter allows you to come face to face with sharks by walking through a 57-foot acrylic tube. The sharks are swimming above you and next to you in a 280,000-gallon tank. Wild Arctic's ice tunnel gives you a sense of what it's like in the Arctic, while the Penguin Encounter includes 300 penguines. Flamingo Cove is another sight.
Admission: adults $65, children 3-9 $55, children 2 and under free. Daily; hours vary by season.

SERRA MUSEUM

2727 Presidio Drive, San Diego, 619-232-6203; www.sandiegohistory.org

Located in Presidio Park, this museum, which interprets the Spanish and Mexican periods of the city's history, stands on top of the hill recognized as the site where California's first mission and presidio were established in 1769. This is where Spanish Franciscan missionary, Father Junípero Serra, established California's first mission and presidio (fort).
Admission: Adults $5, seniors $4, children 6-17 $2, children under 6 free

SPRECKELS ORGAN CONCERTS

Spreckels Organ Society, 1549 El Prado, San Diego, 619-702-8138; www.sosorgan.com

The magnificent Spreckels organ, nestled in an ornate pavilion in the heart of Balboa Park, is a sight to see and hear with its 4,446 individual pipes ranging from less than a half inch to more than 32 feet in length. The organ has been in almost continuous use since brothers John and Adolph Spreckels gave it to the city in 1914. Free hour-long concerts are held on Sundays at 2 p.m., with seating for 2,400. In summer, a 12-week Organ Festival takes place on Monday evenings.

STARLIGHT BOWL/STARLIGHT THEATRE
2005 Pan American Drive, San Diego, 619-232-7827; www.starlighttheatre.org

Since the first strands of *The Naughty Marietta* played in 1946, the San Diego Civic Light Opera Association has staged 120 musicals in this open-air theater. The company employs union actors, musicians and stagehands, but also hires local actors and technicians who are able to get a start in Starlight's apprentice and internship programs. The season runs from mid-June to September. If you attend a performance, be sure to look for the legendary red box: on opening night in 1946, a costume designer took her red sewing box, tied it with a gold tassel and gave it to the stage manager as something regal for the bride to carry when she ran off to get married in a performance of *The Mikado*. The show was so successful the red box has been on stage ever since.

Box office: Monday-Friday 10 a.m.-5 p.m., Saturday-Sunday noon-4 p.m.

TIMKEN MUSEUM OF ART
1500 El Prado, San Diego, 619-239-5548; www.timkenmuseum.org

Located in Balboa Park, the Timken has a collection of European Old Masters, 18th- and 19th-century American paintings, and Russian icons dating back to the 15 century. Among its most celebrated pieces are paintings by John Singleton Copley and Eastman Johnson.

Admission: Free. Tuesday-Saturday 10 a.m.-4:30 p.m., Sunday 1:30 p.m.-4:30 p.m.

VETERANS MEMORIAL CENTER MUSEUM
2115 Park Blvd., San Diego, 619-239-2300; www.sdvmc.org

The memorial/museum is housed in a building in Balboa Park that was once the chapel of the U.S. Naval Hospital. It almost became a parking lot extension for the San Diego Zoo, but is now on the National Register of Historic Places. Go there to see historical objects, artifacts, documents and memorabilia dating to the Civil War. Dedicated to veterans of all conflicts, the the museum covers all brances of service and includes exhibites on all the major conflicts, including World War I, World War II, Pearl Harbor, the Korean and Vietnam wars.

Tuesday-Sunday 10 a.m.-4 p.m.

WHALE-WATCHING TRIPS
San Diego

For three months each year (mid-December to mid-February), California gray whales make their way from Alaska's Bering Sea to the warm bays and lagoons of Baja, passing only a mile or so off the San Diego shoreline. As many as 200 whales a day have been counted during the peak of the migration period. Trips to local waters and Baja lagoons are scheduled by the San Diego Natural History Museum. For information on other whale-watching trips, inquire at local sport-fishing companies (try San Diego Harbor Excursion, 619-234-4111; www.sdhe.com), or at the International Visitors Information Center.

HIGHLIGHT

WHAT ARE SOME SPECIAL EVENTS IN SAN DIEGO?

MISSION FEDERAL ARTWALK

734 W. Beech St., San Diego, 619-615-1090; www.missionfederalartwalk.org

Those in town during April should check out this lively event that fills the streets of Little Italy with art, music and dance, and delicious food. The event has been taking place in San Diego for 25 years and attracts more than 100,00 visitors. The festival is free.

Last weekend in April.

BALBOA PARK DECEMBER NIGHTS-THE ANNUAL CELEBRATION OF CHRIST-MAS ON THE PRADO

Balboa Park, 1549 El Prado, San Diego, 619-239-0512;
www.balboapark.org/decembernights

On the first Friday or Saturday of December, Balboa Park is transformed into a winter wonderland with walkways and buildings adorned with beautiful lights and decorations, including a 50-foot-tall tree and Nativity scenes. All the museums are open until 9 p.m. and are free. Entertainment includes an eclectic mix of bell choirs, Renaissance and baroque music, African drums and barbershop quartets.

Early December.

CORPUS CHRISTI FIESTA

Mission San Antonio de Pala, San Diego

Held annually since 1816, this festival includes an open-air mass and procession, games, dances and entertainment, plus a Spanish-style pit barbecue.

First Sunday in June.

ETHNIC FOOD FAIR

10410 Corporal Way, San Diego, 619-234-0739; www.sdhpr.org/events.html

In the mood to sample something different? Perhaps Hungarian, Austrian or Lithuanian cuisine? Head for the International Cottages at Balboa Park's House of Pacific Relations during Memorial Day weekend. Each of these 32 tiny cottages representing a different nation is decorated and laid out with the traditional foods of that country. Every cottage is staffed with at least two people, one inside to explain customs and the other outside to talk about food and hand out recipes.

Memorial Day weekend.

FESTIVAL OF BELLS

Mission Basilica San Diego de Alcala, 10818 San Diego Mission Road, San Diego, 619-283-7319; www.festivalofbells.com

The weekend-long festival commemorates the July 16, 1769, founding of the mission and celebrates the beginning of Christianity in the western United. States. All five misson bells are rung during the festivities.

Mid-July.

SAN DIEGO BAY PARADE OF LIGHTS

1220 Rosecrans St. San Diego, 619-224-2240; www.sdparadeoflights.org

For two Sunday evenings each December, the San Diego Bay is flooded with color when at least 100 boats adorned with lights and other decorations follow one another on a semicircular path through the calm waters of the bay.

Early December.

WILD ANIMAL PARK

15500 San Pasqual Valley, Escondido, 760-747-8702; www.sandiegozoo.org/wap

More than 3,500 exotic animals wander in herds and packs through this 1,800-acre wild animal preserve, which was opened to the public in 1972 and still operates as a preservation area for endangered species. Go on the Kilimanjaro Safari Walk, journey through the Heart of Africa, visit a Nairobi village and come close to lions in the Lion Camp. Several different tours are conducted daily, such as the highly popular Photo Caravan Tours, which travel right into the field exhibits, where visitors can feed the animals. Special events are also held all summer, including sleepovers.

Admission: Adults one-day pass $37, children 3-11 $27, Passes are also available that include the zoo. Mid-June-early September, daily 9 a.m.-8 p.m.; early September-mid-June, daily 9 a.m.-5 p.m.

WILLIAM HEATH DAVIS HOME

410 Island Ave., San Diego, 619-233-4692; www.gaslampquarter.org

The William Heath Davis House, the oldest structure in the Gaslamp Quarter, was shipped from Portland, Maine, in 1850. The structure of the house has remained unchanged for 120 years and is an excellent example of a prefabricated saltbox family home—a small, square structure with two stories in front and one in back. A museum occupies the first and second floors. The house is also home to the Gaslamp Quarter Historical Foundation, which gives daily walking tours of the historic area. Call ahead for tour times.

Admission: adults $5, seniors $4. Tuesday-Saturday 10 a.m.-6 p.m., Sunday 9 a.m.-3 p.m.

WHERE TO STAY

★★★ANDAZ HOTEL

600 F St., San Diego, 619-849-1234;
www.sandiego.andaz.hyatt.com

Formerly the Ivy Hotel, the Andaz offers contemporary, luxurious style within San Diego's bustling Gaslamp Quarter. Rooms feature sumptuous bed linens, flat-panel televisions and glass-enclosed bathrooms. Enjoy complimentary wireless Internet and a minibar with nonalcoholic beverages and snacks. You can easily spend an entertaining evening right within the hotel's four walls. Start with cocktails and a sunset view at the Ivy Rooftop bar, followed by dinner at the Quarter Kitchen, which serves up upscale American fare made with locally grown produce. Then play bartender among the self-service wine stations that offer 88 vintages at the Ivy Wine Bar, and wrap up your night at the sultry four-level Ivy Nightclub.

159 rooms. Restaurant, bar. Fitness center. Pool. $189-463

★★★BRISTOL HOTEL

1055 First Ave., San Diego, 619-232-6141, 800-662-4477; www.thebristolsandiego.com

This downtown boutique hotel lures young professionals and couples who are drawn to the funky, contemporary vibe. A pop art collection includes works by Andy Warhol, Roy Lichtenstein and Keith Haring. Rooms are decorated with black and white and pops of colors, and include free Internet access, salon-style hair dryers, honor bars and CD players. The top-floor ballroom features a retractable roof, and the bistro is a favorite among locals who come here for the signature martini, the Craizi Daizi.

102 rooms. Restaurant, bar. Fitness center. Pets accepted. $151-250

★★★★THE GRAND DEL MAR

5300 Grand Del Mar Court, San Diego, 858-314-2000; www.thegranddelmar.com

This palatial Mediterranean-style resort has a mind-boggling array of amenities, including world-class golf at the Tom Fazio-designed course and a five-star spa. Foodies can indulge in everything from afternoon tea to gourmet dining at six different venues, and there are four beautiful pools to lounge by, complete with underwater speakers and luxurious cabanas. Even the kids can relax in style; the Explorer's Club keeps them busy with crafts and educational activities. The turn-of-the-century style rooms (dark wood furnishing, crown moldings) have European-style soaking tubs, feather beds and LCD televisions. Service is professional and polished, with a friendly staff on hand to cater to just about every need.

280 rooms. Restaurant, bar. Business center. Fitness center. Pool. Spa. $351 and up

★★★HILTON AIRPORT/HARBOR ISLAND

1960 Harbor Island Drive, San Diego, 619-291-6700, 800-774-1500; www.sandiegoairport.hilton.com

If you need a place to stay near the airport, this comfortable hotel should do the trick. With its waterfront setting on Harbor Island, the hotel has rooms with views of Big Bay, Harbor Island marina and Point Loma. Rooms have work desks and Hilton Serenity Suite Dreams beds with down duvets. If you have time, sailboat and bicycle rentals are available nearby, as are golf courses and the beach. There's a fully equipped fitness center with sauna and an outdoor heated pool.

211 rooms. Restaurant, bar. Fitness center. Pool. $151-250

★★★HILTON SAN DIEGO GASLAMP QUARTER

401 K St., San Diego, 619-231-4040, 800-774-1500; www.hilton.com

This modern hotel is in the historic Gaslamp Quarter, and across from the San Diego Convention Center. Opting to stay at the hotel's Lofts on Fifth Avenue will get you a residential space with 14-foot ceilings, Frette linens and robes, a whirlpool tub and a private entrance. Amenities include a spa

---

WHAT ARE SAN DIEGO'S MOST LUXURIOUS HOTELS?

The Grand Del Mar:
This palatial Mediterranean-style resort offers world-class golf, a five star spa, plenty of fine dining and beautiful pools to lounge by.

U.S. Grant:
The opulent U.S. Grant has charmed visitors since its inception since 1910. Guests are pampered with turn-of-the-century elegance, serene guest rooms and excellent service.

Andaz Hotel:
The Andaz offers
contemporary,
luxurious style within
San Diego's bustling
Gaslamp Quarter.
You'll never run out of
things to do right inside
the hotel, whether it's
cocktails at the Ivy
Rooftop bar, dinner at
Quarter Kitchen, or
sipping from among
the self-service wine
stations at the Ivy
Wine Bar.

Se San Diego:
Located in the trendy
Gaslamp district, this
newer hotel furthers
the area's reputation for
swanky surroundings.
Guest rooms look more
like fancy design store
showrooms with dark
exotic wood floors, sleek
furniture and luxurious
bone finished restrooms.
The infinity-edged Siren
pool located on the
fourth floor is where lazy
days are best spent.

Tower 23:
This boutique hotel
makes the most of its
waterfront location with
"pads" that open to the
surf and sand below.
Suites are spacious and
feature Kohler whirlpool
tubs with chromatherapy
lighting (which means
you can turn your bath
bubbles violet, aqua and
other colors according to
your mood).

and fitness center, outdoor heated pool and hot tub, and adjacent walking trails that border Big Bay. The outdoor fire pit is a nice spot for cocktails and appetizers or dessert.

282 rooms. Restaurant, bar. Fitness center. Pool. Spa. $251-350

★★★HILTON SAN DIEGO MISSION VALLEY

901 Camino del Rio South, San Diego, 619-543-9000;
www.sandiegomissionvalley.hilton.com

This family-friendly hotel is set on the hillside of Mission Valley's business district, surrounded by trees and gardens. Popular Southern California tourist destinations are nearby, including SeaWorld, the historic Gaslamp Quarter and Balboa Park. Relax in spacious, modern rooms that feature Serta luxury mattresses and Crabtree & Evelyn bath products.

51 rooms. Restaurant, bar. Business center. Fitness center. Pool. $151-250

★★★HILTON SAN DIEGO RESORT

1775 E. Mission Bay Drive, San Diego, 619-276-4010, 800-345-6565; www.sandiegohilton.com

The family-friendly Hilton San Diego Resort is on Mission Bay, just steps from the beach and only one mile from SeaWorld. The hotel was recently remodeled, and the result is an airy, beachy feel. There is also a new spa and state-of-the-art fitness center. Enjoy concerts on the lawns of the garden by the bay in summer.

357 rooms. Restaurant, bar. Fitness center. Spa. $251-350

★★★HYATT REGENCY MISSION BAY SPA AND MARINA

1441 Quivira Road, San Diego, 619-224-1234;
www.missionbay.hyatt.com

This towering fixture in the heart of Mission Bay Park is the closest hotel to SeaWorld and offers panoramic views of the marina. A recent renovation resulted in a spa, a water playground with multiple slides and new restaurants. Downtown San Diego and the airport are six miles away.

430 rooms. Restaurant, bar. Business center. Fitness center. Pool. Spa. $151-250

★★★THE KEATING

432 F St., San Digeo, 619-814-5700; www.thekeating.com

Rev up your design quotient while winding down at the swanky boutique hotel designed by Pininfarina Extra, the Italian automobile manufacturer. Located in a historic building dating from 1890, The Keating presents guests with European intrigue and 24-hour personal concierge services. Rooms feature high ceilings, exposed brick, Lavazza espresso makers and a personalized sip and crave bar. Techies will enjoy wall-mounted plasma televisions, in-room Bang & Olufsen entertainment systems and complimentary high-speed Internet. If you need a bite to eat, nibble on tapas at the Sway lounge or California-inspired Italian cuisine at The Merk.

35 rooms. Restaurant, bar. Pool. Spa. Pets accepted. $151-250

★★★KONA KAI HOTEL & SPA

1551 Shelter Island Drive, San Diego, 619-221-8000, 800-566-2524; www.shelterpointe.com

Just five minutes from SeaWorld and downtown, this hotel on the tip of Shelter Island strikes a balance between offering convenience and being a quiet retreat for travelers of all types. Rooms feature elegant, contemporary décor with amenities such as data ports and coffeemakers as well as patios or balconies with bay or coastal views.

206 rooms. Restaurant, bar. Fitness center. Pool. Spa. Pets accepted. $151-250

★★★MANCHESTER GRAND HYATT SAN DIEGO

1 Market Place, San Diego, 619-232-1234, 800-223-1234; www.manchestergrand.hyatt.com

Combining a resort-like atmosphere with the convenience of a downtown location, this luxury property on San Diego Bay is adjacent to the convention center and Seaport Village. Each room offers at least a partial view of the city or bay with windows that open up to enjoy the fresh air. The full-service Regency Spa and Salon staffs skilled therapists, aestheticians and stylists.

1,625 rooms. Restaurant, bar. Fitness center. Pool. Spa. $251-350

★★★MARRIOTT SAN DIEGO HOTEL & MARINA

333 W. Harbor Drive, San Diego, 619-234-1500, 800-228-9290; www.marriott.com

Adjacent to the convention center and the Seaport Village, this waterfront hotel is in a convenient spot. Rooms are spread between two, 25-story towers and offer bay and marina views. Rooms have pops of bright nautical colors and comforable beds and work desks. Suites have ample space with plenty of seating and furnished patios.

1,362 rooms. Restaurant, bar. Fitness center. Pool. Spa. Pets accepted. $251-350

★★★MARRIOTT SAN DIEGO MISSION VALLEY

8757 Rio San Diego Drive, San Diego, 619-692-3800, 800-842-5329; www.sandiegomarriottmissionvalley.com

This resort-style hotel with Spanish accents is about seven miles northwest of downtown and less than two miles from Qualcomm Stadium. It features a host of amenities for both business travelers and vacationers. Many of the modern and whimsical guest rooms overlook the hotel's beautiful courtyard pool and tropical landscaping, and include conveniences like high-speed Internet access. Concierge, secretarial and childcare services are available. The downtown trolley stop is just steps way.

350 rooms. Restaurant, bar. Fitness center. Pool. $151-250

WHICH HOTELS ARE BEST FOR FAMILIES?

Paradise Point Resort & Spa:
This hotel is down the road to SeaWorld and has a number of pools that kids can enjoy as well as beach activities. Plus, roomy bungalows have kitchens and are on Mission Bay.

The Hotel Del Coronado:
Kids will love the candy store and an ice cream shop right on the premises. The hotel also has kiddie bike and boogie board rentals, offers a kit to make s'mores on the beach, and has a kids' camp.

Loews Coronado Bay:
Kids will never get bored, thanks to the game library, Fisher-Price welcome gifts, kiddie cabanas near the pool and kids' camps.

Rancho Bernardo Inn:
Kids receive goodies at check-in and can borrow tents to camp in the rooms.

The Hyatt Regency Mission Bay:
There's a kids' camp, a kiddie poolside movie, three waterslides and a water taxi to nearby SeaWorld. Being a Hyatt, it also has the Babies Travel Lite program—just place an order for what you need a week before your trip and it will be there when you check-in.

★★★PACIFIC TERRACE HOTEL
610 Diamond St., San Diego, 858-581-3500, 800-344-3370; www.pacificterrace.com

This seaside hotel in northern San Diego is the perfect place to revel in the Southern California beach atmosphere. Old Spanish style characterizes the exterior and the common areas. The upscale guest rooms feature cheery prints and rattan furnishings with private patios or balconies and fully stocked minibars. Some rooms have fully equipped kitchenettes, and most have fabulous views of the ocean.

73 rooms. Complimentary breakfast. Business center. Fitness center. $251-350

★★★PARADISE POINT RESORT & SPA
1404 W. Vacation Road, San Diego, 858-274-4630, 800-344-2626; www.paradisepoint.com

This 44-acre private island on Mission Bay offers cabana-style accommodations, making it the perfect spot for those looking for a little relaxation. The light-filled rooms have bright color, comfortable beds and beautiful views of the gardens or bay. The spa incorporates gentle Indonesian body treatments, while those looking for some recreation can enjoy tennis, volleyball and basketball courts; marina rentals; an 18-hole putting green; and bike trails.

460 rooms. Restaurant, bar. Fitness center. Pool. Spa. $251-350

★★★RANCHO BERNARDO INN
17550 Bernardo Oaks Drive, San Diego, 858-675-8500; www.ranchobernardoinn.com

The guest rooms at this inn are warm and inviting, with antiques, original artwork and private patios or balconies. Suites also have wood-burning fireplaces. The hotel offers two excellent options for dining: the Veranda Grill, an outdoor restaurant that overlooks the onsite golf course, and El Bizcocho, known by locals for its French cuisine.

287 rooms. Restaurant, bar. Business center. Spa. Pets accepted. Golf. $151-250

★★★SE SAN DIEGO
1047 5th Ave., San Diego, 619-515-3000; www.sesandiego.com

The soaring 23-story glass-and-steel structure is a stunning contrast to the soft, sensual experience offered inside the Se San Diego. Pacific and Zen-inspired design elements draw guests into another world, punctuated by Nepali carpets, plush upholstery and breathtaking architecture. Guest rooms and suites are equipped with iPod/MP3 players, serene beds and

400-thread count linens. Hotel staff offers complimentary luxury SUV transportation within three miles of the hotel, personal chef and captain service for suites and penthouses, and laptop computers upon request. Dine on seafood and steak at the Suite & Tender restaurant or get an edible molecular-gastronomy cocktail at the rooftop Siren Pool and Uber Lounge.

161 rooms. Restaurant, bar. Business center. Fitness center. Pool. Spa. $251-350

★★★SHERATON SAN DIEGO HOTEL AND MARINA

1380 Harbor Island Drive, San Diego, 619-291-2900, 877-734-2726; www.sheraton.com

This dual-tower waterfront landmark offers panoramic views and fresh, contemporary furnishings. Rooms have custom-designed beds with pillow-top mattresses, oversized desks and private patios or balconies. The East Tower has four restaurants and lounges, including Tapatinis, which serves a tapas menu and martinis. The West Tower features an outdoor heated pool and the restaurant Alfiere's, which specializes in Mediterranean cuisine.

1,053 rooms. Restaurant, bar. Fitness center. Spa. $151-250

★★★SHERATON SUITES SAN DIEGO AT SYMPHONY HALL

701 A St., San Diego, 619-696-9800, 800-962-1367; www.sheraton.com/sandiego

Sharing a roof with Symphony Hall, this downtown all-suite hotel offers rapid access to the convention center, baseball stadium and the historic Gaslamp District. The spacious and contemporary rooms feature living rooms, minibars and custom-designed beds with pillow-top mattresses. The Sky Lobby lounge, with views of the skyline, is a nice place for a cocktail.

264 suites. Restaurant, bar. Business center. Pool. Pets accepted. $151-250

★★★TOWER 23

4551 Ocean Blvd., San Diego, 858-270-2323; www.tower23hotel.com

Tower 23 is a spring-break-inspired locale for adults wanting relaxation and some serious time lounging in the sand. The contemporary oceanfront property offers breathtaking views of Pacific Beach, which is the real reason to stay at this hotel. The rooms mirror the site's natural elements through minimalist decor and an oceanic color palette. Enjoy a private patio or balcony, teak furnishings and flat-screen TVs. Bathe in a therapeutic chromatherapy bath designed by Kohler and rest your head upon a Tempur-Pedic Serenity bed. JRDN Surf features casually sophisticated California fare and a contemporary, 70-foot-long "wave wall" as the restaurant backdrop. The restaurant becomes an upbeat hangout for locals and tourists in the evenings.

44 rooms. Restaurant, bar. Fitness center. Business center. $251-350

★★★★U.S. GRANT HOTEL

326 Broadway, San Diego, 866-837-4270, 800-237-5029; www.usgrant.net

The opulent U.S. Grant has charmed visitors since its inception in 1910 (the historic hotel was opened in 1910 by Ulysses S. Grant Jr. and his wife, Fannie, and is now part of Starwood's Luxury Collection). Entering the grand lobby, guests are greeted with turn-of-the-century elegance: silk carpets, crystal chandeliers and lush green potted palms. Find serenity in the chic guest rooms, which feature nine-foot ceilings, crown moldings, empire-style furnishings and contemporary art. Creature comforts such as Italian linens, plush robes and marble showers offer an escape from the everyday. The Art Deco-style Grant Grill provides farm-to-table California cuisine, while the GG lounge is a prime spot for an end-of-day aperitif. Visit Wednesdays or Thursday nights for live jazz.

270 rooms. Restaurant, bar. Business center. Fitness center. $351 and up

★★★W SAN DIEGO
421 W. B St., San Diego, 619-398-3100; www.whotels.com

Taking its cues from the city's beachfront location, this downtown W hotel is lighter and brighter in design than others in the chain. The rooftop Beach bar (though located far from the sand) has a pool and cabanas ideal for lounging and sipping cocktails, while the hotel's living room is filled with rattan arm chairs and board games. Rooms have sea-blue walls and down duvets, flat-screen TVs with CD/DVD players and Bliss bath products. The onsite Rice restaurant is a favorite with locals for its sultry look and spicy Asian-influenced food.

258 rooms. Restaurant, bar. Fitness center. Pool. Spa. Pets accepted. $251-350

★★★WESTGATE HOTEL
1055 Second Ave., San Diego, 619-238-1818, 800-221-3802; www.westgatehotel.com

Located downtown in the Gaslamp District, this sumptuous hotel is a treasure trove of antiques, French tapestries, crystal chandeliers and Persian carpets. The accommodations have Richelieu furniture, distinctive artwork and a bounty of fresh flowers. The dining is top-notch, particularly at Le Fontainebleau, a favorite choice for special occasions where afternoon tea is a tradition.

223 rooms. Restaurant, bar. Complimentary breakfast. Fitness center. Spa. Pets accepted. $251-350

★★★WESTIN HORTON PLAZA
910 Broadway Circle, San Diego, 619-239-2200; www.westin.com/hortonplaza

This Westin hotel is next to the Horton Plaza shopping mall, which features 182 stores and restaurants. It's also within minutes of the historic Gaslamp Quarter, the San Diego Convention Center, Balboa Park, SeaWorld and the San Diego Zoo. Spacious guest rooms are decorated in neutral tones and feature mahogany furnishings, pillow-top mattresses with all-white bedding, sitting areas and minibars.

450 rooms. Restaurant, bar. Business center. Fitness center. Pool. Pets accepted. $151-250

★★★WESTIN SAN DIEGO
400 W. Broadway, San Diego, 619-239-4500; www.starwoodhotels.com/westin.com

Designed with an urban flair, the Westin San Diego offers a retreat to business and leisure travelers in the heart of downtown. The location means this hotel is minutes away from just about everything: SeaWorld, the zoo, conventions, Old Town, the Padres. The contemporary guest rooms are warm and inviting, with buttery tones and the signature fluffy Westin beds.

436 rooms. Restaurant, bar. Fitness center. Pool. Spa. $151-250

WHERE TO EAT

★★★★★ADDISON

5200 Grand Del Mar Way, San Diego, 858-314-1900; www.addisondelmar.com

Gourmands and style seekers alike will delight in Addison, The Grand Del Mar's signature restaurant. The atmosphere is sophisticated with European-style furnishings, brick-covered floors and grand arched windows overlooking the golf course, but it goes far beyond looks at this award-winning restaurant. Chef William Bradley takes diners on a culinary adventure, offering seasonal and ever-changing four-course menus highlighting his contemporary French cooking style. The impressive, exhaustive wine list carries everything from little-known finds to well-known favorites.

French. Dinner. Closed Sunday-Monday. Reservations recommended. Bar. $86 and up

★★★BACI

1955 W. Morena Blvd., San Diego, 619-275-2094;
www.sandiegobaci.com

This local favorite, which serves classic Northern Italian fare, has lots of Old World charm, from the tuxedo-clad waiters to the romantic dining room and elegant patio. The hearty Italian menu includes dishes such as scampi lobster over angel hair pasta, grilled calamari and penne arrabbiata.

Italian. Lunch (Monday-Friday), dinner. Closed Sunday. $36-85

★★★BERTRAND AT MISTER A'S

2550 Fifth Ave., San Diego, 619-239-1377; www.bertrandatmisteras.com

The most spectacular views of San Diego can be seen atop downtown Mr. A's restaurant. For lunch, join local professionals as they sample the Dungeness crab and asparagus risotto or the multicolored young beet salad. Dinner is a celebratory affair showcasing a menu as good as the views—both land and sea. Your best bets are the Mediterranean-style paella, juicy Angus steaks and the fresh bass. Take advantage of the patio during happy hour, served 2:30 to 6 p.m. Monday through Friday; drinks are just $5 and appetizers $7.

American. Lunch, dinner. $36-85

★★★BLUE POINT COASTAL CUISINE

565 Fifth Ave., San Diego, 619-233-6623; www.cohnrestaurants.com

Lounge on the black banquettes inside this oyster bar and seafood restaurant, or enjoy dinner—and people-watching—at one of the intimate sidewalk tables. The fresh and flavorful cuisine includes a superb blue point lobster pot pie, spicy calamari and crab and pancetta stuffed whole trout.

Seafood. Dinner. $36-85

★★★BUSALACCHI'S ON FIFTH

3707 Fifth Ave., San Diego, 619-298-0119; www.busalacchis.com

Enjoy the authentic Southern Italian cuisine in one of the gems in the Busalacchi family-owned group of Italian eateries in the area. This site occupies a Victorian-style home and features a variety of steaks, seafood, pasta and antipasti. The homey atmosphere, friendly service and satisfying fare keep locals and visitors happy.

Italian. Dinner. $36-85

★★★CALIFORNIA CUISINE

1027 University Ave., San Diego, 619-543-0790;
www.californiacuisine.cc

The chefs here mine the local markets daily to find the freshest ingredients. Dine on dishes such as Niman Ranch pork chops with sweet potato gratin, or filet mignon with roasted-garlic smashed Yukon potatoes and Gorgonzola-pinot noir glaze. This elegant restaurant showcases new artwork each season from local artists.

Californian. Dinner. $36-86

★★★EL BIZCOCHO

17550 Bernardo Oaks Drive, San Diego, 858-675-8550, 800-770-7637; www.ranchobernardoinn.com

Prepare for an unforgettable experience at this elegant restaurant that's been earning raves in San Diego for three decades. The place is full of Old World charm, but the menu is definitely new, with lots of locally grown produce and handcrafted artisan products. A tasting menu might begin with scallop carpaccio, move on to baby octopus and then a duo of ribeye and 36-hour slow rib, and conclude with pomegranate cheesecake.

French. Dinner, Sunday brunch. $36-85

★★★THE OCEANAIRE SEAFOOD ROOM

400 J St., San Diego, 619-858-2277; www.theoceanaire.com

The stuffed fish on the walls and blackboards marked with daily specials set the stage for a delicious, super-fresh (delivered daily) seafood dinner prepared every way imaginable. The lounge is a nice locale for a pre- or post-dinner drink and a few oysters.

Seafood. Dinner. $36-85

★★★THE PRADO AT BALBOA PARK

1549 El Prado Way, San Diego, 619-557-9441; www.balboapark.org

This lively, eclectic restaurant is in the historic 1915 Spanish Colonial House of Hospitality building. The attractive interior features colorful glass-blown sculptures, mosaic-tiled tables and beautiful chandeliers. Chef Jeff Thurston offers a delicious menu focusing on Italian-American and Latin American cuisine. The outdoor patio is lovely for kicking back and enjoying the surrounding views and a mojito.

Italian-American, Latin American. Lunch, dinner. $36-85

★★★PREGO

1370 Frazee Road, San Diego, 619-294-4700;
www.pregoristoranti.com

Prego brings a piece of the Italian countryside to San

Diego with its Tuscan-inspired dining room with arches and columns. The bustling open kitchen turns out authentic pizzas baked in a brick-fired oven, and fresh pasta and seafood.

Italian. Lunch, dinner. $36-85

★★★RAINWATER'S

1202 Kettner Blvd., San Diego, 619-233-5757; www.rainwaters.com

Prime Midwestern beef and fresh seafood are among the specialties at this clubby chophouse with cherry wood accents, leather seating and crisp white linens. The superb wine list, with selections from around the world, and the professional, personalized service make this the perfect spot for a power lunch or an elegant dinner.

American, steak. Lunch, dinner. $86 and up

★★★RUTH'S CHRIS STEAK HOUSE

1355 N. Harbor Drive, San Diego, 619-233-1422; www.ruthschris.com

Born from a single New Orleans restaurant that Ruth Fertel bought in 1965 for $22,000, the chain is a favorite among steak lovers. Aged prime Midwestern beef is broiled at 1,800 degrees and served on a heated plate sizzling with butter and with sides like creamed spinach and au gratin potatoes.

Steak. Dinner. $36-85

★★★SALLY'S

1 Market Place, San Diego, 619-358-6740; www.sallyssandiego.com

Although it's on the Boardwalk adjacent to the Manchester Grand Hyatt, this is no tourist trap. Lots of locals come here to enjoy the beautiful waterfront views and ultra-fresh seafood, which includes pan-fried diver scallops with lychee relish and ahi tuna with miso-mustard. The crab cakes, which are grilled (not fried), are said to be some of the best in the city. For those looking for something besides seafood, dishes such as Asian-style tofu lasagna and Colorado lamb loin marinated in Chinese black beans are a sure bet.

American. Lunch, dinner. $36-85

★★★SALVATORE'S

750 Front St., San Diego, 619-544-1865; www.salvatoresdowntown.com

A longtime favorite for locals, Salvatore's has been serving consistently good Italian food since 1987. Perfectly prepared plates of homemade lasagna or eggplant-and-mushroom-filled ravioli are delivered to tables swathed in crisp white linens and set with fine china by a friendly and efficient staff.

Italian. Dinner. $36-85

★★★TAKA

555 Fifth Ave., San Diego, 619-338-0555; www.takasushi.com

This gem in San Diego's Gaslamp District is popular for its traditional, no-frills sushi and delicious seafood that's brought in fresh everyday. In addition to its sushi menu, the restaurant offers tasty appetizers, salads and hot dishes including baked black cod. There's mochi ice cream for dessert, as well as green tea cream brulee or the black sesame creme brulée.

Japanese. Dinner. $16-35

★★★THEE BUNGALOW

4996 W. Point Loma Blvd., San Diego, 619-224-2884; www.theebungalow.com

Executive chef Paul Niles strives to please the loyal following here with his pan roasted duck with white corn polenta bars, sampler of veal sweetbreads with homemade picked vegetables and swoon-worthy dessert soufflés. A warm setting, outstanding wine list and friendly service have made the restaurant a long-time favorite in San Diego.

American, French. Dinner. $36-85

★★★TOP OF THE MARKET

750 N. Harbor Drive, San Diego, 619-232-3474; www.thefishmarket.com

Top of the Market sits atop The Fish Market, a popular fish market/restaurant, which operates its own fishery and has a partnership with an oyster farm. The restaurants have become so popular that there are now several locations in Southern California, two of which feature separate Top of the Market restaurants upstairs where guests get an expanded wine list, seafood specialities and desserts. The seafood is indeed fresh and the views of the Coronado Bridge make for an ideal setting to enjoy chef Michael McDonald's seasonal menu.

Seafood. Lunch, dinner. $36-85

★★★WINESELLAR AND BRASSERIE

9550 Waples St., San Diego, 858-450-9557; www.winesellar.com

With crisp white linens and a candlelit atmosphere, this is the perfect destination for wine lovers. Enjoy a romantic dinner of seasonal, contemporary French cuisine. Start with something like the marinated olive with Meyer lemons or a date salad, then indulge in steak frites, duck confit or a smoked shaved prosciutto salad with toasted pumpkin seed. Pick up a bottle of wine from the lower-level wine shop to drink with your meal or let the servers suggest a pairing, and if you really like it, pick it up on your way out. Tasting menus with wine pairings are also offered.

French. Lunch, Dinner. Closed Sunday. $36-85

RECOMMENDED

CUCINA URBANA

500 Laurel St., Downtown, 619-239-2222; www.cucinaurbana.com

This downtown bistro boasts a chic city atmosphere without big-city prices. Creative, satisfying fare covers all the basics from pizzas and salads to pasta and meats. The chefs support local, sustainable and organic practices whenever possible, while the bartenders get creative with seasonal cocktails. Imbibe with the Italian screw (vodka, orange juice, grapefruit and ginger beer) or the savory macho gazpacho (gazpacho vodka, cucumber, basil, lime and tomato juice). Try the daily specials served between 5 to 6 p.m., but no matter what time of day, all menu items cost less than $20.

Italian. Lunch (Tuesday-Friday), dinner. Bar. $16-35

ZOCALO GRILL

2444 San Diego Ave., San Diego, 619-298-9840; www.brigantine.com

The casually rustic and upbeat atmosphere of Zocalo Grill makes it a great spot for group get-togethers in the heart of San Diego's Old Town. The menu is Latin-focused, but influences from Mexico, the Caribbean and California can be seen in dishes like honey-porter braised carnitas with warm flatbreads, mango salsa and avocado salad; and cornmeal-crusted calamari, with lemon-cilantro aioli and spicy tomato dipping sauce. Live Brazilian guitar music is featured nightly, and a harpist plays during Sunday brunch. A quaint outdoor dining area features a lovely and inviting fireplace.

American. Lunch, dinner, Sunday brunch. $36-85

SPA

★★★SPA SE

Se San Diego, 1047 5th Ave., San Diego, 619-515-3000; www.sesandiego.com

You know this isn't your typical spa from the moment you walk in and you're offered a choice between a traditional blooming flower hot tea or a shot of the hotel's signature vodka with honey and pomegranate. Once you down your treat, try one of the signature treatments, such as the Vibe Swedish massage, which uses unusual and unexpected sound vibrations to soothe your muscles. Or if you prefer a more traditional massage, why not double the effectiveness with the four-hand massage. Afterward, retreat to one of the nine private treatment rooms and indulge in your own personal steam shower. Although San Diego's weather is second to none, this is one place that makes staying indoors rival the sunniest of days.

WHERE TO SHOP

FASHION VALLEY

7007 Friars Road, San Diego, 619-688-9113; www.simon.com

This high-end outdoor shopping center is a showcase of more than 200 retailers, including anchors Nordstrom, Bloomingdales and Saks Fifth Avenue and boutiques by Gucci, Hermes, Kate Spade and Jimmy Choo. Check out specialty stores like Intimacy, the only West Coast outpost of Oprah's favorite bra store, or Copia, the place for magazine-style art.

G-STAR RAW

470 5th Ave., San Diego, 619-238-7088; www.theswimminghorses.com

Cutting-edge style is at your fingertips at this Gaslamp-area boutique for men and women. From its conception in 1989, G-Star has been known for its innovative approach to denim. The Dutch clothing company takes inspiration from military apparel from around the world.

Monday-Thursday 10:30 a.m.-8 p.m., Friday-Saturday 10:30 a.m.-9 p.m., Sunday 11 a.m.-7 p.m.

HILLCREST

University Avenue and 5th Avenue, San Diego

Adjacent to San Diego's 1,200-acre Balboa Park, Hillcrest is a diverse neighborhood that calls for exploration. It is a hub of art, design and self-expression, featuring a number of independent restaurants, cafes, art galleries, bookshops, boutiques and furniture stores. For one of the largest collection of men and women's footwear in San Diego, check out **Mint Shoes** *(525 University Ave. 619-291-6486; www.mintshoes.com)* The mint-green shop offers unique kicks that you probably won't see duplicated anyplace else, and be sure to buy whatever you fall in love with because there's usually a limited supply of every style. For style in the home, stop by **Cathedral** *(435 University Ave., 619-296-4046; www.shopcathedral.com)*, where you can treat yourself and your place with some chic candles and of-the-moment décor accessories. You'll find artful displays of items from Jonathan Adler and Chilewich, along with exquisite candles from Diptyque and home fragrances.

HORTON PLAZA
324 Horton Plaza, San Diego, 619-239-8180; www.westfield.com/hortonplaza

If you're downtown, there's no way to avoid Horton Plaza, the multi-level, open-air shopping center that spans several city blocks. Like something out of a Dr. Seuss book, the building's maze-like walkways will have you discovering stores through the center's whimsical twists and turns. Here you will find all your favorite mid- to upper-end retailers, including Nordstrom, BCBG, Louis Vuitton and Levi's. Grab a coffee or check out a movie here at the theater, too.
Monday-Saturday 10 a.m.-9 p.m., Sunday 11 a.m.-7 p.m.

SEAPORT VILLAGE
849 West Harbor Drive, San Diego, 619-235-4014; www.seaportvillage.com

Spend an afternoon exploring the bustling 14-acre waterfront shopping, dining and entertainment district along the San Diego's glistening harbor. The center, a popular stop-off for cruises, features 54 one-of-a-kind shops such as **Urban Girl Accessories** *(837 West Harbor Drive Suite A, 619-231-8845)* to shop for unique accessories and Bungalow 360 bags. Get your spice on at **Hot Licks**, *(865 West Harbor Drive, 619-235-4000)* which showcases an array of hot sauces from all over the world.
Daily 10 a.m.-9 p.m.

SPANISH VILLAGE ARTS CENTER
1770 Village Place, San Diego, 619-233-9050; www.spanishvillageart.com

Pick up a treasure for yourself or a friend at the Spanish Village Arts Center, home to more than 250 artists from the San Diego area. Discover local photography, handmade jewelry, pottery, watercolors, vibrant textile arts and glass. On weekends, artists line up their wares in an outdoor bazaar, giving the entire experience a festival-like atmosphere.

UNIVERSITY TOWN CENTER
4545 La Jolla Village Drive, San Diego, 858-546-8858; www.westfield.com/utc

If you are looking for some big chain stores and some smaller well-known shops, head to the University Town Center. This outdoor locale is anchored by Nordstrom, Macy's and Sears and offers 120 boutiques, including Anthropologie, Bare Escentuals, Restoration Hardware and Williams-Sonoma. Toys Etc. offers classic, family-oriented games for kids of all ages. If you need a break from shopping, head to Ice Town, an year-round ice rink that's open seven days a week.
Monday-Saturday 10 a.m.-9 p.m., Sunday 11 a.m.-7 p.m.

SIDE TRIPS

BORREGO SPRINGS

This old dessert community is located northeast of San Diego and is surrounded by the Anza-Borrego State Park. In the winter and spring, wildflowers transform the desert's valleys, canyons and washes into a rainbow of colors, creating an oasis in the midst of the desert. The area is so quiet and uncomplicated, you won't even find a single stoplight.

WHAT TO SEE

ANZA-BORREGO DESERT STATE PARK

200 Palm Canyon Drive, Borrego Springs, 760-767-5311; www.parks.ca.gov

The largest state park in California has 600,000 acres of desert wilderness. The best time to visit is November to mid-May, when 600 species of flowering plants are in bloom. Elephant trees reach the northernmost limits of their range and rare smoke trees and fan palms grow here around natural seeps and springs. The park also provides a refuge for wildlife, including roadrunners, rare bighorn sheep and kit foxes. There are miles of hiking trails and campsites scattered throughout the park. Naturalist programs, tours and campfire programs are offered on weekends.

Sunrise-sunset.

WHERE TO STAY

★★★LA CASA DEL ZORRO

3845 Yaqui Pass Road, Borrego Springs, 760-767-5323, 800-824-1884; www.lacasadelzorro.com

This historic resort dates back to 1937 and is in the heart of San Diego County's majestic Anza Borrego Desert. The region's Spanish history inspires the décor at this serene resort. The 44 deluxe poolside rooms include marble baths and sitting areas with fireplaces and patios or balconies. The private casitas, each with its own pool or spa, range from one to four bedrooms.

63 rooms. Restaurant, bar. Business center. Fitness center. Pool. Spa. $251-350

★★★THE PALMS AT INDIAN HEAD

2220 Hoberg Road, Borrego Springs, 760-767-7788, 800-519-2624; www.thepalmsatindianhead.com

This historic hotel was built in classic Mid-century style with Mondrian influences. The lobby features floor-to-ceiling windows, terrazzo floors and historical photos of the property and its famous former guests, including Marilyn Monroe, Bing Crosby and Cary Grant. The cozy guest rooms are minimalist—no phones, no TVs. Warm cookies are delivered around sunset. Enjoy the Zen garden or go for an invigorating hike.

12 rooms. Restaurant. Complimentary breakfast. Pool. $61-150

WHERE TO EAT

★★★BUTTERFIELD ROOM

3845 Yaqui Pass Road, Borrego Springs, 760-767-5323; www.lacasadelzorro.com

Beautiful oil paintings of the Old West Butterfield Stageline adorn the white-washed adobe walls of this elegant restaurant. Candlelight and sparkling table settings create a romantic atmosphere in which to enjoy creative California cuisine. The menu changes throughout the year, taking advantage of the freshest seasonal ingredients. Previous offerings include a grilled ahi tuna sandwich with cucumber-cilantro salad or Colorado rack of lamb glazed with Dijon mustard, wildflower honey and Provencal herbs.

American. Breakfast, lunch, dinner. $35-85

CARLSBAD

Named for a famous European spa in Karlsbad, Bohemia (now in the Czech Republic), this beach-oriented community is a playground for golfers, tennis players, water-skiers and fishing enthusiasts. Every year in March, more than 150,000 visitors head to Flower Fields at Carlsbad Ranch (5704 Paseo Del Norte, Carlsbad, 760-431-0352; www.theflowerfields.com) to see the beautiful tecolote giant ranunculus. A British immigrant and horticulturist brought this Asian relative of the buttercup to California, where it now grows on 50 acres. Locals consider the March flowering to be a harbinger of spring. Families will want to make a trip here to visit Legoland.

WHAT TO SEE

LEGOLAND

1 Legoland Drive, Carlsbad, 760-918-5346; www.legoland.com

Visitors are greeted by a 9-foot dinosaur of bright red blocks at the entrance to Legoland, and that's just the start. Everything here is made of Legos, from the characters along Fairy Tale Brook to the horses that kids ride through an enchanted forest. Designed for children ages 2-12, the 128-acre park has 60 family rides, hands-on attractions and shows, plus a special area designed for toddlers. The park's centerpiece is Miniland, which replicates areas of New York; Washington, D.C.; the California coastline; New Orleans; and an interactive New England harbor scene using 20 million Lego bricks.

Daily; hours vary.

WHERE TO STAY

★★★LA COSTA RESORT AND SPA

2100 Costa Del Mar Road, Carlsbad, 760-438-9111, 800-854-5000; www.lacosta.com

Guests come to La Costa Resort and Spa to hit the links, relax in the spa, feast on mouthwatering meals and lounge by the pool. Designed to resemble a Spanish Colonial village, La Costa has a warm, inviting spirit. Golfers love the two PGA 18-hole courses, while the 21-court tennis center is a favorite of players. The resort is also home to the renowned Chopra Center, which helps guests achieve well-being through Ayurvedic principles. The dazzling spa with a Roman waterfall offers a variety of pampering treatments.

480 rooms. Restaurant, bar. Business center. Fitness center. Pool. Spa. $251-350

RECOMMENDED

PARK HYATT AVIARA RESORT

7100 Four Seasons Point, Carlsbad, 760-448 1234; www.parkaviara.hyatt.com

The Park Hyatt Aviara is a Spanish colonial-style building designed to blend into the Southern California landscape. Each guest room opens to a private balcony or ground-level landscaped terrace. Most rooms have views, of the Pacific or the Batiquitos Lagoon, but those that don't overlook the gardens, swimming pools or golf greens. Oversized marble tubs, down bedding and twice-daily housekeeping keep guests comfortable. Take advantage of complimentary beach butler service, which transports you to the shore with all the necessary amenities: chairs, umbrellas, towels and blankets. A full-day children's program is also available.

329 rooms. Restaurant, bar. Business center. Fitness center. Pool. Tennis. Golf. $351 and up

WHERE TO EAT

★★★VIVACE

Park Hyatt Aviara Resort, 7100 Four Seasons Point, Carlsbad, 760-603-6800; www.parkaviara.hyatt.com

Dine on Central Italian cuisine with a twist at this chic restaurant. Creative dishes include black spaghetti with rock shrimp and calabrese sausage, and handmade orecchiette with braised capon. A large light stone fireplace fills the dining room with warmth while the floor-to-ceiling windows allow breathtaking views of the ocean and lagoon.

Italian. Dinner. $36-85

CORONADO

Known as the Crown City, Coronado lies across the bay from San Diego and is connected to the mainland by a long, narrow sandbar called the Silver Strand by the beautiful Coronado Bridge. It is the site of the famous Hotel del Coronado.

WHERE TO STAY

★★★HOTEL DEL CORONADO

1500 Orange Ave., Coronado, 619-435-6611, 800-468-3533; www.hoteldel.com

Walking into the historic Hotel Del feels like part museum, part amusement park. Situated on the glistening sands of Coronado, the hotel's iconic red turrets, as seen in the film *Some Like It Hot*, are magnets for tourists, families and wedding parties alike. The hotel's original Victorian building offers couples a graceful locale for romance. Each room in this building comes in a unique size and shape and is decorated in rich colors and traditional furnishings. The resort rooms, located in the adjacent Ocean Towers and California Cabana buildings, offer casual elegance and a tropical décor that is practical for families and social gatherings. Opt for the premium resort rooms for an ocean view. The new Beach Village suites offer 78 beachfront guestrooms complete with gourmet kitchens and spacious living, dining and outdoor entertainment areas. The newly redone Spa at the Del provides coed relaxation areas, a hydrotherapy tub, 21 treatment rooms and a private terrace with fire pit and vanishing-edge pool. Thirteen dining options, including room service, will satisfy any craving.

679 rooms. Restaurant, bar. Business center. Fitness center. Pool. Spa. $251-350

★★★LOEWS CORONADO BAY RESORT
4000 Coronado Bay Road, Coronado, 619-424-4000, 800-235-6397; www.loewshotels.com

Ocean views, outdoor sports and proximity to Silver Strand State Beach provide a welcome escape at the Loews Coronado. The family-friendly resort boasts three lighted bayside tennis courts, three outdoor swimming pools and bicycle, rollerblade, wave runner, sailboat and paddleboat rentals. A marina provides convenient access for watercraft. Head there to climb aboard one the hotel's gondolas and ride around in the water. If you're not the outdoorsy type, unwind at the Sea Spa, complete with 15 treatment rooms, a steam room, a sauna, a relaxation lounge and a fitness center. Or retreat to one of the contemporary guest rooms, which provide pillow-top mattresses, flat-screen TVs, 24-hour room service, coffee makers and minibars.

439 rooms. Restaurant, bar. Business center. Fitness center. Pool. Spa. Tennis. $151-250

★★★GLORIETTA BAY INN
1630 Glorietta Blvd., Coronado, 619-435-3101, 800-283-9383; www.gloriettabayinn.com

The Glorietta Bay Inn consists of the historic John D. Spreckles mansion—built in 1908 and located across from the Hotel Del Coronado—and several other buildings constructed in the 1950s. Eleven of the 100 rooms are in the original Edwardian-style mansion and feature traditional furnishings and fresh flowers. The newer rooms are spacious, reasonably priced accommodations that are cozy (if a bit dated). Families will want to opt for the two-bedroom, two-bath suites with kitchenettes. All rooms include continental breakfast delivered daily, complimentary wireless Internet, heated pool and whirlpool spa access.

100 rooms. Complimentary breakfast. Business center. Pool. $151-250

★★★MARRIOTT CORONADO ISLAND RESORT
2000 Second St., Coronado, 619-435-3000; www.marriott.com

This waterfront resort, just across the bay from downtown San Diego, sits on 16 tropical acres dotted with waterfalls, koi ponds and strolling flamingos. For a special getaway, reserve a villa with a private entrance and pool.

100 rooms. Complimentary breakfast. Business center. Pool. $151-$250

WHERE TO EAT

★★★MISTRAL AT LOEWS CORONADO BAY REORTS
Loews Coronado Bay Resort, 4000 Coronado Bay Road, Coronado, 619-424-4000;
www.loewshotels.com

Dine overlooking the beautiful views of Coronado Bay and the San Diego skyline at Mistral. Chef Patrick Ponsaty creates modern French cuisine with herbs plucked from the Loews Coronado Bay Resort garden. Each season, the chef concocts a signature sparkling cocktail best sipped alongside a savory first course, such as beef carpaccio with tarragon vinaigrette. Try the rocket salad, made with farmer's market arugula, asparagus and avocado and dressed with citrus vinaigrette. For the main course, savor Baja white shrimp with angel hair pasta or seared scallops with basil pesto sauce.

California. Dinner. Closed Monday. Reservations recommended. Bar. $36-85

DEL MAR

This village by the sea offers beautiful white beaches and brilliant sunsets. It's also an attractive area for year-round ballooning. From July to mid-September, visitors and locals head to the Del Mar Thoroughbred Club (*2260 Jimmy Durante Blvd., Del Mar, 858-755-1141; www.dmtc.com*) to put their bets in and enjoy an afternoon of thoroughbred horse racing.

WHERE TO STAY

★★★HILTON SAN DIEGO/DEL MAR

15575 Jimmy Durante Blvd., Del Mar, 858-792-5200; www.hilton.com

This comfortable hotel is next to the Del Mar Thoroughbred Club and just minutes from the beach, though the pool may tempt guests to skip the sand. The rooms include Internet access, new Serenity beds and Web TV.

256 rooms. Restaurant, bar. Business center. Fitness center. Pool. Pets accepted. $151-250

★★★L'AUBERGE DEL MAR RESORT AND SPA

1540 Camino del Mar, Del Mar, 800-245-9757; www.laubergedelmar.com

Tucked within the picturesque village of Del Mar, the L'Auberge Del Mar Resort and Spa combines a casual elegance and panoramic coastal views that's perfect for a romantic getaway. It also offers easy access to art galleries, boutique shopping and championship golf. The hotel features two lighted championship tennis courts, a state-of-the-art fitness facility, an outdoor whirlpool spa and a pool. The relaxed yet elegant rooms are plush with billowy duvets and walk-in showers. Some rooms feature fireplaces, balconies or private patios. The full-service European spa is the place for facials, massages and body treatments. The signature restaurant Kitchen 1540 serves seasonal fare cooked with hormone free meats, locally grown produce and sustainable seafood.

120 rooms. Restaurant, bar. Fitness center. Pool. Spa. $351 and up

SPA

★★★★★THE SPA AT THE GRAND DEL MAR

5300 Grand Del Mar Court, San Diego, 858-314-2020; www.thegranddelmar.com

With its gleaming Carrera marble and crystal glass tiles, The Spa at The Grand Del Mar is elegance personified. The confident staff guides guests through each pampering, indulgent appointment. Unwind with the signature Renaissance treatment, which blends a mineral-rich mud wrap, rosemary-infused shower and relaxing massage. From rosemary and sage herbal salt scrubs and herbal reflexology to renewal facials using pomegranate and pumpkin, the focus is on nature-based ingredients. Triad treatments, combining a series of three treatments, are an indulgent way to experience this opulent spa.

LA JOLLA

Named for the word "jewel" in Spanish, the oceanside neighborhood of La Jolla is home to the legendary Salk Institute, the Birch Aquarium and the renowned Torrey Pines Golf Course. But the crown jewel here is downtown La Jolla, bordering the town's expansive beach. North Torrey Pines Road will take you downtown by way of winding roads and a slow, downhill approach of the beach. To get there, take La Jolla Shores Drive and turn on Camino del Oro. Downtown La Jolla's best street to browse is Girard Avenue, where there are high-end boutiques, including Ralph Lauren. Park anywhere you can find a spot and begin walking. This portion of La Jolla is packed with art galleries, restaurants and hotels. On Girard, you'll spot a small passage with the sign "Arcade Building," which mimics Parisian-style passage shopping. From Girard, you can walk to La Jolla Cove, where the avenue grows narrow and winds slightly downhill until you see an expanse of sapphire-blue ocean and a large, brightly manicured lawn. Grab a coffee from one of La Jolla's cafés and head down to the sea.

WHAT TO SEE

BIRCH AQUARIUM AT SCRIPPS

2300 Expedition Way, La Jolla, 858-534-3474; www.aquarium.ucsd.edu

At the Scripps Institution of Oceanography, see undersea creatures in realistic habitats at this aquarium situated on a hill with spectacular ocean views. Check out the tide pool exhibit. Beach and picnic areas are nearby.

Admission: adults $11, seniors $9, children 3-17 $7.50, children 2 and under free. Daily 9 a.m.-5 p.m.

LA JOLLA COVE

1100 Coast Blvd., La Jolla, 619-221-8901; www.sannet.gov

An ideal place for picnicking, the La Jolla Cove provides a marvelous backdrop of the Pacific Ocean and sandy cliffs, and is an ideal place to see the water crash against the craggy rocks at the cove's point. The churning sea perfumes the air with the scent of seaweed. After taking a walk along the sidewalk, relax on the lawn and drink in the sun. Located at the southern edge of the San Diego-La Jolla Underwater Park, the cove is an ecologically protected area. The tiny beach is a great place to sunbathe, snorkel or scuba dive and check out the seals, which are often seen sunbathing on the Cove's rocky edge. Divers can enjoy visibility of more than 30 feet and the waters are ideal for photography.

Daily.

LA JOLLA PLAYHOUSE

2910 La Jolla Village Drive, La Jolla, 858-550-1010; www.lajollaplayhouse.com

This Tony Award-winning venue has long been one of America's premier regional theaters. Gregory Peck, Dorothy McGuire and Mel Ferrer founded it in 1947. Located on the campus of the University of California, San Diego, the playhouse puts on six shows per season. Although *Thoroughly Modern Millie* and *Rent* played here, the playhouse is best known for taking chances on new work.

Days and times vary.

LA JOLLA SHORES

8200 Camino del Oro, La Jolla

This beach is a favorite among locals for its tame shore. The sand is silky with glints of false gold and is distinctly darker than the sands of beaches farther north in Orange County and Los Angeles. The beach has several barbecue pits for evening bonfires.

MUSEUM OF CONTEMPORARY ART

700 Prospect St., La Jolla, 858-454-3541; www.mcasd.org

Exhibits focus on contemporary paintings, sculptures, design, photography and architecture. The museum also offers a sculpture garden, a bookstore, films and lecture programs.

Admission: adults $10, seniors $5, ages 25 and under free. Thursday-Tuesday 11 a.m.-5 p.m.; third Thursday of the month 11 a.m.-7 p.m.

TORREY PINES GLIDERPORT

2800 Torrey Pines Scenic Drive, La Jolla, 858-452-9858; www.flytorrey.com

Soar 50 to 150 feet above the pines. Instructors give 20 minutes of paragliding lessons on the ground before sending guests up in tandem with their teachers. Hang gliding is offered as well, but eight lessons are needed to earn a beginner rating before taking flight.

Daily.

TORREY PINES STATE RESERVE

12000 N. Torrey Pines Road, La Jolla, 858-755-2063; www.torreypine.org

The 1,750-acre Torrey Pines State Reserve was established to protect the world's rarest pine tree, the gnarly, malformed Torrey pine, which hundreds of years ago covered Southern California. Today, they are found only on Santa Rosa Island off the coast of Santa Barbara and in the La Jolla reserve. There are miles of unspoiled beaches and eight miles of hiking trails here. The visitors' center and museum are open daily 9 a.m. to sunset. Go on a guided nature walk, weekends and holidays, 10 a.m. and 2 p.m.

Daily 8 a.m.-sunset.

WINDANSEA BEACH

6800 Neptune Place, La Jolla, 619-221-8874; www.beachcalifornia.com

Windansea Beach is best known for surfing, as its intense breaks created by underwater reefs. The only drawback: everyone knows about it. On the best days, Windansea's concentrated surf breaks get crowded very quickly and even ambitious amateurs are advised to stay out of the way.

WHAT IS THE MOST LUXURIOUS RESORT RIGHT OUTSIDE SAN DIEGO?

The Lodge at Torrey Pines:
Sitting on a rocky cliff and surrounded by protected forest and unspoiled beaches, The Lodge at Torrey Pines is a quiet escape to luxury. But don't think for a minute that you'll be bored; in addition to a myriad of amenities, the lodge neighbors the 18th hold of the acclaimed Torrey Pines Golf Course. Or, you can just sit and admire the views.

WHERE TO STAY

★★★HILTON LA JOLLA TORREY PINES
10950 N. Torrey Pines Road, La Jolla, 858-558-1500, 800-762-6160; www.hilton.com

This full-service resort overlooks the famed oceanfront links of the Torrey Pines Golf Course in the heart of La Jolla. Advance reservations at the coveted course are available to guests. Rooms boast a private balcony or deck overlooking the links, ocean or garden. The Torreyana Grille serves up steaks and seafood prepared Pacific -Rim-style.

394 rooms. Restaurant, bar. Business center. Fitness center. $151-250

★★★HOTEL PARISI
1111 Prospect St., La Jolla, 858-454-1511, 877-454-1511; www.hotelparisi.com

This hotel goes above and beyond to help visitors relax, from the award-winning feng shui design to the wide range of Eastern-inspired bodywork in the spa—there's even an on-call psychologist. The elegant rooms have goose-down comforters, Egyptian cotton sheets and gourmet coffee makers. Luxury apartments with full-size kitchens are also available for extended stays.

20 rooms. Complimentary breakfast. $251-350

★★★HYATT REGENCY LA JOLLA AT AVERTINE
3777 La Jolla Village Drive, San Diego, 858-552-1234; www.lajolla.hyatt.com

Situated on 11 acres, this elegant hotel is minutes away from beaches, golf and museums. The rooms have been recently remodeled and include down comforters and Portico bath products. The biggest draw may be the Sporting Club and the Spa, a 32,000-square-foot fitness center that includes a full-size basketball court, two lighted tennis courts and a variety of classes, in addition to pampering treatments.

419 rooms. Restaurant, bar. Business center. Fitness center. Pool. $251-350

★★★★LODGE AT TORREY PINES
11480 N. Torrey Pines Road, La Jolla, 858-453-4420; www.lodgetorreypines.com

The Lodge sits on a rocky cliff overlooking the Pacific Ocean and is surrounded by protected forest and unspoiled beaches. The view is gorgeous, but many are drawn by another aspect of the location: the lodge neighbors the 18th hole of the Torrey Pines Golf Course, one of the most acclaimed courses in the world. Tee times are guaranteed for guests for the championship course. The resort itself is a celebration of the American Craftsman period, from its stained glass and hand-crafted woodwork to its Stickley-style furnishings. The warm guest rooms boast custom-designed furniture, and spectacular views of the golf course or courtyard.

171 rooms. Restaurant, bar. Fitness center. Spa. Golf. $251-350

WHERE TO EAT

★★★★A.R. VALENTIEN
The Lodge at Torrey Pines, 11480 N. Torrey Pines Road, La Jolla, 858-453-4220; www.arvalentien.com

La Jolla's Lodge at Torrey Pines may be best known for its golf, but its much-lauded restaurant, A.R. Valentien, is a show-stopper. Named after an impressionist California artist, the dining room is a showcase of stained glass lighting and Mission-style furnishings with large windows overlooking the 18th hole. Chef Jeff Jackson delivers stand-out traditional American cooking focusing on the quality of the ingredients. Settle in and sample dishes like chicken and dumplings, spaghetti and meatballs or the drugstore style hamburger. The outstanding creations of West Coast producers dot the superlative cheese list, so be sure to save room for a taste.

American. Dinner. Reservations recommended. $36-85

★★★FLEMING'S PRIME STEAKHOUSE & WINE BAR

8970 University Center Lane, La Jolla, 858-535-0078; www.flemingssteakhouse.com

In addition to the usual steaks, you'll find some delicious surprises on the menu, such as tuna mignon and the Australian lamb chops with a champagne meat sauce. The potatoes with cream, jalapeños and cheddar are as good as they sound.

American, steak. Dinner. $36-85

★★★MARINE ROOM

2000 Spindrift Drive, La Jolla, 858-459-7222, 866-644-2351; www.marineroom.com

In operation since 1941, this restaurant owned by the La Jolla Beach & Tennis Club has been a favorite among locals who come here for the fresh global cuisine that's rooted in the French classics, superb wine list, spectacular ocean views and professional service. The menu features such delights as spinach-wrapped oysters and pistachio butter basted Australian lobster tail.

International. Dinner. $16-35

★★★PIATTI RISTORANTE

2182 Avenida de la Playa, La Jolla, 858-454-1589; www.piatti.com

With its open kitchen and stone pizza hearth, this warm restaurant resembles an Italian trattoria. Sit in the terra-cotta dining room or out on the fountain patio while enjoying the lush salads, rustic pizzas and flavorful pastas.

Italian. Lunch, dinner. $16-35

★★★ROPPONGI

875 Prospect St., La Jolla, 858-551-5252; www.roppongiusa.com

Restaurateur Sami Ladeki has hit the jackpot with this popular dining spot. The tapas—Polynesian

---

WHAT IS THE BEST OVERALL RESTAURANT OUTSIDE SAN DIEGO?

A.R. Valentien:
Named after an impressionist California artist, A.R. Valentien is a showstopper with its stained glass lighting and Mission-style furnishings and stand-out traditional American cooking focusing on the quality of the ingredients.

crab stack, crispy buttermilk onion rings and local halibut carpaccio, to name a few—are irresistible. There's also a sushi and regular dinner and lunch menus.
Asian fusion. Lunch, dinner. $36-85

★★★SANTE RISTORANTE
7811 Herschel Ave., La Jolla, 858-454-1315; www.santeristorante.com
After a popular run in New York at La Fenice, Tony Buonsante brought his authentic Northern Italian cooking to La Jolla in this intimate, elegant space. Dishes include eggless ricotta dumplings with Gruyère cheese and hearty lasagna Bolognese. Dine on the sidewalk terraces, in the elegant dining room with white tablecloths or at the cozy bar where you can browse the celebrity photographs.
Italian. Lunch, dinner. $16-35

★★★THE STEAKHOUSE AT AZUL LA JOLLA
1250 Prospect St., La Jolla, 858-454-9616; www.azul-lajolla.com
Settle into this warm and welcoming restaurant overlooking the Pacific and dig into the all-dressed up burger with crisp bacon, caramelized onions and aged white cheddar cheese or the prime aged beef with any of the outstanding sides, including crispy artichoke hearts or Parmesan risotto, while taking in the sweeping views of the Pacific. The menu also features a milk-fed veal chop, Colorado rack of lamb, free-range chicken and fresh seafood.
American. Lunch (Saturday), dinner, Sunday brunch. $36-86

★★★TAPENADE
7612 Fay Ave., La Jolla, 858-551-7500; www.tapenaderestaurant.com
The first item to arrive at your table when you dine at this restaurant is, of course, tapenade. What follows is expertly prepared Southern French food meant to evoke a summer day in Provence. Dishes include aged sirloin with black peppercorn sauce made with cognac and pommes frites and roasted duck breast with Yukon gold garlic mashed potatoes. Be sure to save room for the cheese plate or coconut crème brûlée.
French. Lunch (Monday-Friday), dinner. $36-85

SPA

★★★★THE SPA AT TORREY PINES
The Lodge at Torrey Pines, 11480 N. Torrey Pines Road, La Jolla, 858-453-4420, 800-656-0087; www.spatorreypines.com
This spa at the Lodge at Torrey Pines has an oceanfront setting and a surrounding forest that influence many of the treatments. There are numerous water treatments, including balneotherapy, a seawater bath in a hydrotherapy tub. Body scrubs use coastal sage and pine for exfoliation. Several facials combat aging, including a champagne facial that uses yeast extracts and bubbly. The spa also has a list of rituals on the menu, which blend body treatments with massage. The Aromasoul Ritual, for instance, uses Chinese massage techniques to increase the flow of energy and replenish vitality.

RANCHO SANTA FE

This idyllic town (you'll often see people riding their horses on trails) is modeled after a Spanish village. The Inn at Rancho Sante Fe was once a destination for Hollywood stars, including Bette Davis and Bing Crosby. Today, many people visit to play the Rancho Santa Fe Golf Course, which is considered one of the best courses in Southern California, while the Rancho Valencia is a well-known tennis resort.

WHERE TO STAY

★★★INN AT RANCHO SANTA FE

5951 Linea Del Cielo, Rancho Santa Fe, 858-756-1131, 800-843-4661;
www.theinnatranchosantafe.com

With several small cottages dotting the 20-acre property, guest accommodations are available in three varieties: deluxe rooms, suites and private cottages. The deluxe rooms have patios or decks, and many have fireplaces, wet bars, kitchenettes or sitting areas (some of the older rooms have hardwood floors). Suites are one- or two-bedroom cottages, each with a living room, kitchen and fireplace, plus a patio or deck. The one-, two- and three-bedroom private cottages have a full-sized kitchen and guest bath. A full-service spa, a fitness program (offering guided runs and walks, swimming lessons, water aerobics and weight training classes), tennis courts, a croquet lawn and walking and jogging trails provide plenty of recreation.

87 rooms. Restaurant. Fitness center. Pool. Spa. Pets accepted. $151-250

★★★MORGAN RUN RESORT & CLUB

5690 Cancha de Golf, Rancho Santa Fe, 858-756-2471, 800-378-4653;
www.morganrun.com

The Morgan Run Resort & Club is both a club for area residents and a resort for guests. Travelers can take full advantage of the club and its facilities, including a 27-hole championship golf course, tennis courts and a fitness center offering Pilates and yoga classes. The guest rooms are traditional and elegant, and each has its own private patio or balcony. The resort is only five miles from the beach community of Del Mar with its sandy shores, boutiques and Del Mar Race Track, where's there's plenty of horse-racing action.

90 rooms. Restaurant, bar. Fitness center. Spa. $151-250

★★★★RANCHO VALENCIA RESORT & SPA

5921 Valencia Circle, Rancho Santa Fe, 858-756-1123, 800-548-3664;
www.ranchovalencia.com

Located in the canyon of Rancho Santa Fe on 40 manicured acres of rolling hills, this relaxing retreat is just minutes from the charming boutiques and cafés of La Jolla. If you're looking for something secluded, this is it. The resort is made up of 20 pink casitas, which house only 49 suites, each featuring fireplaces with hand-painted tiles, beamed ceilings and private garden patios and large bathrooms, some with bathtubs and steam showers. There's also an award-winning tennis program, spa and privileges at local golf courses. An outstanding restaurant makes for a perfect stay.

49 suites. Restaurant, bar. Fitness center. Spa. Pets accepted. $251 and up

WHERE TO EAT

★★★MILLE FLEURS

6009 Paseo Delicias, Rancho Santa Fe, 858-756-3085; www.millefleurs.com

This elegant restaurant serves such unforgettable dishes as vegetable ravioli with cave-aged Gruyère and venison loin from New Zealand. Many of the fruits and vegetables come from a farm just down the road, which the chef visits every morning. An outdoor patio, seasonal music and a piano bar make for a perfect evening.

French. Lunch (Tuesday-Friday), dinner. Bar. $36-85

★★★THE RESTAURANT RANCHO VALENCIA

Rancho Valencia, 5921 Valencia Circle, Rancho Santa Fe, 858-759-6216; www.ranchovalencia.com

Just off the mission-style courtyard of the Rancho Valencia resort, you'll find Valencia, a romantic dining experience reminiscent of the French countryside, with whitewashed walls, beamed ceilings, live palms and a tiered patio. The menu features seafood, fresh vegetables and aged beef. Highlights include the Diver scallops; a Colorado lamb rib eye with escargots, garlic, and shallots; and the Valencia veal picatta with olive oil mashed potatoes and broccoli rabe. Save room for one of the decadent desserts or the artisan cheese plate. The restaurant also offers an outstanding Sunday brunch.

Seafood. Breakfast, lunch, dinner, Sunday brunch. $86 and up

SPA

★★★THE SPA AT RANCHO VALENCIA

Rancho Valencia, 5921 Valencia Circle, Rancho Santa Fe, 858-756-1123; www.ranchovalencia.com

This spa's mosaic-tiled décor echoes the Spanish mission-style look of the Rancho Valencia Resort. The 10 treatment rooms, outfitted with showers and private patios, are luxurious retreats where the staff delivers massages, exfoliations, masks and wraps that make full use of the area's natural bounty, from Pacific sea salt to seaweed, sweet citrus fruits and cypress.

PALM SPRINGS AND THE DESERT

Palm Springs and its sister desert communities have long been a getaway of the rich and famous. Located 120 miles east of Los Angeles and 135 miles north of San Diego, the desert oasis is complete with spectacular resorts, fine dining and unique Mid-century modern desert architecture. Recently, the town's resorts have been undergoing a renovation revival, with star designers such as Jonathan Adler and Kelly Wearstler called in to dream up funky, colorful and stylish interiors. The area known as Palm Desert is located approximately 10 miles from Palm Springs. Many people come to live here in the winter, especially in the surrounding areas of Indian Wells, Rancho Mirage and La Quinta. Of course, scores of people visit to play golf.

Others come to explore the desert. There is much to behold in the Southern California desert. The most popular trip is from Palm Springs to Joshua

HIGHLIGHT

WHAT ARE THE TOP THINGS TO DO IN PALM SPRINGS?

GOLF
Palm Springs is the place to play golf. There are more than 100 golf courses within a 15-mile radius of Palm Springs. Add in amazing weather year round and you have a serious golf destination.

SHOP
Around Palm Springs you'll find everything from great vintage stores to premium outlets. High-end boutiques line Palm Canyon Drive.

SEE THE ARCHITECTURE
Palm Springs has some of the best examples of Mid-Century modern architecture. Visit psmodern.com for information on famous architects and their works around the area.

Tree National Park, about an hour away on the rugged Twenty-Nine Palms Highways (CA-62). Hit the road early and you can see much of the park in a day, and then head back to Palm Springs. Death Valley National Park is another fascinating getaway about 200 miles from Los Angeles.

WHAT TO SEE

PALM DESERT
CLASSIC CLUB
75200 Classic Club Blvd., Palm Desert, 760-601-3601; www.classicclubgolf.com
Gaining fame in 2006 and 2007 by hosting the PGA's Bob Hope Chrysler Classic, this semiprivate club presents a challenging course of rolling terrain, wide landing areas, and 30 acres of water elements. Five sets of tees makes Classic Club playable for golfers of all levels.

DESERT WILLOW GOLF RESORT
38-995 Desert Willow Drive, Palm Desert, 760-346-7060; www.desertwillow.com
The resort, one of the best public access facilities in Southern California, has two championship courses: The tougher of the two, Firecliff, has more than 100 bunkers and numerous water hazards. Mountain View has wider fairways, sloping greens and less sand. Both have environmentally smart designs and construction.

SPECIAL EVENT

BOB HOPE CLASSIC

39000 Bob Hope Drive, Rancho Mirage, 760-346-8184; www.bhcc.com
The well-known golf tournament has been taking place since 1960 when it was called the Palm Springs Golf Classic. Bob Hope played in the inaugural tournament (Arnold Palmer won that first year and played in 42 tournaments). It was renamed the Bob Hope Desert Classic in 1965, and Bob Hope continued to host and play for more than 30 years. Golf pros and celebrities play at four country clubs. In 2010, these were: La Quinta Country Club, Nicklaus Private at PGA West, SilverRock Resort and Palmer Private at PGA West. The tournament is played over five days each January.

LIVING DESERT
47-900 S. Portola Ave., Palm Desert, 760-346-5694; www.livingdesert.org
This 1,200-acre wildlife and botanical park contains interpretive exhibits from the world's deserts. The park also has Native American exhibits, picnic areas, nature trails, a gift shop, a café and a nursery. Check out the special weekend programs.
September-mid-June, daily 9 a.m.-5 p.m.; mid-June-August, daily 8 a.m.-1:30 p.m.

PALM SPRINGS
INDIAN CANYONS
38520 S. Palm Canyon Drive, Palm Springs, 760-325-1862; www.indian-canyons.com
The remains of the ancient Cahuilla people, the first to inhabit this area, include rock art, mortars ground into bedrock, pictographs and shelters built atop high cliff walls. Spot bighorn sleep and wild ponies along the hiking trails. Rangers give interpretive walks.
Daily 8 a.m.-5 p.m.

KNOTT'S SOAK CITY WATER PARK PALM SPRINGS
1500 Gene Autry Trail, Palm Springs, 760-327-0499; www.knotts.com
This 22-acre water park has 13 water slides, an inner tube ride and a wave pool.
Admission: adult $29.99, seniors $19.99, children under 48" $19.99. Late March-August, daily; hours vary.

MOORTEN'S BOTANICAL GARDEN
1701 S. Palm Canyon Drive, Palm Springs, 760-327-6555; www.palmsprings.com/moorten
Approximately 3,000 varieties of desert plants reside in this botanical garden. It also features the world's first "cactarium," which contains several hundred species of cactus and desert plants from around the world.
Admission: adults $3, children $1.50. Monday-Tuesday, Thursday-Saturday 9 a.m.-4:30 p.m., Sunday 10 a.m.-4 p.m.

PALM SPRINGS AERIAL TRAMWAY
1 Tramway Road, Palm Springs, 760-325-1449, 760-325-1391; www.pstramway.com
Take a ride along the world's longest double-reversible, single-span aerial tramway. Two 80-passenger revolving cars make the 2½-mile trip (ascending to 8,516 feet) to the top of Mount San Jacinto. There are also opportunities for

picnicking, camping in the summer and a bite to eat at the cafeteria at the summit.

Admission: adults $22.95, seniors $20.95, children 3-12 $15.95. Monday-Friday every half-hour from 10 a.m., Saturday-Sunday from 8 a.m.

PALM SPRINGS AIR MUSEUM

745 N. Gene Autry Trail, Palm Springs, 760-778-6262; www.air-museum.org

Vintage World War II aircraft are on display at this museum. You'll also see period photographs and video documentaries.

Admission: adults $12, seniors and children 13-17 $10, children 6-12 $5, children under 7 free. Daily 10 a.m.-5 p.m.

PALM SPRINGS DESERT MUSEUM

101 Museum Drive, Palm Springs, 760-325-4490; www.psmuseum.org

Enjoy diverse art collections of world-renowned artists, science exhibitions with interactive elements and educational programs for the whole family. The Annenberg Performing Arts Theater features jazz, classical, dance and Broadway performances.

Admission: adults $12.50, seniors $10.50, children free. Free every Thursday 4-8 p.m. Tuesday-Wednesday, Friday-Sunday 10 a.m.-5 p.m., Thursday noon-8 p.m.

PALM SPRINGS HISTORICAL SOCIETY ON VILLAGE GREEN

221 S. Palm Canyon Drive, Palm Springs, 760-323-8297; www.palmsprings.com/history

The historical society is composed of two 19th-century buildings that exhibit artifacts from early Palm Springs. McCallum Adobe (circa 1885) is the oldest building in the city and it houses an extensive collection of photographs, paintings, clothes, tools, books and Native American wares. The Cornelia White House (circa 1893) was partially constructed of rail ties from the defunct Palmdale Railway and is furnished with authentic antiques.

Mid-October-late May, Wednesday, Sunday noon-3 p.m., Thursday-Saturday 10 a.m.-4 p.m.

TAHQUITZ CREEK GOLF RESORT

1885 Golf Club Drive, Palm Springs, 760-328-1005; www.tahquitzgolfresort.com

The club features two 18-hole courses: the Legend course and the Resort course. The Legend course has a traditional layout, with tree-lined fairways and

The resort city of Palm Springs is a golfer's dream destination, but the **The PGA West Stadium Course** (*55-955 PGA Blvd., La Quinta, 800-742-9378, 760-564-7111; www.pgawest.com*) stands out from the crowd and should not be missed. Regarded as one of the toughest courses to play, PGA West has hosted the Bob Hope Classic and the PGA Grand Slam of Golf. With five sets of tees, architect Pete Dye designed the course for players of all levels—however, high handicappers should be forewarned that their skills will be tested here. There are water hazards on nine holes and massive bunkers everywhere, so there is little margin for error. The course has generous landing areas and large, undulating greens. Inspired by the Scottish seaside courses, its design is rugged and dramatic.

40 bunkers, but was designed with severely sloped greens from back to front. The Resort course is a desert links-style layout, with rolling terrain, strategically placed sand and eye-catching mountain views.

WHERE TO STAY

PALM DESERT

★★★DESERT SPRINGS JW MARRIOTT RESORT & SPA

74855 Country Club Drive, Palm Desert, 760-341-2211, 800-255-0848; www.desertspringsresort.com

The policy here is the bigger the better, as the largest resort and convention complex in the southwestern United States. The guest rooms and suites are located in wings surrounding swimming pools, lakes, verdant fairways, lush English gardens and manicured lawns. Spacious guest rooms have luxury beds, and granite, limestone and Italian marble bathrooms with separate tubs and showers. Two Ted Robinson championship golf courses provide a total of 36 rounds of golf, plus there are tennis courts (hard, clay and grass), basketball courts, a European spa, and lawn croquet. It's almost too much to take in at once. Did we mention the gondola rides from the lobby?

884 rooms. Restaurant, bars. Business center. Fitness center. Spa. $251-350

PALM SPRINGS

★★★COLONY PALMS HOTEL

572 N. Indian Canyon Drive, Palm Springs, 800-557-2187; www.colonypalmshotel.com

Some hotels rely on marketing to conjure up images of good times and suave guests, but the Colony Palms Hotel only needs to look to its history. Open since the 1930s, the Colony Palms has enjoyed several lifetimes of good, but not always clean, fun (it once included a brothel). Today's guests can expect laid-back luxury in this newly renovated hotel where Turkish suzani headboards and a Morocco-inspired spa provide a sexy international vibe. The poolside Purple Palm Restaurant & Bar is the place to be if you're into delicious Mediterranean fare. Beds feature Italian linens and down duvets, to ensure that the nap that'll inevitably follow the food coma is a good one.

71 rooms. Restaurant, bar. Fitness center. Pool. Spa. $351 and up

★★★DORAL DESERT PRINCESS RESORT

67-967 Vista Chino, Cathedral City, 760-322-7000, 888-386-4677; www.doralpalmsprings.com

The panoramic mountain views from this sprawling resort set the mood for a true California golf weekend. All of the comfortable guest rooms are spacious enough, but should you choose to bunk with your golf buddies, suites have an extra bedroom, dining room, wet bar and wraparound balconies to take in the above-mentioned view. You can also squeeze in games of golf right here on the resort's PGA-rated 27-hole golf course. Work out knots afterward at the spa—or if you're not already sore enough, squeeze in a game of tennis. Feast on hearty portions of herb roasted chicken or "carb friendly" pasta alfredo at the Fairway Café, which specializes in California cuisine and also offers lovely views of the San Jacinto Mountains.

285 rooms. Restaurant, bar. Fitness center. Spa. Pets accepted. Golf. $61-150

★★★HILTON PALM SPRINGS RESORT

400 E. Tahquitz Canyon Way, Palm Springs, 760-320-6868, 800-522-6900;
www.hiltonpalmsprings.com

From its dramatic setting at the foot of the steeply rising San Jacinto Mountains to the grand rooms with Italian travertine flooring, contemporary furnishings and cozy sitting areas, this is a popular resort for business travelers and vacationing families. It's less than two miles from the airport and within walking distance of cafés, galleries, boutiques, a casino and the Palm Springs Desert Museum.

261 rooms. Restaurant, bar. Business center. Fitness center. Pool. Spa. Pets accepted. $61-150

★★★HYATT REGENCY SUITES PALM SPRINGS

285 N. Palm Canyon Drive, Palm Springs, 760-322-9000, 800-223-1234;
www.palmsprings.hyatt.com

This Hyatt hotel is set in a prime downtown location overlooking the San Jacinto Mountains. Guest rooms feature separate sitting areas with pull-out sofas and dining tables, and furnished balconies give way to views of the mountains, pool or city. There are plenty of onsite activities, including jogging paths, bicycle trails, a heated pool and putting green. The hotel's restaurant, the Palm Court Café, is in the center of the six-story atrium and serves eclectic California cuisine in a casual setting.

194 suites. Restaurant, bar. Business center. Fitness center. Pool. Spa. $151-250

★★★INGLESIDE INN

200 W. Ramon Road, Palm Springs, 760-325-0046, 800-772-6655; www.inglesideinn.com

Everyone from Rita Hayworth to Arnold Schwarzenegger has stayed at this quiet inn fashioned from an early-1900s estate. Today it's a throwback to 1920s Hollywood with individually-decorated suites and villas with old world décor and modern amenities like steam baths and whirlpool tubs. Melvyn's Restaurant is perfect for those who don't like to fuss: For a flat $70 a day, you can eat all your meals in the restaurant or in your room. The Casablanca Room is an intimate piano bar.

30 rooms. Restaurant, bar. Pool. $151-250

★★★RANCHO LAS PALMAS RESORT AND SPA

41-000 Bob Hope Drive, Rancho Mirage, 760-568-2727, 866-423-1195;
www.rancholaspalmas.com

This family-friendly hotel is in the heart of Rancho Mirage on 240 acres surrounded by mountains, lakes and gardens. Activities include a Ted Robinson-designed golf course, a 25-court tennis center, a 100-foot water slide and a 20,000-square-foot European spa. The warm and bright Spanish-style guest rooms feature plush bedding and French doors that open up to furnished patios or balconies overlooking the breezy flower-filled grounds.

466 rooms. Restaurant, bar. Fitness center. Pool. Spa. $151-250

★★★SPA RESORT CASINO

401 E. Amado Road, Palm Springs, 888-999-1995, 800-854-1279; www.sparesortcasino.com

The rooms here are less luxurious than those found in other hotels in the area. But if your idea of the perfect vacation is golf by day and blackjack by night, you've found a place to rest your head. This is the only full-service resort/

casino in Palm Springs, and has more than 1,000 slots and 30 tables (plus a private room for serious betters) to try your luck. The resort also has all the dining options of a typical casino: two Asian restaurants, a New York-style deli, a large buffet-style restaurant and several bars. Plus, you are just a block from Palm Canyon Drive where there are numerous shopping and dining options.

228 rooms. Restaurant, bar. Spa. Casino. $61-150

★★★VICEROY PALM SPRINGS
415 S. Belardo Road, Palm Springs, 760-320-4117, 800-670-6184; www.viceroypalmsprings.com

Built in 1929 and updated by designer Kelly Wearstler to reflect the Hollywood Regency style popular during the city's original glamour era, this boutique hotel located in the historic district is a great way to spoil yourself on a golf weekend with your spouse. Luxurious rooms, suites and villas, which look like they jumped out of the pages of a magazine, are surrounded by gorgeous gardens and are outfitted with Italian linens, custom beds and all the fun accessories: speaker phones, LCD televisions and mini-refrigerators stocked with gourmet snacks. Villas have private patios and full kitchens. The full-service spa will make you feel pampered with its specialty outdoor treatments. Mani/ pedis and massages are delivered poolside in cabanas. Gourmet restaurant Citron dishes up delicious California cuisine in a bright, outdoorsy setting with lemon yellow walls and white, marble-tiled floors.

68 rooms. Restaurant, bar. Pets accepted. $151-250

★★★THE VILLA ROYALE INN
1620 S. Indian Trail, Palm Springs, 760-327-2314, 800-245-2314; www.villaroyale.com

Just a mile from downtown, this hotel combines the pampered privacy of a bed and breakfast with the amenities of a full-service hotel. Individually appointed Mediterranean-style suites and villas nestled amid tranquil, lushly landscaped courtyards and two heated pools are decorated with European antiques and feature down duvets, luxurious robes and herbal bath products. Larger rooms also have fireplaces, open-beam ceilings, kitchens and private patios. The intimate restaurant, Europa, serves award-winning continental cuisine under the stars.

30 rooms. Restaurant, bar. Complimentary breakfast. Pool. $151-250

★★★THE WESTIN MISSION HILLS RESORT AND SPA
71333 Dinah Shore Drive, Rancho Mirage; www.westin.com/missionhills

Set on 360 acres surrounded by mountains, palm trees and lush landscaping, there's almost no need to leave the resort. Activities are plentiful, with two championship golf courses, three swimming pools—one with a 60-foot water slide—a 14,000-square-foot spa with a state-of-the-art fitness center and seven lighted tennis courts. Handsome guest rooms have private patios and sitting areas with a couch and coffee table.

472 rooms. Restaurant, bar. Fitness center. Pool. Pets accepted. $251-350

★★★THE WILLOWS HISTORIC PALM SPRINGS INN
412 W. Tahquitz Canyon Way, Palm Springs, 760-320-0771; www.thewillowspalmsprings.com

Built in 1924, this legendary Mediterranean villa in the heart of Old Palm

Springs has hosted everyone from Marion Davies to Albert Einstein, and is a great choice if you're looking for something small and intimate. The inn has only eight guest rooms, each with its own style, from the slate flooring in the Rock Room to the coffered ceiling in the Library, where Clark Gable and Carole Lombard spent their honeymoon.

8 rooms. Pool. $251-350

INDIAN WELLS

★★★HYATT GRAND CHAMPIONS RESORT AND SPA
44-600 Indian Wells Lane, Indian Wells, 760-341-1000, 800-554-9288; www.grandchampions.hyatt.com

This classic California Palm Desert resort has luxury accommodations with furnished balconies and marble baths with separate tubs and showers. Duffers will enjoy the 36 holes of the Golf Resort at Indian Wells, which surrounds the hotel. The sprawling resort also includes a 30,000-square-foot spa, seven pools, an espresso bar and a café offering light fare.

530 rooms. Restaurant, bar. Business center. Fitness center. Pool. Pets accepted. Golf. Tennis. $251-350

★★★INDIAN WELLS RESORT HOTEL
76661 Highway 111, Indian Wells, 760-345-6466, 800-248-3220; www.indianwellsresort.com

This European boutique-style hotel surrounded by the Indian Wells Golf Course features spacious accommodations and personalized service and is close to top shopping and recreation. The pool overlooks the golf course.

155 rooms. Restaurant, bar. Complimentary breakfast. Fitness center. Pool. Golf. Tennis. $151-250

★★★MIRAMONTE RESORT AND SPA
45-000 Indian Wells Lane, Indian Wells, 760-341-2200, 800-237-2926; www.miramonteresort.com

Just 15 minutes from Palm Springs, this charming resort is nestled at the base of the Santa Rosa Mountains. The lovely grounds are dotted with courtyards and manicured rose gardens. Order lunch from the restaurant and someone will hop on a bike and deliver it to your room or wherever you are. Three golf courses surround the property and there's a superb spa for pampering.

215 rooms. Restaurant. Fitness center. Tennis. Pool. Business center. $251-350

★★★RENAISSANCE ESMERALDA RESORT
44-400 Indian Wells Lane, Indian Wells, 760-773-4444; www.renaissanceesmeralda.com

This luxurious resort has a full-service spa, championship golf, tennis, plus a camp for kids with arts and crafts activities, swimming and poolside play. Each of the cheerful and contemporary rooms has a private balcony, with a view of the surrounding mountains, golf courses and desert.

560 rooms. Restaurant, bar. Business center. Fitness center. Pool. Golf. Tennis. $151-250

WHERE TO EAT

INDIAN WELLS
★★★LE SAINT GERMAIN
74-985 Highway 111, Indian Wells, 760-773-6511; www.lestgermain.com

This is a charming and elegant restaurant where classic French and California flavors fuse to create an eclectic dining experience. Dine on roasted chicken with lemon and honey au jus, or grilled Black Angus beef with a Roquefort crust. There's also an extensive wine list.

French, Mediterranean. Dinner. Closed Sunday, June-August. $36-85

PALM DESERT
★★CUISTOT

72-595 El Paseo, Palm Desert, 760-340-1000;
www.cuistotrestaurant.com

Chef/owner Bernard Dervieux serves up inventive dishes inspired by his upbringing in France. Look for quail stuffed with sweetbreads with black rice and Chablis sauce, or skillet-roasted veal chop with mushrooms, roasted garlic and fresh thyme. The restaurant is reminiscent of a French farmhouse, with beamed cathedral ceilings, a large stone fireplace and candlelight.

French. Lunch, dinner. Closed Monday. $36-85

★★★JILLIAN'S

74-155 El Paseo, Palm Desert, 760-776-8242; www.jilliansfinedining.com

Housed in a 1948 hacienda, this restaurant features a beautiful garden through which guests pass to reach the dining area, where tables are set with fresh flowers and candles. Selections from the lengthy and impressive wine list perfectly accompany the eclectic menu, which includes creations like prime boneless short ribs braised in California cabernet and rack of Colorado lamb with a Dijon herb crust. Featured desserts, like chocolate brioche pudding and blueberry cheesecake, are made daily.

International. Dinner. Closed Sunday and mid-October-mid-June. Reservations recommended. $36-85

★★★RISTORANTE MAMMA GINA

73-705 El Paseo, Palm Desert, 760-568-9898; www.mammagina.com

This sister restaurant to one in Florence carries on the decades-old tradition of serving freshly prepared, traditional Tuscan fare. Pappa al pomodoro (authentic Florentine-style thick tomato bread soup), spaghetti alla Bolognese and risotto Mamma Gina (arborio rice with imported wild porcini mushroom sauce) are a few dishes on the menu that keep customers coming back. An award-winning wine list and a number of decadent desserts add to the authentic Tuscan experience.

Italian. Dinner. $36-86

★★★RUTH'S CHRIS STEAK HOUSE

74-740 Highway 111, Palm Desert, 760-779-1998; www.ruthschris.com

Born from a single New Orleans restaurant that Ruth Fertel bought in 1965 for $22,000, the chain is a favorite among steak lovers. Aged prime Midwestern beef is broiled at 1,800 degrees and served on a heated plate sizzling with butter and with sides like creamed spinach and au gratin potatoes.

Steak. Dinner. $36-86

★★★TUSCANY

74855 Country Club Drive, Palm Desert, 760-341-2211;
www.desertspringsresort.com

One of the many restaurants in the JW Marriott Desert Springs Resort and

Spa, this eatery has a seasonal menu that features dishes like ravioli stuffed with fresh Maine lobster, minestrone with pesto and housemade tiramisu. The mile-long wine list is comprehensive and has bottles from around the world. Soft music and frescoes add to the authentic vibe.

Italian. Dinner. $36-86

PALM SPRINGS

★★★EUROPA
1620 Indian Trail, Palm Springs, 760-327-2314; www.villaroyale.com

Housed in the Villa Royale Inn, this restaurant is beloved by locals for its delightful continental cuisine, inspired by the sun-basked countries of Southern Europe, and strong wine list. Dine on duck confit or osso bucco poolside by the fountains or enjoy a bottle of wine fireside in the cozy dining room.

Continental. Dinner. Closed Monday. Bar. $36-85

★★★LE VALLAURIS
385 W. Tahquitz Canyon Way, Palm Springs, 760-325-5059; www.levallauris.com

Housed in a 1924 home with Louis XV furniture, rich tapestries and an enchanting tree-shaded garden surrounded by flowers, Le Vallauris transports you to the French countryside. Daily selections—from rack of lamb to Grand Marnier soufflé—are written on a board brought to the table. The impressive wine list includes bottles from France and California as well as Italy, New Zealand and Spain.

French. Lunch, dinner. Closed July-August. Bar. $36-85

★★★MELVYN'S
200 W. Ramon Road, Palm Springs, 760-325-0046; www.inglesideinn.com

Located in the Ingleside Inn, this classic steakhouse is a long-standing Palm Springs tradition. Start with drinks at the fully restored carved oak and mahogany bar before sitting down to select from the extensive American menu that features a variety of beef, seafood, pasta and poultry dishes. Wine aficionados will especially appreciate Melvyn's two well-stocked wine cellars.

Continental. Lunch (Monday-Friday), dinner, Saturday-Sunday brunch. Reservations recommended. Bar. $36-85

★★★SAMMY G'S TUSCAN GRILL
265 S. Palm Canyon Drive, Palm Springs, 760-320-8041; www.sammygsrestaurant.com

Located in the heart of downtown Palm Springs, Sammy G's features a variety of Italian dishes from pastas to chicken, seafood and meats. They include housemade pastas and risottos such as gnocchi with either a tomato basil sauce, a four-cheese sauce or pesto; lasagna Bolognese; and risotto with shrimp and a tomato-cream sauce. Enjoy live music Thursday through Saturday evenings.

Italian. Dinner. Closed Monday. Bar. $36-85

SPA

★★★THE WELL SPA AT MIRAMONTE RESORT
45000 Indian Wells Lane, Indian Wells, 760-341-2200; www.miramonteresort.com

This Tuscan-inspired jewel will awaken your senses with a setting that is distinctive and tranquil. Outdoor and indoor treatment rooms are available to ensure the ultimate spa experience. Services incorporate therapeutic mud, wine extracts, pure essential oils and refreshing waters. A fitness center with an array of classes, full-service salon, spa boutique and smoothie bar round out the relaxing experience.

JOSHUA TREE NATIONAL PARK

Covering more than 1,236 square miles, this park preserves a section of the Mojave and Colorado deserts that is rich in vegetation. The park shelters many species of desert plants. The Joshua tree, which gives the park its name, was named by the Mormons for its upstretched "arms" reaching for heaven. A member of the lily family, this giant yucca attains heights of more than 40 feet. The area consists of a series of block mountains ranging in altitude from 1,000-5,800 feet and separated by desert flats. The summer gets very hot and in the winter, the temperature drops below freezing. Water is available only at the Black Rock Canyon Visitor Center/Campground, Cottonwood Campground, the Indian Cove Ranger Station and the Twenty-nine Palms Visitor Center. Pets are permitted on leash only and not on trails. Take one of the guided tours and campfire programs. Picnicking is permitted in designated areas and campgrounds, but no fires may be built outside the campgrounds.

WHAT TO SEE

JOSHUA TREE'S UPRISING ADVENTURE GUIDES
Joshua Tree, 760-366-3799, 888-254-6266; www.uprising.com

This outdoor rock-climbing gym offers training and climbing for all ages. Night climbing is also available.

HIDDEN VALLEY NATURE TRAIL
74485 National Park Drive, Joshua Tree National Park, 760-367-5500; www.nps.gov/jotr

This trail is a one-mile loop. Access it from the picnic area across Hidden Valley Campground. The valley is enclosed by a wall of rocks.

KEYS VIEW
74485 National Park Drive, Joshua Tree National Park, 760-367-5500; www.nps.gov/jotr

Here you'll get a sweeping view of the Coachella valley, desert and mountain. A paved path leads off the main road.

LOST PALMS CANYON
74485 National Park Drive, Joshua Tree National Park, 760-367-5500; www.nps.gov/jotr

This eight-mile round-trip hike is reachable by four-mile trail from Cottonwood Spring. It shelters the largest group of palms (120) in the park.
Daily sunrise-sunset.

OASIS VISITOR CENTER
74485 National Park Drive, Joshua Tree National Park, 760-367-5500; www.nps.gov/jotr

At this visitors' center, you'll find exhibits and a self-guided nature trail through the Oasis of Mara, discovered by a government survey party in 1855.
Daily.

DEATH VALLEY NATIONAL PARK

Scorching heat, frigid cold, the driest atmosphere you can imagine. The 49ers would have never dreamed that this would someday be a tourist destination. But that's exactly what this inhospitable, 5,200 square miles of rugged desert, peaks and depressions officially became when President Herbert Hoover designated it a national monument in 1933. Located approximately 300 miles northeast of Los Angeles, Death Valley was so named for a party of gold hunters who took a shortcut through here and many of them perished. The discovery and subsequent mining of borax, hauled out by the famous 20-mule teams, kept tourists away until the mid-1920s.

The park is one vast geological museum. Millions of years ago, this was part of the Pacific Ocean. Violent uplifts of the earth occurred, creating mountain ranges and draining water to the west. Today, 200 square miles of the valley are at or below sea level. The lowest point on the continent (282 feet below sea level) can be found here. Telescope Peak, at 11,049 feet, towers directly above it. The average rainfall is less than two inches a year. The climate is pleasant from October to May, but it's very hot in summer—a maximum temperature of 134° F has been recorded.

Venturing off paved roads in this area in the summer can be dangerous. Carefully obey all National Park Service signs and regulations and make sure that your vehicle has plenty of gas and oil. Carry water when you explore this park, especially in hot weather.

WHAT TO SEE

20-MULE-TEAM CANYON
Lone Pine, 760-786-2331; www.nps.gov/deva
Named for the 20 mule teams that carried loads of borax out of the desert, this canyon is viewed from an unpaved, twisting road that leads you past some of the best scenery in the park.

ARTIST'S PALETTE
Death Valley National Park, 760-786-2331; www.nps.gov/deva
This is one of the most spectacular sights in Death Valley National Park. Artist's Drive, a nine-mile loop, leads you (on a narrow, topsy-turvy road) past a kaleidoscope of colors from all the volcanic deposits.

DANTE'S VIEW
Death Valley National Park, 760-786-2331; www.nps.gov/deva
The view from this lookout located at 5,000 feet is mind-boggling. That small black dot way down below? That would be Badwater Basin, which is 282 miles below sea level, the lowest spot in the Western Hemisphere.

DEVIL'S GOLF COURSE
Death Valley National Park, 760-786-2331; www.nps.gov/deva
It was said that only the devil could play golf on this terrain, thanks to the vast beds of rugged salt crystals that make up the surface.

GOLDEN CANYON
Death Valley National Park, 760-786-2331; www.nps.gov/deva

A one-mile trail provides access to the canyon, which displays a range of colors from deep red to rich gold.

RHYOLITE GHOST TOWN
Death Valley National Park, 760-786-2331; www.nps.gov/deva

Once the largest mining town in Death Valley in the early 1900s, by 1911, it was a ghost town. One structure still left standing from that era is the "bottle house," constructed of beer and liquor bottles.

SCOTTY'S CASTLE
Death Valley National Park, 760-786-2331; www.nps.gov/deva

This desert mansion from the early 1920s was designed as both a work of art and a winter home for Chicago millionaire Albert Johnson, and is one of the most popular tourist attractions in the park. The furnishings are typical of the period and many were specially designed and handcrafted for this house. Costumed interpreters lead living history tours.

Daily 9 a.m.-6 p.m.

TELESCOPE PEAK
Death Valley National Park, 760-786-2331; www.nps.gov/deva

You'll have to hoof it to reach the highest peak in the Panamint Range—it's a 3,000-foot-climb to the 11,049-foot summit and a 14-mile round trip.

UBEHEBE CRATER
Death Valley National Park, 760-786-2331; www.nps.gov/deva

A volcanic steam explosion left this colorful crater.

ZABRISKIE POINT
Death Valley National Park, 760-786-2331; www.nps.gov/deva

Catch one of the most scenic views here, especially at sunrise or sunset, when the multicolor hills are bathed in natural light.

WHERE TO STAY

ALSO RECOMMENDED
FURNACE CREEK RESORT
Hwy. 190 S. Death Valley, 760-786-2345;
www.furnacecreekresort.com

Furnace Creek is two resorts: the Inn and the Ranch, which was a working range in the 1880s and where the famous twenty mules teams stayed. The resort is home to the world's lowest golf course (at at 214 feet below sea level), shops, tennis courst, four restaurants, and much more. Activities range from horseback riding to children's activities to bike rentals. The Wrangler Steakhouse is a great spot for dinner.

290 rooms. Restaurant, bar. Golf. Pool.

ORANGE COUNTY

Orange County is so much more than a mass of suburbs. The area has wide, beautiful beaches and charming coastal towns with gorgeous harbors (Newport), art galleries (Laguna) and tree-lined coves shading beautiful yachts (Dana Point). You could definitely spend an idyllic vacation here, especially considering that the area is also home to luxurious resorts—several Forbes Five or Four Star resorts are located here. These resorts have top-notch spas and restaurants, making a stay here relaxing and pampering.

Catalina Island is also in Orange County and it's a place that locals and tourists both love. Catalina doesn't have the white sand and blue-green water of typical island vacation spots, but it has a charm of its own. The island's landscape is identical to the mainland, with the dry, chaparral topography that characterizes most of Southern California. You'll see more craggy cliffs and shores than wide-open beaches, and the water is a deep navy blue where it meets the island's edge. So while it may not be a sunbathing mecca, Catalina's warm, clear water (with temperatures in the mid to high 60s) and scenery make it ideal for kayaking, windsurfing, scuba diving and snorkeling. The island's hilly landscape also provides excellent terrain for hiking, bicycling and horseback riding. The quaint town of Avalon is home to the charming Inn on Mt. Ada, the former colonial-style home of chewing gum magnate William Wrigley, Jr.

Of course, Orange County is also known for major attractions such as Disneyland and Knott's Berry Farm. Sure, there are Disney attractions in Orlando, Paris and even Japan. But the Anaheim location is the original Disney theme park. If you have time, you can also hop over to Disney's California Adventure, a theme park that specializes in more intense rides and is the new host to Disney's Electrical Parade, a nighttime event that showcases light-bulb-encrusted Disney floats. Knott's Berry Farm is another fun diversion for the family with rides and games.

If business is bringing you to Orange County, you may very well be headed to Irving, the area's business hub. It is also home to the University of California, Irvine.

Whatever brings you to Orange County, be sure to make a stop at Richard Nixon's former home and library in nearby Yorba Linda. The museum includes a gallery related to the Watergate Scandal. Many visitors also head to San Juan Capistrano to see the Mission San Juan Capistrano, which was founded in 1776.

ANAHEIM

Once part of a Spanish land grant, Anaheim was bought and settled by German colonists as a place to tend vineyards and make wine. The town's name reflects its dual heritage: "Ana" is derived from the nearby Santa Ana River, while "heim" is from the German word for "home." Today, the area's best-known settlers include Mickey, Minnie, Donald and Goofy and all the other loveable residents of Anaheim's Disneyland.

WHAT TO SEE

DISNEYLAND
1313 S. Disneyland Drive, Anaheim, 714-781-4565; disneyland.disney.go.com

If you're traveling with kids (or you just still dream of being whisked away by

HIGHLIGHT

WHAT ARE THE TOP THINGS TO DO IN ORANGE COUNTY?

VISIT AVALON

This charming town located on Catalina Island is the perfect escape whether it's for a weekend or an afternoon. You can walk around the tiny town in less than an hour and it's filled with cute seafood places and quirky little shops.

STROLL THROUGH DOWNTOWN LAGUNA

If you love art, you'll want to stop and peruse all the charming little galleries that fill the downtown Laguna area. The best way to see them is on a Friday night when they all throw open their doors and host free wine and cheese receptions.

SHOP FASHION ISLAND

This is one of Southern California's best malls. The outdoor mall is anchored by Neiman's and Saks and has more than 150 stores.

SPEND AN AFTERNOON ON BALBOA ISLAND

Residents live on this island, which you can get to via ferry from the pier off Newport Lane. The town is famous for it's cute shops and most of all, chocolate covered frozen bananas, a Balboa treat.

GO TO DISNEY

What's a trip to Southern California without visiting the Happiest Place on Earth. Disney is a must on your travel itinerary if you have kids—or even if you don't. The park is divided into seven lands, each packed with fun-filled rides, games and, of course, your favorite characters.

Prince Charming or secretly wish you could abandon your career and become a pirate), don't bypass the Happiest Place on Earth. Sure, there are Disney attractions in Orlando, Paris and even Japan. But the Anaheim location is the original Disney theme park. The park is divided into various "lands," including Fantasyland, Tomorrowland, Adventureland and Frontierland. The candy-colored Fantasyland gives you the classic Disney experience with Sleeping Beauty's Castle, the Mad Hatter's Tea Cups and the pleasant Dumbo ride. Take a spin on the ride that inspired Johnny Depp's blockbuster film trilogy, *Pirates of the Caribbean*. The ride has been updated to feature elements of the pirate movies. The boat is part musical show and part water ride as it shimmies along a shallow waterway while pirate robots sing those familiar chanties. After the ride, grab lunch at the Blue Bayou (714-781-3463), a Creole-style restaurant bedecked with rainbow lanterns and housed inside the Pirates ride. Then head to the Haunted House, a surprisingly spooky and surreal display of ghost-story horror that is a welcome break from Disney's signature smiles and songs. The theme park glitters after dark. The "Main Street" portion of the park is particularly wondrous when the white lights turn on, and the Castle glows in pink and blue lights.

Admission: adults $69, children 3-9 $59, children under 3 free. Monday-Thursday 10 a.m.-8 p.m., Friday-Sunday 8 a.m.-midnight. Hours vary for holidays or special events.

DISNEY'S CALIFORNIA ADVENTURE

1313 S. Harbor Blvd., Anaheim, 714-781-4565; disneyland.disney.go.com

California Adventure may be Disneyland's smaller, younger sibling, but that doesn't mean you should overlook it. Located a hop, skip and a jump from Disneyland Park, California Adventure specializes in more intense rides. You'll feel like you're rafting down an actual California river on Grizzly River Run, get a simulated bird's-eye view of the California landscape on Soarin' Over California, and get jostled around on mini-roller coaster Mulholland Madness. If you're really feeling brave, get in line for The Twilight Zone Tower of Terror, where you'll free-fall 13 stories in the fictional Hollywood Tower Hotel. The park is also the new host to the Main Street Electrical Parade, a nighttime event that showcases light bulb-encrusted Disney floats.

Admission: adults $69, children 3-9 $59, children under 3 free. Monday-Friday 10 a.m.-6 p.m., Saturday-Sunday 10 a.m.-8 p.m. Hours vary for holidays and special events.

WHERE TO STAY

★★★DISNEY'S GRAND CALIFORNIAN

1600 S. Disneyland Drive, Anaheim, 714-956-6425, 800-207-6900; disneyland.disney.go.com

Conveniently situated between Disney's California Adventure theme park and the vibrant Downtown Disney entertainment complex, this giant alpine lodge is designed in an early-20th-century Arts and Crafts style. The Napa Rose, a gourmet restaurant with an extensive list of California wines, is a lovely place to dine after a day in the park.

751 rooms. Restaurant, bar. Business center. Fitness center. Pool. $151-250

★★★HILTON SUITES ANAHEIM/ORANGE

400 N. State College Blvd., Orange, 714-938-1111; www.anaheimsuites.hilton.com

Located on the border of Anaheim and Orange, this comfortable property is within walking distance of Angel Stadium and minutes from Disneyland. Rooms feature plush beds and spacious bathrooms with separate tubs and Crabtree & Evelyn products. An indoor and outdoor pool, whirlpool, sundeck and dry sauna help guests relax.

230 rooms. Complimentary breakfast. Restaurant, bar. Business center. Fitness center. Pool. Tennis. Golf. $151-250

★★★HYATT REGENCY ORANGE COUNTY

11999 Harbor Blvd., Garden Grove, 714-750-1234, 800-233-1234; www.hyatt.com

Business and leisure clientele mingle at this hotel, brushing up their golf swings on the adjacent driving range, dipping in the rooftop pool or sipping drinks beneath the soaring 17-story atrium. Suites offer convenience and comfort. Knott's Berry Farm, Crystal Cathedral and the Discovery Science Center are among the top attractions within a 10-mile radius; popular Southern California beaches are a short drive away. There's also a complimentary shuttle to the Anaheim Convention Center and Disneyland Resort.

654 rooms. Restaurant, bar. Business center. Fitness center. Tennis. Pool. $151-250

★★★SHERATON ANAHEIM HOTEL

900 S. Disneyland Drive, Anaheim, 714-778-1700, 325-3535; www.sheraton.com

This English manor-style lodge may seem misplaced so close to Disneyland, but its grand rotunda, stone fireplace and koi pond, which runs through the lobby to the outside rose garden, makes it the perfect post-theme-park refuge.

489 rooms. Restaurant, bar. Pets accepted. $151-250

★★★SHERATON CERRITOS HOTEL

12725 Center Court Drive, Cerritos, 562-809-1500, 800-598-1753; www.sheraton.com

This hotel is among the Towne Center shops and is adjacent to the Cerritos Center for Performing Arts. Many corporate offices (Siemens, Yamaha) are nearby, making this hotel a convenient choice for business travelers. The elegant, contemporary guest rooms and suites have large windows (some with park views), dark wood furniture, comfortable chairs and ottomans, large work desks and ergonomic chairs. The onsite restaurant, Grille 91, offers a California menu in a casual, bistro-style setting.

203 rooms. Restaurant, bar. Business center. Fitness center. Pool. $151-250

WHERE TO EAT

★★★ANAHEIM WHITE HOUSE

887 S. Anaheim Blvd., Anaheim, 714-772-1381; www.anaheimwhitehouse.com

Many celebrities have visited this converted 1909 Victorian-style mansion. Twelve intimate dining rooms bring back Hollywood glamour with fabric-draped ceilings. A roaring fireplace warms the Reagan Room, while those who prefer a porch setting can reserve a table in the Nixon Room. The wine list includes more than 200 selections. Free shuttle service is offered to and from area hotels.

French, Italian. Lunch, dinner. $36-85

HIGHLIGHT

RICHARD NIXON LIBRARY AND BIRTHPLACE

18001 Yorba Linda Blvd., Yorba Linda, 714-993-5075; www.nixonfoundation.org

This tribute to Richard Nixon includes a gallery devoted to the Watergate scandal, a World Leaders section showcasing priceless gifts the Nixons received from governments around the world, the restored farmhouse in which Nixon was born in 1913 and the memorial burial sites of both the president and his wife. The library and birthplace both provide a fascinating look into the life of the 37th president. Did you know that the home in which Nixon was born was built by his father using a catalog kit? Nixon wrote that he was very happy in this home, and that it was full of love. It's these sort of interesting facts that reveal another side to this very multi-faceted man. The tour of the museum itself begins with a short film titled "Never Give Up: Richard Nixon in the Arena" and takes visitors on the Road to the Presidency. The site is just 15 minutes from Disneyland.

Admission: adults $9.95, seniors $6.95, children 7-11 $3.75, children 6 and under free. Monday-Saturday 10 a.m.-5 p.m., Sunday 11a.m.-5 p.m.

★★★THE CELLAR

305 N. Harbor Blvd., Fullerton, 714-525-5682; www.cellardining.com

The path to this restaurant—literally a cellar underneath Villa del Sol (the old California Hotel)—is down a set of dimly lit stairs. Once there, visitors are transported to what feels like an old European restaurant. The cave-like walls are decorated with wine casks and lanterns. The French cuisine includes roasted pheasant and filet of ostrich.

French. Dinner. Closed Sunday-Monday. $36-85

★★★SUMMIT HOUSE RESTAURANT

2000 E. Bastanchury Road, Fullerton, 714-671-4111; www.summithouse.net

This cozy, friendly inn is on the hilltop of Vista Park, offering one of the best views in Orange County while diners dig into filet mignon or Colorado lamb.

American. Lunch, dinner. $36-85

CATALINA ISLAND

Catalina Island is a favorite with locals for its quaint charm. The island thrived with unusual native plants and animals until the 16th century, when European explorers found the place. The land then suffered from the ensuing efforts at mining and raising livestock. But chewing gum magnate William Wrigley Jr. bought Catalina in the early 20th century and beautified it, making it the scenic spot it is today. Catalina doesn't have the white sand and blue-green water of typical island vacation spots, but it has a charm of its own. The island's landscape is identical to the mainland, with the dry, chaparral topography that character- izes most of Southern California. You'll see more craggy cliffs and shores than wide-open beaches, and the water is a deep navy blue where it meets the island's edge. So while it may not be a sunbathing mecca, Catalina's warm, clear water (with temperatures in the mid to high 60s) and scenery make it ideal for kayaking, windsurfing, scuba diving and snorkeling. The island's hilly landscape also provides excellent terrain for hiking, bicycling and horseback riding.

When you visit the 22-mile-long island, you'll hit up Avalon, its only city. Avalon's signature building is the Art Deco-inspired Catalina Casino (800-626-5440; www.visitcatalinaisland.com), which is not a gambling venue but a grand ballroom and theater. The large circular structure gives the island's harbor a distinctive resort air and adds elegance to Catalina's rustic surroundings.

William Wrigley, Jr. established a program of conservation on the island that still applies today. Tourism is its only industry, and scuba diving, kayaking, golf, tennis, horseback riding, swimming and hiking are all popular. Avalon, Catalina's quaint harbor town, offers sport fishing and is dotted with resorts. Daily air or boat service to the island is available year-round from Long Beach and San Pedro; boat service available from Newport Beach.

WHAT TO SEE

BUFFALO SAFARI
310-510-4205; www.visitcatalinaisland.com

While Avalon is the most populous section of the island, you may opt to go northwest of the city to Two Harbors for camping. Here, you can also go on a safari that takes you to the island's canyons in hopes of spotting some buffalo, which were originally placed on the island during 1920's film shoots, and have since been allowed to become permanent residents. A four-hour tour costs $99 while a two-hour tour costs $74. All this activity is sure to leave you hungry; stop by Armstrong's Fish Market and Seafood Restaurant (306-510-0113; www.armstrongseafood.com) for oysters, clams, mussels and other fresh seafood on the outdoor patio.

CATALINA TOURS AND TRIPS
150 Metropole Ave., Avalon, 310-510-2500

Two major companies offer tours of the island. Santa Catalina Island Company Discovery Tours (www.scico.com) has a variety of fun tours, including a GPS-led walking tour, underwater adventures (a boat cruises five feet underwater so you can see all of Catalina's marine life), a zip line tour and more. Catalina Adventure Tours (www.catalinaadventuretours.com) has been around for more than 20 years and offers semi-submersible beat rides, glass bottom boats, and walking tours led by guides who share the history of Catalina.

Prices vary. See websites for details.

WRIGLEY MEMORIAL AND BOTANICAL GARDEN
1400 Avalon Canyon Road, Avalon, 310-510-2595; www.catalinaconservancy.org

The memorial honors the memory of native William Wrigley Jr., who lived her for part of the year. He was passionate about the island and was instrumental in developing much of it, including these lovely botanical gardens, which include native trees, cacti, succulent plants and flowering shrubs on 37.85 acres. Self-guided tours are available.

Admission: adults $5, seniors $3, children free. Daily 8 a.m.-5 p.m.

WHERE TO STAY

★★★HOTEL METROPOLE

205 Crescent Ave., Avalon, 310-510-1884, 800-300-8528;
www.hotel-metropole.com

Only steps from the beach, this charming hotel features cottage-style guest rooms with a choice of ocean, mountain or courtyard views. Each room is different but all have a beach decor; VIP suites are very luxurious with plasma TVs and Jacuzzi tubs.

48 rooms. Complimentary breakfast. $251-350

★★★★THE INN ON MT. ADA

398 Wrigley Road, Avalon (Catalina Island), 310-510-2030,
800-608-7669; www.innonmtada.com

This colonial-style mansion, with its sparkling white exterior and hunter-green shutters, recalls the grand summer residences more often seen on the East Coast. It is the highest point on the island, and rests amid beautiful shrubbery and landscaping. Completed in 1921, the former home of chewing gum magnate William Wrigley, Jr. hosted important social gatherings during its heyday. Nowadays, you're the guest of honor in the cozy Inn's six guest rooms and suites, which feature ocean or harbor views (some rooms have fireplaces and others have terraces or decks). Floral-patterned wallpaper, bed coverings and window treatments lend a New England ambience, while high ceilings and large windows make the rooms feel spacious.

7 rooms. No children under 14. Complimentary breakfast and lunch. $351 and up

IRVINE

In the heart of Orange County, Irvine is the home of the University of California, Irvine, and several large corporations.

WHAT TO SEE

WILD RIVERS WATERPARK

8770 Irvine Center Drive, Irvine, 949-788-0808;
www.wildrivers.com

One of Southern California's biggest water parks (20 acres), Wild Rivers offers rides designed for children, teens and adults.

Mid-May-late September; hours vary.

SAN JUAN CAPISTRANO

26801 Ortega Highway, San Juan Capistrano, 949-234-1300; www.missionsjc.com
San Juan Capistrano developed around the Catholic mission for which it was named. Many of the buildings in town resemble the Spanish architecture of the church.

Founded by Fray Junipero Serra in 1776 and named for the crusader St. John of Capistrano, the church was built in the form of a cross and was one of the most beautiful of all California missions. A self-guided tour includes the Serra Chapel, which is one of the oldest buildings in California, the padres' living quarters and three museum rooms exhibiting artifacts from Native American and early Spanish cultures.
The mission is also famous for its swallows, which depart each year on St. John's Day (in October) and return on St. Joseph's Day (in March).
Admission: adults $9, seniors $8, children 4-11 $5, children 3 and under free. Daily 8:30 a.m.-5 p.m.

WHERE TO STAY

★★★HYATT REGENCY

17900 Jamboree Road, Irvine, 949-975-1234, 800-233-1234; www.irvine.hyatt.com

Centrally located to the business districts of Irvine and Newport, all rooms at this hotel feature luxury bedding and pillow-top mattresses. Opting for the business plan rooms will provide free breakfast and local calls and 24-hour access to copying, printing and business supplies, plus city mountain views and marble baths.

536 rooms. Restaurant, bar. Complimentary breakfast. Fitness center. Pool. $151-250

WHERE TO EAT

★★★RUTH'S CHRIS STEAK HOUSE

2961 Michelson Drive, Irvine, 949-252-8848; www.ruthschris.com

Born from a single New Orleans restaurant that Ruth Fertel bought in 1965 for $22,000, the chain is a favorite among steak lovers. Aged prime Midwestern beef is broiled and served on a heated plate sizzling with butter and with sides like creamed spinach and au gratin potatoes.

Steak. Dinner. $36-86

★★L'HIRONDELLE

31631 Camino Capistrano, San Juan Capistrano, 949-661-0425; www.lhirondellesjc.com

This charming restaurant located across from San Juan Capistrano Mission features a variety of salads and sandwiches for lunch, but you'll also find tasty alternatives such as fresh salmon scramble and the picnic plate, with fresh fruit, pate, chicken and cheese. Dinner offers roasted duck, herb crusted rack of lamb and fresh fish.

French. Lunch, dinner, Sunday brunch. $16-35

ORANGE COUNTY COASTAL TOWNS

Some of the most charming towns in Southern California are located in Orange County about one hour outside of Los Angeles along the Pacific Ocean. You will come across one after the other heading north to south: Newport Beach, Laguna and Dana Point. Newport Beach may be the most exclusive enclave. The Resort at Pelican Hill is in Newport Beach and many come here to play the Tom Fazio designed golf courses. Laguna Beach is more bohemian. Galleries and restaurants dot the beach and the atmosphere is very relaxed. Right past Laguna is Dana Point where along the coast you'll find the Ritz Carlton Laguna Niguel and a little inland, The St. Regis Monarch Beach.

WHAT TO SEE

NEWPORT BEACH
BALBOA ISLAND

www.balboaisland.com

This tiny, densely populated man-made island is one of Orange County's most popular attractions. You can drive onto the island via Jamboree Road or hop the ferry from Balboa Peninsula. The pretty island has some of the most expensive real estate in the country and the main street, Marine Avenue, is lined with boutiques, restaurants and ice cream shops selling the popular Balboa Bars, vanilla ice cream dipped in chocolate and then covered with nuts or candy, or the frozen chocolate bananas.

BALBOA FUN ZONE
600 E. Bay Ave., Newport Beach, 949-673-0408; www.thebalboafunzone.com
Go round and round on the Ferris wheel, hop on some rides, play video games or visit the arcade—it's all in a day's worth of fun at this amusement park surrounding the Balboa Pavilion.
Sunday-Thursday 11 a.m.-9 p.m., Friday-Saturday 11 a.m.-10 p.m.

CORONA DEL MAR
www.orangecounty.net
Newport Beach's stretch of Highway 1 is packed with restaurants, bars and boutiques, and also leads to one of the locals' favorite beaches, Corona del Mar, which is made up of two beaches: Little Corona and Big Corona. Colorful reefs make it an ideal spot for snorkelers. You'll also find volleyball courts, fire pits and food stands.

CRYSTAL COVE STATE PARK
www.crystalcovestatepark.com
Crystal Cove State Beach, between Corona del Mar and Laguna, attracts beachgoers who are looking for a more secluded area and is one of the loveliest beaches you'll see. You can access Crystal Cove beach from Highway 1 and parking costs $10 per day.

ORANGE COUNTY MUSEUM OF ARTS
850 San Clemente Drive, Newport Beach, 949-759-1122; www.ocma.net
The OCMA showcases modern and contemporary art, with an emphasis on Californian art since World War II.
Admission: adults $12, seniors and students $10, children under 13 free. Free second Sunday of the month. Wednesday, Friday-Sunday 11 a.m.-5 p.m., Thursday 11 a.m.-8 p.m.

LAGUNA BEACH
LAGUNA ART MUSEUM
307 Cliff Drive, Laguna Beach, 949-494-8971; www.lagunaartmuseum.org
Artists have flocked to Laguna since the 1800s for inspiration, and there remains no better place to see the fruits of their labor than the Laguna Art Museum. With perhaps the largest permanent collection of artwork by California artists and ever-changing exhibitions, this museum is a great option for those looking to experience Laguna's early days.
Daily 11 a.m.-5 p.m.

LAGUNA PLAYHOUSE
606 Laguna Canyon Road, Laguna Beach, 949-497-2787; www.lagunaplayhouse.com
The oldest running playhouse on the West Coast, this 1920s-era theater presents every kind of theatrical event imaginable, from dramas and comedies

SPECIAL EVENTS

CHRISTMAS BOAT PARADE

Newport Beach Harbor, Newport Blvd., Newport Beach, 949-729-4400;
www.christmasboatparade.com
Hundreds of yachts, boats, kayaks and canoes sail around the harbor decked out in
Christmas lights, and many go all out with holiday scenes, music and costumed carolers.
Mid-December.

TASTE OF NEWPORT

Newport Center Drive, Newport Beach, 949-729-4400; www.tasteofnewport.com
For three days, 75,000 people attend this festival to taste countless culinary creations
from some of the area's best-loved restaurants. In addition to pizza, tacos, gyros and ribs,
you'll find prime rib, crab cakes and sushi. The Sound Stage features live music throughout the festival. Sample wines from premium California wineries.
Mid-September.

to musicals and children's theater. Make time for a performance before or after
dinner and don't forget your swimsuit; the theater is just steps from the beach.
Main stage: Mid-July-June, Tuesday-Sunday.

REDFERN GALLERY AT MONTAGE RESORT

30801 S. Coast Highway, Laguna Beach, 949-715-6193; www.redferngallery.com
In addition to impeccable accommodations and spectacular views, the Montage
Resort also houses the Redfern Gallery, which features early California impres-
sionist painting. Here, you'll find the likes of Granville Redmond's *Patch of
Poppies*, a lovely painting that is reminiscent of Claude Monet's *The Poppy
Field, near Argenteuil.*

FESTIVAL OF ARTS AND PAGEANT OF THE MASTERS

650 Laguna Canyon Road, Laguna Beach, 949-494-1145, 800-487-3378;
www.foapom.com
Exhibits by 160 artists are highlighted in the festival.
Mid-July-August.

SAWDUST FINE ARTS AND CRAFTS FESTIVAL

935 Laguna Canyon Road, Laguna Beach, 949-494-3030; www.sawdustartfestival.org
More than 175 Laguna Beach artists create paintings, photographs, sculptures,
jewelry, ceramics, hand-blown glass and other works of art.
July-early September.

DANA POINT

DOHENY STATE BEACH

Del Obispo/Dana Harbor Drive (just south of Dana Point Marina), 914-496-6171;
www.dohenystate.beach
Surfers come for the waves—Doheny State Beach is regarded as one of Southern
California's premier surfing beaches—but it's fun in the sun for everyone at this

bustling, picture-perfect beach. Doheny is also known as a great camping site (with some spots right on the beach), and there are volleyball courts, a pier for fishing, tide pools, food stands and picnic areas.

Call ahead to reserve a camping spot, which can fill up months in advance.

WHERE TO STAY

NEWPORT BEACH
★★★BALBOA BAY CLUB & RESORT
1221 W. Coast Highway, Newport Beach, 888-445-7153; www.balboabayclub.com

Set on 15 waterfront acres, the rooms at this comfortable and whimsical resort feel like private bungalows with their furnished patios and plantation shutters. Sit back and watch the yachts in the bay, hit the spa or enjoy the numerous attractions nearby. The First Cabin Restaurant offers a seasonal menu of California cuisine in a cozy setting with panoramic views of the bay.

160 rooms. Restaurant, bar. Spa. Pets accepted. $251-350

★★★FAIRMONT NEWPORT BEACH
4500 MacArthur Blvd., Newport Beach, 949-476-2001, 800-810-3039; www.fairmont.com

This hotel's exterior replicates a Mayan temple with a stacked semi-pyramid design. While an ocean view doesn't come with the room rate here (the ocean is about eight miles away from the hotel), don't let this sway any plans to stay. The hotel recently completed a $32 million renovation and the result is a new high-end spa, a redesigned sky pool and luxurious new rooms with Egyptian cotton sheets and flat-screen TVs. And be sure to visit the pool, located next to the spa on the hotel's third floor, where the cabanas are sheathed in golden curtains the color of egg yolks.

440 rooms. Restaurant, bar. Fitness center. Pool. Spa. Pets accepted. $151-250

★★★HYATT REGENCY NEWPORT BEACH
1107 Jamboree Road, Newport Beach, 949-729-1234, 800-633-7313; www.hyatt.com

This Spanish-style hotel sits on 26 lush acres overlooking Newport Beach. The rooms echo the surroundings with tropical-inspired décor, and there's plenty to do: golf, volleyball, a relaxing spa and three outdoor pools.

403 rooms. Restaurant, bar. Business center. Fitness center. Pool. Spa. $151-250

WHAT ARE THE OC'S MOST LUXURIOUS HOTELS?

Montage Laguna Beach:
The stylish Montage Laguna Beach blends an arts and crafts style with all the luxury of a full-service resort, including a fantastic spa, luxurious rooms and a cliff-top location.

The Resort at Pelican Hill:
This gorgeous Tuscan-style resort features supremely comfortable rooms, world-glass golf, a super-luxurious spa and a circular pool that's almost too pretty to swim in.

The Ritz-Carlton, Laguna Niguel:
Situated atop a 150-foot bluff overlooking the ocean, this stylish resort offers beautiful views at every turn, a fabulous spa, a wine tasting room and luxe guest rooms.

St. Regis Monarch Beach:
A luscious, secluded setting lures travelers to this Tuscan-insprired resort which includes a Michael Mina restaurant, swank cabanas by the pool and spacious and contemporary guest rooms

★★★★THE ISLAND HOTEL, NEWPORT BEACH

690 Newport Center Drive, Newport Beach, 866-554-4620;
www.theislandhotel.com

This 20-story tower is angled toward the Pacific Ocean
and is only minutes from the beach. Guest rooms are
spacious and comfortable with marble bathrooms,
luxurious Italian linens and well-appointed workspaces.
The private balconies in some suites and furnished
patios offer exceptional views of the Pacific Ocean and
Newport Harbor. You may never want to leave the pool
with its lush landscaping, 17-foot fireplace for chilly
evenings and dataports and telephone jacks to stay in
touch. Overlooking the nearby islands of Balboa, Lido
and Catalina, this Newport Beach gem is only minutes
from upscale shopping and golf facilities.

*383 rooms. Restaurant, bar. Business center. Pool. Spa. Golf. Pets
accepted. $251-350*

★★★NEWPORT BEACH MARRIOTT BAYVIEW

500 Bayview Circle, Newport Beach, 949-854-4500, 800-228-9290;
www.marriott.com

This all-suite hotel features separate bedrooms and
living areas, balconies and oversized marble bathrooms.
Some rooms have views of Upper Back Bay, so be sure
to ask when making a reservation.

254 suites. Restaurant, bar. Pool. $151-250

★★★NEWPORT BEACH MARRIOTT HOTEL AND SPA

900 Newport Center Drive, Newport Beach, 949-640-4000,
800-228-9290; www.newportstay.com

A $70 million renovation turned this into a sleek and
modern hotel. Nautical-inspired rooms have feather
beds, Egyptian cotton sheets, flat-screen televisions
and glass enclosed showers. The hotel is just blocks
from Newport Harbor and next door to the high-end
Fashion Island mall. Onsite Pure Blue Spa is a haven
for relaxation.

*532 rooms. Restaurant, bar. Fitness center. Spa. Pets accepted.
$151-250*

★★★★THE RESORT AT PELICAN HILL

22701 Pelican Hill Road South, Newport Coast, 949-467-6800,
800-315-8214;
www.pelicanhill.com

The area's newest place to stay is located in the small
enclave of Newport Coast. The Resort at Pelican Hill
resembles a beautiful (and very large) Tuscan villa. The
property has 204 hillside bungalows and private villas
that overlook the world class Tom Fazio-designed golf

courses. Each bungalow has its own patio (a perfect spot for your morning cup of coffee from the well-sourced beans in your room), large bathroom and plush bedding. The pool is supposedly the largest circular pool in the world—it certainly looks as if it could be the largest—and you will likely want to spend all day there as the staff delivers fruit-scented water and food from the Coliseum Restaurant. If you prefer the beach, the friendly staff will send you off with your own tote bag full of everything you need for a day under the sun. (Shuttles take you back and forth to Crystal Cove Beach.) End the day with a visit to the luxurious Spa at Pelican Hill and a meal at Andrea, which serves delicate, homemade pasta in an elegant setting (try to get a seat on the terrace while the sun is setting). Throughout your stay, indulge is creamy scoops of the housemade gelato in the café.

332 rooms. Restaurant, bar. Spa. Pool. Fitness Center. $351 and up

LAGUNA BEACH

★★★★MONTAGE LAGUNA BEACH

30801 S. Coast Highway, Laguna Beach, 949-715-6000, 877-782-9821;
www.montagelagunabeach.com

Reigning over Laguna Beach from its rugged cliff-top location, this stylish getaway blends arts and crafts style with the luxury of a full-service resort. Rooms, suites and bungalows feature 400-thread-count linens and marble bathrooms with a large shower and tub, and private balconies or patios with ocean views. Dining at Montage takes sophisticated California cuisine to a new level, particularly at the romantically cozy oceanfront bungalow restaurant, Studio. The full-range spa has more than 20 treatment rooms and the poolside cabanas are decked out with flat-screen TVs and DVD/CD players.

262 rooms. Restaurant, bar. Pets accepted. $351 and up

★★★SURF & SAND RESORT

1555 S. Coast Highway, Laguna Beach, 949-497-4477, 877-786-6835;
www.surfandsandresort.com

This resort blends coastal elegance with West Coast cool. Guest rooms feature marble tiled entryways and private balconies with ocean views. The Aquaterra Spa offers a wide variety of treatments and the fitness center and yoga studio will get guests in shape. The restaurant and lounge serve up signature Southern California views with a Mediterranean-inspired menu.

152 rooms. Restaurant, bar. Fitness center. Pool. Spa. $351 and up

DANA POINT

★★★LAGUNA CLIFFS RESORT & SPA BY MARRIOTT

25135 Park Lantern, Dana Point, 949-661-5000, 800-533-9748; www.lagunacliffs.com

Located on cliffs above the bay, this hotel sits on 42 acres and has great views of the Pacific Ocean. Rooms have a beachy décor and pop with color. There's also a nice pool with chaise lounges to relax and soak up the California sunshine, and the property is within walking distance of the harbor's restaurants and shops. A new 14,000-square-foot spa offers several invigorating orange-based treatments.

376 rooms. Restaurant, bar. Business center. Fitness center. Pool. Spa. Pets accepted. Tennis. $251-350

★★★★★ST. REGIS RESORT, MONARCH BEACH

1 Monarch Beach Resort, Dana Point, 949-234-3200, 800-722-1543; www.stregismb.com

Even seasoned travelers will swoon over the luscious, secluded setting and the Tuscan-inspired design of this resort, which is tucked away on 200 acres high above the Pacific Ocean. Elegant marble floors, plush carpets and massive sofas grace the public areas. The spacious guest rooms have dramatic contemporary décor with wood shutters, marble bathrooms, private balconies, goose down comforters and 300-thread count sheets. The resort has an 18-hole championship golf course, swank poolside cabanas, award-winning spa, beach club (with surfing lessons) and nature trails. Restaurants include Michael Mina's acclaimed StoneHill Tavern.

400 rooms. Restaurant, bar. Business center. Fitness center. Pool. Spa. Pets accepted. Tennis. Golf. $351 and up

★★★★THE RITZ-CARLTON, LAGUNA NIGUEL

1 Ritz-Carlton Drive, Dana Point, 949-240-2000, 800-241-3333; www.ritzcarlton.com

Situated atop a 150-foot bluff overlooking the ocean, this Mediterranean style villa is an elegant retreat. Guest rooms have been decorated in a palette of cream and soft blue to reflect the beach setting and have ocean, pool or garden views. The resort has three restaurants, including the unique wine tasting room, ENO, which offers an extensive menu of wines, cheeses and chocolates from around the globe. Surfing lessons are available at the beach, and the spa is fabulous with its contemporary California-glam décor and full menu of luxurious treatments. Golfers come to play several spectacular courses nearby.

393 rooms. Restaurant, bar. Business center. Fitness center. Pool. Spa. Pets accepted. Tennis. $351 and up

WHERE TO EAT

NEWPORT BEACH
★★★★ANDREA

The Resort at Pelican Hill, 22701 Pelican Hill Road South, Newport Coast,
949-467-6800, 800-315-8214; www.pelicanhill.com

With an elegant interior of natural colors, lush potted trees and a covered terrace providing unparalleled views of the ocean and golf greens, you may think you are in Tuscany, and that's before the fresh northern Italian dishes and unique pastas made in the restaurant's own temperature controlled pasta rooms even hit your table. The friendly service will lead you to believe this is a more casual restaurant than it is, but make no mistake, the food served here is carefully executed and well-sourced. The typical prosciutto, for example, is elevated with a Zibbibo wine-marinated melon. This kind of simple yet refreshing bite provides the perfect lead in to the delicate hand-rolled pasta. Standout pasta selections when we visited included the ravioli di ricotta, a simple ravioli filled with fresh spinach and ricotta and finished in a heavenly sage butter sauce. Pasta is not the only item that gets special billing here, however, as all meals should end with a scoop of the artisan gelato.

Italian. Dinner. Bar. Reservations recommended. $36-85

★★★THE RITZ

880 Newport Center Drive, Newport Beach, 949-720-1800;
www.ritzrestaurant.com

The moment you step inside this epicurean eatery, you'll feel transported. Dim lighting is not a bother but a comfort; its mellow but rich glow is ideal for a romantic dinner or drink. The restaurant's ambience achieves European charm through its dark wood walls, black leather booths and giant bottles of Moët & Chandon champagne that stand behind one particular booth. The Escoffier Room (a pavilion-style space with Georgian accents and portraits of the renowned Paris Ritz Hotel chef Auguste Escoffier) is in contrast to the darker, more subdued and private Wine Cellar (a vaulted brick chamber accessed through an oval tunnel that seats large parties of up to 32 people). The menu encompasses French, Italian and American styles. For lunch, try the wild mushroom "cappuccino," along with the enormous Ritz salad, and leave room for the Harlequin soufflé, made with Belgian chocolate and Grand Marnier served with a Marnier crème anglaise sauce.

American, French. Lunch, dinner. Reservations recommended. Bar. $36-85

★★★TRADITION BY PASCAL

1000 N. Bristol St., Newport Beach, 949-263-9400;
www.pascalnewportbeach.com

Much-lauded chef/restaurateur Pascal Olhats showcases his French countryside cuisine in this rose-filled, farmhouse-style space. The light French food includes beet salad with lemon flavored goat cheese and roasted hazlenuts, and dijon crusted lamb with celery root purée. A three-course prix fixe menu is available, as well as two lavish four-course meals.

French. Lunch (Monday-Friday), dinner (Tuesday-Sunday). $36-85

LAGUNA BEACH

★★★RAYA

1 Ritz Carlton Drive, Dana Point, 949-240-2000;
www.ritzcarlton.com

Located 162 feet above sea level, this restaurant inside the luxurious Ritz Carlton provides a spectacular oceanside view. The restaurant by acclaimed chef Richard Sandoval with chef de cuisine Greg Howe at the helm features pan-latin coastal cuisine using sustainable seafood, local produce, grass fed meats and vibrant Latin flavors. Dinner includes

---

WHAT ARE THE BEST OVERALL RESTAURANTS IN ORANGE COUNTY?

Andrea:
The fresh pasta made daily by hand in this serene restaurant is wonderful. The chef mixes up sauces that are flavorful and bright and the homemade gelato is perfection.

Stonehill Tavern:
Famed San Francisco chef-turned-restaurateur Michael Mina's urban bistro, located in the St. Regis, is a sleek, intimate spot designed by Tony Chi with comfortable couches, glass-enclosed booths and a large terrace from which to enjoy the chef's delicious cuisine.

Studio:
This cozy restaurant is a study in understated elegance, featuring contemporary California cuisine made with the freshest local ingredients.

starters such as a ceviche tasting and lobster tacos. Sandwiches (available at blunch at dinner) include short rib sliders with pickled onion, cucumbers adn pobalos, while entrees feature dishes such as miso blad cod. Be sure to save room for some of the churros at the end of your meal.

Latin. Breakfast, lunch, dinner. $36-85

★★★★STONEHILL TAVERN

1 Monarch Beach Resort, Dana Point, 949-234-3318; www.michaelmina.net/stonehill

Famed San Francisco chef-turned-restaurateur Michael Mina's urban bistro, located in the St. Regis, is a sleek, intimate spot designed by Tony Chi with comfortable couches, glass-enclosed booths and a large terrace. The menu includes Mina's signature appetizer trios—three different preparations of one ingredient, such as tuna, lobster or duck, as well as twists on American classics (think fried chicken with mascarpone polenta and a root beer float for dessert). An impressive wine program focuses on boutique California producers, but also includes a diverse selection from Austria and Burgundy.

American. Dinner. Closed Monday-Tuesday. $86 and up

★★★★★STUDIO

Montage Laguna Beach, 30801 S. Coast Highway, Laguna Beach, 949-715-6000; www.studiolagunabeach.com

Housed in a cozy arts and crafts cottage overlooking the ocean, this restaurant at Montage Laguna Beach is a study in understated elegance. The menu features contemporary California cuisine made with the freshest local ingredients. Settle in for a supper made up of divine dishes such as pan-seared John Dory with baby fennel, cipollini onions and caramelized cauliflower and madras curry, or vinegar-braised short ribs with butter-roasted asparagus. The wine cellar features more than 2,200 bottles with plenty of California selections and wines available by the glass.

American. Dinner. Closed Monday-Tuesday. Bar. $36-85

SPAS

NEWPORT BEACH
★★★★THE SPA AT THE ISLAND HOTEL

690 Newport Center Drive, Newport Beach, 949-759-0808, 866-554-4620; www.theislandhotel.com

Slip away to the Spa at the Island Hotel for a muscle-relieving massage or detoxifying volcanic clay treatment that is said to reenergize the body from head to toe. Spacious and modern, the spa's elegant touches—granite floors, silver tea pitchers and a calming water wall—instantly set a tranquil and tasteful tone. The spa's signature rituals use rejuvenating elements from India, Bali and the Hawaiian Islands to smooth, soften and invigorate skin. The Island Tropical Splendor is a full-body scrub blending fresh coconut, rice and vetiver—a perennial grass native to India known for its medicinal and aromatic properties.

★★★★★THE SPA AT THE RESORT AT PELICAN HILL

The Resort at Pelican Hill, 22701 Pelican Hill Road South, Newport Coast, 949-467-6800, 800-315-8214; www.pelicanhill.com

If you think the Pelican Hill Resort is transporting, wait until you arrive at the

Spa at Pelican Hill, where they will easily address one of three goals: replenishment, invigoration or relaxation. Prior to your treatments, spend your time in the Aqua Colonnade, the epitome of Tuscan-inspired relaxation complete with an herbal steam room and sauna. Your needs are so tended to that the therapist might offer you lunch from the delectable spa menu while you have your nails carefully polished. Just as in Italy, gelato is everywhere, so give in to the Body Gelato, which is a seasonally-inspired treatment incorporating luxurious herbs and fruit that will leave your skin feeling refreshed and nourished. If a full day is in your future, indulge in The Master's Palette, a nearly six hour affair of the spa's most decadent treatments.

LAGUNA BEACH

★★★★★SPA MONTAGE, LAGUNA BEACH

Montage Laguna Beach, 30801 S. Coast Highway, Laguna Beach, 949-715-6000, 866-271-6953; www.spamontage.com

Spa Montage is a stunning facility that takes advantage of its superior beachfront setting. An indoor-outdoor structure and floor-to-ceiling windows framing 160-degree views alleviate any guilt guests may feel for opting to stay in for a bit of pampering on a sunny day. The spa's holistic, get-back-to-nature approach is evident in its design, as well as in the products it uses. Custom-mixed lotions and oils blend natural ingredients, including eucalyptus, lavender, orange blossoms and citrus. Wrap up in one of the spa's plush robes and try any number of therapies, from a California citrus polish to an algae cellulite massage. Hungry spa-goers can find a cozy spot by the lap pool, where healthy snacks and meals are available from the Mosaic Grille.

DANA POINT

★★★★THE RITZ-CARLTON SPA, LAGUNA NIGUEL

1 Ritz-Carlton Drive, Dana Point, 949-240-2000, 800-241-3333; www.ritzcarlton.com

Eleven treatment rooms, a full-service beauty salon, a circular manicure and pedicure station and a modern fitness center are available to guests at the Ritz-Carlton Spa. Choose from holistic treatments grounded in ancient practices as well as the latest skin treatments, massages and exfoliations. Collagen infusion facials and California citrus body polishes stand out among the spa's signature treatments. There are also seasonal treatments such as a summer chocolate sugar scrub pedicure. Treatments are rooted in the sea's purifying elements: rich minerals, sea salt or nutrient-rich algae and water.

★★★★★SPA GAUCIN

1 Monarch Beach Resort, Dana Point, 949-234-3200, 800-722-1543; www.stregismonarchbeach.com

Spa Gaucin at the St. Regis is the picture of elegance with dark woods, Asian-style accents and three-story waterfalls. The warm cream interior accentuates specially commissioned artwork throughout the space and the 25 treatment rooms offer state-of-the-art amenities (including gas fireplaces to cozy up to). The spa menu includes everything from Mediterranean massage to total vitamin facials to the Chardonnay sugar scrub. Try the Solace Mineral Trio, a hydrating treatment utilizing grapeseed body exfoliation and a volcanic clay wrap, or the Dermal Quench facial to ward off road-lag. There's also an extensive offering of beauty treatments from microdermabrasion to pedicures.

SHOPPING

FASHION ISLAND
2647 E. Pacific Coast Highway, Corona del Mar, 949-721-2000; www.shopfashionisland.com

Get your shopping fix at one of the most popular shopping centers in Southern California. The giant mall includes more than 200 stores, a large food court (with an alfresco dining area) and several upscale chain restaurants, including China Grille and Flemings. Major department stores include Neiman Marcus and Bloomingdale's, while shops range from Anthropologie and Urban Outfitters.

Monday-Friday 10 a.m.-9 p.m., Saturday 10 a.m.-7 p.m., Sunday 11 a.m.-6 p.m.

SIDE TRIP

TEMECULA

Most people associate winemaking in California with Napa and Sonoma valleys. But there's serious Southern California wine tasting in the Temecula Valley, located about an hour from Anaheim. The Temecula Valley, bordered on the west by Camp Pendleton Marine Corps Base and the Cleveland National Forest, is also home to five championship golf courses and casino gambling at the local resorts.

WHAT TO SEE

CALIFORNIA DREAMIN'
33133 Vista Del Monte Road, Temecula, 800-373-3359; www.californiadreamin.com

This company offers sunrise balloon rides over Temecula wine country, as well as spectacular daytime forays over the Pacific and the Del Mar bluffs. The baskets accommodate six, nine or 12 people, making it perfect for families. Adrenaline junkies may prefer to schedule a ride in a World War I-style biplane. *Daily.*

CALLAWAY VINEYARD AND WINERY
32720 Rancho California Road, Temecula, 800-472-2377; www.callawaywinery.com

If the name sounds familiar, that's because founder Ely Reeves Callaway Jr. was a leader in the golf industry, especially after the success of the Big Bertha golf club. He began Callaway Vineyard and Winery in 1969, the first in the area. The wines are in limited production, so it's worth a stop here to taste, and to stock up if you so desire. The onsite restaurant boasts vineyard views and Mediterranean tapas.

Daily 10 a.m.-5 p.m.

FILSINGER WINERY
39050 De Portola Road, Temecula, 951-302-6363; www.filsingerwinery.com

This family-owned and operated winery has been around since 1978 and produces about 3,000 cases of wine a year. The winery has won many awards for their gewurztraminer.

Friday 11 a.m.-4 p.m., Saturday-Sunday 10 a.m.-5 p.m.

SPECIAL EVENT

BALLOON AND WINE FESTIVAL

Lake Skinner, 37701 Warren Road, Temecula, 951-676-6713; www.tvbwf.com
This fest offers wine tastings, a hot-air balloon race, musical entertainment and children's activities.
Early June.

STUART CELLARS
33515 Rancho California Road, Temecula, 888-260-0870; www.stuartcellars.com
This family-run winery is a wonderful retreat. Bring a picnic lunch and enjoy it on the winery grounds with views of the Temecula Valley.
Daily 10 a.m.-5 p.m.

WHERE TO STAY

★★★PECHANGA RESORT & CASINO
45000 Pechanga Parkway, Temecula, 951-643-1819, 888-732-4264;
www.pechanga.com
Designed in the Prairie School style, this resort has spacious rooms with floor-to-ceiling windows and large bathrooms. One-bedroom suites include a wet bar, separate sleeping quarters and one and a half baths. The 188,000-square-foot gaming floor makes this the biggest casino in California. Dining options abound.
517 rooms. Restaurant, bar. Pool. Spa. $151-250

★★★TEMECULA CREEK INN
44501 Rainbow Canyon Road, Temecula, 951-694-1000, 877-517-1823;
www.temeculacreekinn.com
This hotel offers the perfect combination of work and play, with ample meeting space and a 27-hole golf course. Comfortable guest rooms overlook the golf course or mountains. The hotel's Temet Grill offers cuisine to complement wine from the area's many vineyards.
130 rooms. Restaurant, bar. Tennis. Golf. $151-250

WHERE TO EAT

RECOMMENDED
BAILY'S
28699 Old Town Front St., Temecula, 951-676-9567; www.baily.com
This local favorite on top of Front Street Bar & Grill focuses on seasonal ingredients and offers an extensive wine list. The menu is centered around a variety of seafood items, including a fresh fish of the day, as well as several steak selections. Every Tuesday features a four-course prix fixe menu that changes every week and is only $20. Friday and Saturday nights bring a sinful Death by Chocolate buffet.
American. Dinner. $16-35

CAFE CHAMPAGNE
32575 Rancho California Road, Temecula, 951-699-0099; www.thorntonwine.com

Dine inside the warm and cozy French country space or out on the patio overlooking Thorton Winery on a sunny day. The fusion menu includes suggested wine pairings. For example, the crispy roast duck would be lovely with the Thorton 2005 OVOC Zinfandel. A nice selection of appetizers includes warm brie, a vineyard tapas plate with salami, roasted peppers, herbed goat cheese and more, and calamari finished in a Thorton Brut-Dill Beurre Blanc. Lunch includes a variety of sandwiches such as a lamb pita and grilled ham and gouda.
French. Lunch, dinner, Sunday brunch. $36-85

LOS ANGELES

On September 4, 1781, the governor of California, Don Felipe de Neve, marched to the city and founded the town of Our Lady Queen of the Angels of Porciúncula, later thankfully shortened to Los Angeles.

L.A. has often been described as 40 suburbs without a city. Visitors usually stick to four distinct areas. If it's sun and sand you seek, make a beeline for the beach communities of Malibu, Venice and Santa Monica. Malibu is full of surfers and million-dollar homes right on the water; Venice is funky as ever, especially on the honky-tonk boardwalk; Santa Monica is a cross between the two, with a popular amusement park on the pier and a few more homeless people than the city would like. If you've come to shop, you might never leave Beverly Hills. The super-glitzy stores of Rodeo Drive are here, as are some of L.A.'s most fabulously expensive homes. For shopping on a mere mortal's budget, try the Beverly Center or The Grove, L.A.'s premier malls-cum-entertainment-centers, and home to retailers ranging from Gucci to H&M. L.A. does have an actual downtown, which includes Frank Gehry's Walt Disney Concert Hall, several top-flight museums, Chinatown, Little Tokyo and Mexican marketplace Olvera Street. Downtown is undergoing a renaissance, but the sidewalks still roll up at night, so hotels here cater primarily to business travelers.

West Hollywood is (ironically) the most centrally located part of Los Angeles, and home to the hippest restaurants and nightspots of the moment along Melrose Avenue and the Sunset Strip. And unlike Hollywood proper, which is somewhat seedy, you might see movie stars here. Just don't expect to find parking.

WHAT TO SEE

CALIFORNIA SCIENCE CENTER
700 Exposition Park Drive, South Central, 323-724-3623; www.californiasciencecenter.org

This free, hands-on museum is all about making science fun and accessible, even for those who dozed during high school chemistry and physics classes. Learn about the mechanics of man-made inventions, explore how plant and animal life thrives, and discover how space travel works. If that's not hands-on enough, defy gravity by riding the High Wire Bicycle, take a spin in the Motion-Based Simulator or scale the indoor rock-climbing wall ($7 to do all three). Keep an eye out for special exhibits dedicated to everything from race (where you can match your voice with people in photos) to identity (where you can see what you'll look like 30 years from now). Save some time for a movie in the center's IMAX Theater, where you can take 3D tours of all kinds of exotic places, from the bottom of the sea to the Egyptian desert. You'll be a science geek in no time. *Admission: free. IMAX Admission: adults $8.25, seniors and students 13-17 $6, children 4-12 $5. Daily 10 a.m.-5 p.m.*

CENTER THEATRE GROUP

Mark Taper Forum and Ahmanson Theatre at the Music Center, 135 N. Grand Ave., Downtown; Kirk Douglas Theatre, 9820 Washington Blvd., Culver City, 213-628-2772; www.centertheatregroup.org

Center Theatre Group, which includes the Ahmanson Theatre, the Mark Taper Forum and the Kirk Douglas Theatre, is Los Angeles's prized theater company and has been recognized as one of the best in the country. Headed by artistic director Michael Ritchie, the non-profit group has elicited a Tony Award-winning performance in *Angels in America* at the Mark Taper Forum, as well as raves for a *Death of a Salesman* at the Ahmanson. The small, 317-seat Kirk Douglas Theatre in Culver City has put on classics such as *Come Back, Little Sheba,* as well as premieres of new musicals.
Show times vary. See website for details.

DOWNTOWN LOS ANGELES ART WALK

213-784-2598; www.downtownartwalk.com

In 2003, city officials pushed a motion to designate a section of downtown (known as the Historic Core) as "Gallery Row" in order to formally recognize its blossoming art scene. What was once an area largely dominated by gang activity, homelessness and prostitution is now home to dozens of galleries. The best way to explore the downtown art scene is on the second Thursday of the month, when dozens of local galleries throw open their doors for an art walk—or you can hop on one of the 1940s vintage retro-fitted school buses that shuttle people around to the different galleries (just wave to flag one down; they run from 6-10 p.m.). Participating galleries include the Museum of Contemporary Art and the Los Angeles Center for Digital Art, as well as small, independent outfits. The event is self-guided (and free), so start at whichever gallery catches your eye first.
Second Thursday of the month; hours vary by gallery.

LOS ANGELES BALLET

Los Angeles Ballet Center, 11755 Exposition Blvd., Downtown, 310-998-7782; www.losangelesballet.org

The Los Angeles Ballet is relatively new—their premiere performance was a December 2006 production of the *The Nutcracker*—but they've already won rave reviews, finally giving this major city a ballet company of its own. (Very wisely, the founders decided that if the people of this sprawling city wouldn't come to them, they'd go to the people—the company performs in six different theaters all over Los Angeles.) It seems the ballet is here to stay, too. The holiday production of *The Nutcracker* has already become a Southern California tradition. The troupe also tackles contemporary pieces, including Lar Lubovitch's *The Evangelist.*
Show times vary. See website for details.

BEST ATTRACTIONS

WHAT ARE THE TOP THINGS TO DO IN L.A?

HIT THE BEACHES

Whether you want to swim in the ocean, relax on the sand, bike along the ocean-front recreational path or stroll the Venice Boardwalk, the beach is an essential part of any visit to Los Angeles. With more than 20 beaches in Los Angeles, which one you visit depends on what you're looking for. Surfers should head to Zuma beach in Malibu for great waves. The best people watching is, of course, in Venice Beach, which is still as funky as ever. Locals visit Manhattan Beach to play volley-ball, while Santa Monica offers plenty of amusement park fun on the pier.

HOORAY FOR HOLLYWOOD

The super-touristy Hollywood Walk of Fame runs along Hollywood Boulevard from Gower Street to La Brea Avenue and on Vine Street from Sunset Boulevard to Yucca Street. Stars are bought and paid for, which explains why Mabel Taliaferro (who?) has one, but Robert Redford doesn't. Still, just about everybody walks with their heads down until they reach Grauman's Chinese Theatre. While you're matching your hands and feet against the cement molds of your favorite Hollywood stars of past and present, don't forget to check out the theater's elaborate design and architecture. No wonder it's a favorite for film premieres.

CHECK OUT THE CITY'S ART OFFERINGS

The Getty Villa is the perfect museum for Los Angeles. Perched on a prime bluff in Malibu overlooking the ocean, the former estate of oil magnate J. Paul Getty has one of the world's finest collections of Greek, Roman and Etruscan antiqui-ties. But it's the sun-soaked courtyards and gardens that keep the Getty from feeling like a dusty tomb. Outdoor breezeways and patios connect the galleries, making the Getty perhaps the only museum in the world where you might need sunglasses.

VISIT THE FARMER'S MARKETS

L.A.'s farmers' markets are some of the finest in the country. The city's Mediterranean climate means something is always in season: apples and persim-mons in fall, avocados and citrus fruits in winter, peaches and plums in summer, and strawberries year-round. The Los Angeles Farmers Market is open daily;

others are held just once or twice a week. Another good pick is the Santa Monica Farmers Market, which draws foodies and chefs from all over the area every Wednesday, Saturday and Sunday morning to buy the freshest ingredients and stock up on organic goods. It's a great stop whether you're off to prepare a five-course meal or just looking to pick up a few snacks for a day at the beach. You might also spot a celebrity or two doing the same.

SHOP

The world's greatest concentration of luxury stores (Bulgari, Versace, Gucci, etc.) are all in a three-block stretch between Wilshire and Santa Monica boulevards on Rodeo Drive of course. Another cluster of couture shops (including Carolina Herrera and Marc Jacobs) have recently opened on Melrose Avenue which used to be known solely for offbeat and vintage clothing stores. You'll also see celebrities shopping along Robertson Boulevard between Beverly and Wilshire boulevards.

Another great stretch for shopping is on West Third Street between L.A.'s two destination malls, The Beverly Center and The Grove. Third Street has many more independent boutiques, such as Hillary Rush or Scout. This Third Street is not to be confused with Santa Monica's Third Street Promenade, an outdoor mall with dozens of movie theaters, casual restaurants and familiar shops like the Apple Store and Brookstone. For more eclectic shops, try Abbott Kinney Boulevard in Venice. This formerly seedy strip of used furniture shops and dive bars has attracted trendy boutiques, including Heist (1104 Abbot Kinney Blvd., 310-450-6531; www.shopheist.com), which carries designer labels such as Rag & Bone and American Vintage, and The Stronghold (1625 Abbot Kinney Blvd., 310-399-7200), which has a custom denim bar.

DOWNTOWN/CHINATOWN

Yes, there is a downtown in Los Angeles, complete with skyscrapers, traffic-clogged one-way streets and busy professionals scurrying about in suits. Although the streets can empty out at night, there is a burgeoning trend of people moving into high-rise downtown condos. And in hopes of persuading more people to stick around through the evening, city leaders have erected shiny new cultural institutions like Frank Gehry's fanciful Walt Disney Concert Hall, the Nokia Theatre and the Staples Center. At down-town's northeast corner stands Olvera Street, where the city began. Now a Mexican-themed pedestrian promenade, it is home to the oldest standing residence in L.A., the Avila Adobe. Nearby Chinatown (just over the 110 freeway) is a good place for a dim sum brunch.

LOS ANGELES FASHION DISTRICT
90-block area bordered by Seventh Street, I-10, Main and San Petro streets, Downtown; Santee Alley is between Santee Street and Maple Avenue at Olympic Boulevard; www.fashiondistrict.org

If you've been dying to get your manicured hands on some designer labels, then a trip to Downtown L.A.'s Fashion District is in order. You can't visit the Fashion District without hitting up Santee Alley (between Santee Street and Maple Avenue). The alley is a cross between a flea market and Middle Eastern bazaar, with people hawking everything from fake designer purses to gold jewelry. Santee Alley contains more than 150 stores, and the weekend is its busiest time, so go early (alley stores open around 10 a.m.) to avoid the crowds. Remember, bargaining is completely acceptable while shopping in the alley. If you're not a fan of designer knockoffs, then consider heading to the Fashion District on the last Friday of the month, when many designer showrooms hold sample sales that are open to the public.

LA OPERA
Dorothy Chandler Pavilion, 135 North Grand Ave., Downtown, 213-972-7219; www.laopera.com

Legendary opera singer Plácido Domingo leads the company and has been integral to its success; in just under two decades, it has become the fourth largest opera company in the U.S. Housed at the Dorothy Chandler Pavilion (former home of the Oscars), the opera's most recent season featured classic performances of Donizetti's *The Elixir of Love*, Wagner's *Siegfried* and Rossini's *The Barber of Seville*.
Show times vary. See website for details.

MUSEUM OF CONTEMPORARY ART (MOCA)
250 S. Grand Ave., Downtown, 213-626-6222; www.moca.org

MOCA has been providing Los Angeles with cutting-edge contemporary art since 1979. The museum is spread across three facilities (MOCA Grand Avenue, The Geffen Contemporary at MOCA and MOCA Pacific Design Center), but the Grand Avenue location offers the biggest bang for your buck. Besides welcoming exhibits showcasing world-renowned artists such as Jean-Michel Basquiat, Andy Warhol and Robert Rauschenberg, the museum also has an impressive permanent collection. Roy Lichtenstein, Claes Oldenburg, Mark Rothko and Diane Arbus are just a few of the artists whose work can be seen year-round at MOCA. After taking in the art, visit the MOCA Store, which offers modern design-inspired knickknacks and then grab a bite at the new café, Lemonade at MOCA, which offers casual, fresh comfort food and housemade lemonades. Admission is free on Thursday between 5 and 8 p.m.

Admission: adults $10, students and seniors $5, children under 12 free. Monday and Friday 11 a.m.-5 p.m., Thursday 11 a.m.-8 p.m., Saturday-Sunday 11 a.m.-6 p.m. Free Thursday 5-8 p.m.

NATURAL HISTORY MUSEUM OF LOS ANGELES COUNTY

900 Exposition Blvd., South Central, 213-763-3466; www.nhm.org

Confront a Tyrannosaurus rex; look Megamouth, an extremely rare type of shark, in the eye; and discover more than 300 pounds of gold. Make like Indiana Jones and do all of this at the Natural History Museum of Los Angeles County, the third-largest museum of its kind in the United States. The Natural History Museum is a monument to the natural world. After seeing T. rex bones, aquarium-bound predators and precious metal at the Hall of Gems and Minerals, learn some state lore in the Lando Hall of California History. Then explore the cultures of native peoples in the Visible Vault: Archeological Treasures from Ancient Latin America, where artifacts from the Mayan, Aztec and Incan empires are on display. If you're still jonesing for some Indy-type adventure, head to the Ralph M. Parsons Discovery Center and get cozy with all kinds of live insects, reptiles and amphibians.

Admission: adults $9, seniors and children 13-17 $6.50, children 5-12 $2, children under 5 free. Daily 9:30 a.m.-5 p.m.

OLVERA STREET

845 N. Alameda St., Downtown, 213-485-6855; www.lacity.org/elp

To get a glimpse of L.A.'s Latino heritage, seek out Olvera Street. This area, called El Pueblo de Los Angeles Historical Monument, is considered the birth-place of Los Angeles, so there are many historic buildings to explore. Check out the Avila Adobe *(10 E. Olvera St.)*, which was built in the early 19th century by former mayor Francisco Avila; the Pelanconi House *(17 Olvera St.)*, the oldest brick home in the city, which now houses the Casa La Golondrina Mexican restaurant; and the Victorian-style Sepul-veda House *(622-624 N. Main St.)*, built in 1887. Besides touring these local landmarks, you can also shop for traditional Mexican wares and snack on huaraches and other authentic Latin American foods from the dozens of merchants who line the street.

Admission: Free. Avila Adobe: Daily 9 a.m.-4 p.m. Sepulveda House: Daily 9 a.m.-4 p.m.

STAPLES CENTER

1111 S. Figueroa St., Downtown, 213-742-7340; www.staplescenter.com

If you're looking to rub elbows with thousands of Angelenos—or see athletes throw a couple elbows—head to the Staples Center. Located in downtown Los Angeles, Staples is home to some of the city's finest sports teams: the Los Angeles Kings, Los Angeles Lakers, Los Angeles Clippers and Los Angeles Sparks. Besides being able to cheer along with Jack Nicholson, Tobey Maguire and other famous fans, visitors to the Staples Center can also watch some of the biggest performers in the world onstage. Taylor Swift, Lady Gaga and Alicia Keys are just a few of the A-listers who have performed here.

WALT DISNEY CONCERT HALL

111 S. Grand Ave., Downtown, 323-850-2000; www.laphil.com

Designed by architect extraordinaire Frank Gehry, Walt Disney Concert Hall is one of L.A.'s newer landmarks, but that hasn't stopped its shiny, stainless steel curves from becoming synonymous with downtown Los Angeles. Aside from being a fascinating example of modern architecture, the hall also provides the city with a venue equipped with superior acoustics. So even if you end up sitting way in the back of the hall's honey-colored, wood-paneled auditorium, you'll still get an earful. The WDCH serves as the permanent home of the L.A. Philharmonic (except for when they decamp to the Hollywood Bowl for the summer), and also welcomes contemporary acts such as Air and Patti LuPone throughout the year.

WATTS TOWERS

1761-65 E. 107th St., Watts, 213-847-4646; www.wattstowers.us

Originally called Nuestro Pueblo (which translates to "Our Town"), the Watts Towers were built by Italian immigrant Sabato (Simon) Rodia from 1921 to 1954. When he was done, Rodia had created nine major structures, with the two tallest measuring about 100 feet. Using traditional hand tools and window-washing equipment, Rodia constructed the towers out of steel, wire mesh and mortar, and later decorated them with found objects such as ceramic tiles, pottery, porcelain, broken glass and seashell fragments. Today, the hollow, spiraling structures, which resemble a series of small electricity pylons, are National Historic Landmarks. The Watts Towers Arts Center, which was built in 1970, hosts workshops, lectures and exhibits.

Tours: adults $7, seniors and children 13-17 $3, children 12 and under free. Friday 11 a.m.-3 p.m., Saturday 10:30 a.m.-3 p.m., Sunday 12:30-3 p.m.; every half hour hour.

WHERE TO STAY

★★★HILTON CHECKERS LOS ANGELES

535 S. Grand Ave., Downtown, 213-624-0000;
www.hiltoncheckers.com

If you love an evening at the theater but think the experience is reserved for other cities, make a grand entrance at the Hilton Checkers Los Angeles. The refurbished 1920s hotel in L.A.'s newly booming Downtown offers dinner guests complimentary shuttles to the theater district, stopping at places such as the Mark Taper Forum and the Walt Disney Concert Hall. If you're in town for business, relax on the rooftop pool deck between meetings, and absorb the contrasting cityscape or partake in easy-to-squeeze-in "Express" spa treatments.

188 rooms. Restaurant, bar. Fitness center. Pool. Spa. $151-250

★★★LOS ANGELES MARRIOTT DOWNTOWN

333 S. Figueroa St., Downtown, 213-617-1133; www.marriott.com

The hotel's décor lacks personality and skews a bit corporate, but the Los Angeles Marriott Downtown is perfect for business travelers needing easy access to the L.A. Convention Center, Staples Center, Financial District and more. Recently upgraded, the hotel features plush goose-down bedding, highlighted views of the Downtown skyline and mile-high lobby ceilings with skylights. Forgo the hotel's numerous casual eateries and head to one of the many good restaurants now located downtown, including Water Grill and Church and State.

469 rooms. Restaurant, bar. Fitness center. Pool. $151-250

★★★MILLENNIUM BILTMORE HOTEL LOS ANGELES

506 S. Grand Ave., Downtown, 213-624-1011; www.millenniumhotels.com

In the days before downtown resurged and boomed once more with contemporary lofts and trendy new hotels popping up everywhere, Millennium Biltmore made its reputation as one of L.A.'s classiest hotel experiences. Wandering into the lobby is like happening upon a museum, as mile-high ceilings are ornately gilded with images of cherubs. At least it's palatial enough for Hollywood royalty: Eight of the first Academy Awards ceremonies in the 1930s and '40s were held at the Biltmore Bowl, the hotel's opulent ballroom. Whether you cozy up to the Gallery Bar and Cognac Room or have high Victorian tea in the Rendezvous Court, you'll feel transported to another era. Modern in-room amenities like MP3 hook-ups plus the innovative Sai Sai restaurant (serving dishes such as a grilled pork chop with sweet potato mash, onion confit, asparagus and pear and lychee compote, or Maine diver scallops with edamame polenta and sake shrimp) shepherd you back to the present day.

683 rooms. Restaurant, bar. Business center. Fitness center. Pool. $151-250

★★★OMNI LOS ANGELES HOTEL AT CALIFORNIA PLAZA

251 S. Olive St., Downtown, 213-617-3300; www.omnihotels.com

As Downtown's most luxe convention hotel, Omni Los Angeles offers standard business-related amenities such as hotel-wide wireless Internet access. But Omni created some unusual services for travelers, too. Because frequent travel can lead to an unbalanced lifestyle and even weight gain, the hotel has an Ideal Living program for eating healthfully, Get Fit suites with exercise equipment such as treadmills, and even Get Fit kits with dumbbells, a yoga mat and more. For families, the hotel offers a

WHAT ARE L.A.'S BEST CULTURAL VENUES?

Pantages Theater: Southern California's version of Broadway is the Pantages, which puts on shows like *The Color Purple* and *Chicago*.

Walt Disney Concert Hall: Aside from being a fascinating example of modern architecture, the hall is equipped with superior acoustics and is the home of the L.A. Philharmonic.

Kids Fantasy Suite, complete with beanbag chairs, bunk beds and toys galore. For grown-ups, at upstairs fine-dining restaurant Noé (which has a lovely view of California Plaza's Watercourt, a great destination for summer concerts), executive chef Glen Ishii serves lauded contemporary American cuisine. Dishes include shellfish-stuffed Japanese turnip with caviar and ratatouille vinaigrette, and cocktails include pear-lavender martinis and a candied ginger collins.

453 rooms. Restaurant, bar. Business center. Fitness center. Pool. Spa. $151-250

★★★SHERATON LOS ANGELES DOWNTOWN HOTEL

711 S. Hope St., Downtown, 213-488-3500; www.starwoodhotels.com

Once you tear yourself away from meetings at the nearby L.A. Convention Center, Lakers' games at Staples Center and countless events at L.A. Live, you might enjoy hanging out in your room at Sheraton Los Angeles Downtown. Crimson striped carpeting and dark wood welcome you to the high-rise, and the hotel's rooms offer luxuries such as the signature comfy beds. A decked-out club lounge plies you with complimentary breakfast and afternoon hors d'oeuvres, if you should choose to upgrade. The Brasserie, The Italian Grill (open seasonally) and The Lobby Bar offer several other dining options, but rather than partake of the hotel's generically named eateries, explore the great culinary scene nearby.

485 rooms. Restaurant, bar. Business center. Fitness center. Pool. $61-150

RECOMMENDED

JW MARRIOTT

900 W. Olympic Blvd., Downtown, 213-765-8600; www.lalivemarriott.com

Part of Downtown's glitzy new entertainment complex, L.A. Live, the JW Marriott is a welcome addition to the city's hotel scene, providing comfortable accommodations adjacent to the Los Angeles Convention Center and within walking distance of the Staples Center. The hotel features more than 75,000 square feet of meeting space, spacious rooms with comfortable workstations, a rooftop pool and a variety of dining options which includes a restaurant from chef Kerry Simon, LA Market, and a wine bar. A variety of suites are perfect for hosting small business meetings. After a day of meetings, guests can head to the second-floor spa and fitness center.

878 rooms. Restaurant, bar. Business center. Fitness center. Pool. Spa. $251-350

THE RITZ-CARLTON, LOS ANGELES

900 W. Olympic Blvd., Downtown, 213-743-8800; www.ritzcarlton.com

The Ritz-Carlton, Los Angeles, which occupies floors 22-26 (there are just 123 rooms and 14 suites) of the 54-story glass tower which also houses the JW Marriott, is a luxurious new choice in the heart of Downtown Los Angeles. Rooms feature foyers, marble bathrooms and technological features that allow for PDAs to be viewed on the flat-screen televisions. Suites have entertainment areas, studies and formal dining rooms. Dining options include WP24 by Wolfgang Puck. The 7,000-square-foot spa includes an outdoor swimming pool and a terrace with views of the city and mountains.

137 rooms. Restaurant, bar. Business center. Fitness Center. Spa. Pool. $351 and up

WHERE TO EAT

★★★CAFÉ PINOT

700 W. Fifth St., Downtown, 213-239-6500; www.patinagroup.com/cafepinot

For light fare and a casual dining experience, Café Pinot is just the ticket. The restaurant is situated in the charming front garden of the Los Angeles Public Library, making it a natural choice for the business-lunch crowd. Office workers nibble tasty morsels such as the Maryland crab cake with sweet corn, roasted pepper and black olive relish, and the mustard-glazed rotisserie chicken with fries. But sports fans know that it's also a good spot for a pre-Lakers game dinner. Lunch includes a spa menu based on what's available from the farmers' market.

American. Lunch (Monday-Friday), dinner. Reservations recommended. Bar. $36-85

★★★CHURCH AND STATE

1850 Industrial St., Downtown, 213-405-1434; www.churchandstatebistro.com

Located in a space that served as the former loading dock of the Nabisco factory is Church & State, a destination bistro for Francophiles, foodies and hipsters alike. The restaurant, helmed by chef Joshua Smith (formerly of Bastide), has maintained a lot of the features of its former haunt (the original brick flooring remains) but added very French finishings, including wooden furniture, romantic lighting and a chalkboard full of casual scrawlings like: "Bacon bourbon!" That particular bourbon, by the way, is infused in-house along with rosemary bourbon and housemade bitters. Prepare for exciting pairings with Escargots de Bourgogne (snails baked in garlic and parsley butter) and Oreilles de Cochon (pork shoulder and feet, lentils, frisée aux lardons).

Contemporary French. Lunch (Monday-Friday), dinner. Reservations recommended. Outdoor seating. Bar. No valet. $16-35

★★★★PATINA

Walt Disney Concert Hall, 141 S. Grand Ave., Downtown, 213-972-3331; www.patinagroup.com/patina

There are those who still mourn the late, great neighborhood vibe of Patina in its former space on Melrose Avenue. While it has fancy new digs at the Walt Disney Concert Hall, the haute cuisine here imagined by master chef Joachim Splichal is still exquisite. So go ahead and let the detractors complain—that just means you'll have more room to admire the undulating interior walls and seamless service. You can't go wrong with any of the daily or seasonal tasting menus, which may include a warm lobster salad with a barbecued corn sorbet or seared Kobe beef with root beer and avocado purée. Don't pass up dessert, which might include chocolate coulant cake with cane sugar honey, and housemade strawberry and tomato sorbet. Add to that a show at the Frank Gehry-designed concert venue, and your evening couldn't be more magical than if you were a 6-year-old at Disneyland.

French. Dinner. Closed Monday. Hours may change during L.A. Philharmonic concerts. Reservations recommended. Bar. $36-85

★★★WATER GRILL

544 S. Grand Ave., Downtown, 213-891-0900; www.watergrill.com

Given L.A.'s close proximity to the water, there ought to be more seafood restaurants like Water Grill. Easily boasting some of the best seafood in Los Angeles, if not Southern California, Water Grill offers an ever-changing menu of the freshest and best quality seafood from around the world. This includes an extensive array of raw bar foods—in addition to the eight oyster varieties listed, ask for the off-the-menu shucks. Or go ahead and order "The King"-sized iced shellfish platter, which includes oysters, crab nuggets, wild jumbo shrimp, over a pound of lobster, dungeness crab and one whole sea urchin. If you're here on a Sunday, the Lobster Clam Bake is a huge draw. Another plus is the extensive wine program.

Seafood. Lunch (Monday-Friday), dinner. Reservations recommended. Bar. $36-85

RECOMMENDED

NICKEL DINER
524 S. Main St., Downtown, 213-623-8301; www.nickeldiner.com

L.A.'s Downtown district is no stranger to 100-year-old diners. The Nickel, however, is an updated one, paying homage to Fifth Street, known for decades as Skid Row's "the nickel." The menu's drug references are humorous—the "5 cent bag" here is homemade brioche cinnamon toast with butter and homemade jam; the "10 cent bag" is flat iron steak with two eggs, potatoes and grilled tomatoes. The breakfast menu is served all day and features maple bacon donuts and jam tarts. Lunch includes a spicy pulled pork sandwich and the BLTA: bacon, arugula, tomato, avocado and a spicy aioli on grilled country bread. For dinner, there's chicken stuffed with mushrooms and served with old-fashioned stuffing. The interior's décor is pre-WWII, complete with squeaky red booths and old-fashioned signs. Whatever you do, save room for the wonderful desserts such as lemon pie, homemade vanilla creme-filled devil's food cupcakes (basically, really good Hostess cupcakes) and an outrageous red velvet cake.

Contemporary American. Breakfast, lunch, dinner. Closed Monday. $16-35

HOLLYWOOD/WEST HOLLYWOOD/MIDTOWN

Films are rarely made in Hollywood anymore, but that doesn't stop visitors from flocking to the corner of Hollywood and Vine, gawking at the cement prints of the stars in front of Grauman's Chinese Theatre or hunting for their favorite celebrities along the Walk of Fame. Once a year, the red carpet goes down in front of the gorgeous Kodak Theatre for the Academy Awards; on the other 364 days, the Hollywood & Highland entertainment complex is the central attraction in an otherwise seedy neighborhood. It's also an excellent place to take a photograph with the Hollywood sign in the background. West Hollywood pulses with activity at night, especially along Santa Monica Boulevard and Sunset Boulevard (a.k.a. the Sunset Strip), with venues that hold later hours than much of Los Angeles West Hollywood, (or WeHo, as it's sometimes called) is also the center of Los Angeles's gay community, but the clubs cater to audiences of all persuasions.

WHAT TO SEE

BARNSDALL ART PARK
4800 Hollywood Blvd., Hollywood, 323-660-4254; www.barnsdallartpark.com

Heiress Aline Barnsdall donated the Barnsdall Art Park to the city in the 1920s to provide an arts center for the community, and that she did. The park's biggest attraction is the Hollyhock House, which was designed for Barnsdall by Frank Lloyd Wright. The house, which was inspired by the architecture of Colombia's Mayan temples, was Wright's first project in Los Angeles. The architect specifically designed the structure with Southern California's climate in mind, but Hollyhock still manages to evoke his signature style. Besides touring Hollyhock House, you can peruse artworks at the wonderful Los Angeles Municipal Art Gallery, see Shakespeare in the park and catch a show at the Barnsdall Gallery Theatre, a low-priced rental house for theater, dance, music and more. The park also overlooks the city of Los Angeles, providing beautiful views.

Hollyhock House Tours: adults $7, seniors $3, children 17 and under $2. Wednesday-Sunday 12:30 p.m., 1:30 p.m., 2:30 p.m. and 3:30 p.m.

FARMERS MARKET

6333 W. Third St., Midtown, 323-933-9211; www.farmersmarketla.com

Located at Fairfax Avenue and Third Street is one of the U.S.'s first farmers markets, which has been going strong since the 1930s. While there are only a handful of stalls that sell fresh fruit and vegetables here (the market is dominated by restaurant stalls), it's a great destination for an alfresco lunch. Bennett's *(stall 548, 323-939-6786)* offers some of L.A.'s best ice cream and sorbet with fun flavors such as cabernet sauvignon and pumpkin; ¡Loteria! *(stall 322, 323-930-2211; www.loteriagrill.com)* serves lighter versions of Mexican fare, like chiles rellenos stuffed with goat cheese and chorizo; Magee's Kitchen *(stall 624, 323-938-4127)*, one of the oldest stalls in the market, tempts with all-American dishes like roast and corned beef; and Patsy D'Amore's *(stall 448, 323-938-4938; www.patsydamore.com)* New York-style pizza is legendary. The market is a laid-back yet lively place to eat and people-watch. You'll see hipsters eating crêpes, kids clamoring for treats in front of candy stalls and old-timers dunking their doughnuts in cups of joe.

Monday-Friday 9 a.m.-9 p.m., Saturday 9 a.m.-8 p.m., Sunday 10 a.m.-7 p.m.

GRAUMAN'S CHINESE THEATRE

6925 Hollywood Blvd., Hollywood, 323-464-8111; www.manntheatres.com

Grauman's Chinese Theatre is the heart and soul of Hollywood Boulevard. Since it opened in 1927, the theater has become one of the city's most iconic landmarks and a favorite venue for celebrity-studded film premieres. Thanks to the celebrity hand and foot prints embedded in cement outside the theater's entrance, it's also a favorite spot for tourists. If you think the theater's elaborate design and architecture is just another testament to movie magic, think again. When it was constructed, authentic temple bells, pagodas and stone figures were imported all the way from China to decorate the theater—many of those pieces can still be seen today. While Grauman's is a crowded tourist trap, you can't help but be a little moved by all the prints outside this legendary theater, so go ahead and put your hands in Brad Pitt's cement imprints.

Tickets: adults $12.75, seniors and children 3-12 $10.

THE GROUNDLINGS

7307 Melrose Ave., West Hollywood, 323-934-4747; www.groundlings.com

This L.A. institution has been cracking up audiences since 1975, thanks to all the hilarious actors who train at the Groundlings School of Improvisation. Lisa Kudrow, Will Ferrell, Jon Lovitz and many others have all practiced their improvisational skills here. Many alums have also gone on to write for favorite TV comedy shows, including *Cheers*, *Taxi* and *Golden Girls*. Drop by on a Thursday night to see L.A.'s longest running improv show (since 1992), *Cookin' with Gas*, which is based entirely on audience suggestions. Shows take place five days a week.

Box office open daily at 10 a.m., expect for Saturday 2:30 and Sunday 2 p.m. Shows: Wednesday-Thursday 8 p.m., Friday-Saturday 8 p.m. and 10 p.m., Sunday 7:30 p.m.

HOLLYWOOD FOREVER MEMORIAL PARK

6000 Santa Monica Blvd., Hollywood, 323-469-1181; www.hollywoodforever.com

The Hollywood Forever Memorial Park is the final resting place for legendary stars such as Douglas Fairbanks, Rudolph Valentino and Jayne Mansfield. During the day you can take a guided tour *(www.cemeterytour.com; $12)* of the cemetery grounds, which include mausoleums, exhibitions, monuments and gardens. At night, the park hosts another iteration of its name via biweekly summer movie screenings. The outdoor screenings, which are organized by Cinespia *(www.cinespia.org)*, feature cult favorites such as *Rosemary's Baby*, *Harold and Maude* and *The Exorcist*. Make like the locals and bring picnic dinners, blankets and lawn chairs (seating is not provided).

HOLLYWOOD MUSEUM

1660 N. Highland Ave., Hollywood, 323-464-7776; www.thehollywoodmuseum.com

Located in the famous Max Factor Building, this museum is a must for the Hollywood-obsessed. The Art Deco building itself is beautiful and it's where cosmetics genius Max Factor did the actual makeup of icons such as Lucille Ball, Marilyn Monroe and Judy Garland (you can even glance in their private salons). Wander through four floors of exhibits featuring everything from props, photos, memorabilia and costumes from your favorite movies and television shows. The permanent collection features items such as Judy Garland's dress from *A Star is Born*, a Mae West display, and the prison cell used in the film *Silence of the Lambs*. Other items include Rocky's boxing gloves, Marilyn Monroe's dresses and Cary Grant's Rolls-Royce.

Admission: adults $15, seniors and students $12, children under 5 $5. Wednesday-Sunday 10 a.m.-5 p.m.

HOLLYWOOD SIGN

Mount Lee Perch, Hollywood; www.hollywoodsign.org

What was once a glorified real estate sign has turned into one of the world's most recognizable icons. The Hollywood sign has been tampered with a number of times (to read "Hollyweed" and "Ollywood") since it was erected in 1923, but it has since been restored to its original glory. And thanks to a combined force of gates, security cameras and park rangers, the sign will be safe and sound for years to come. Since it's illegal to get anywhere near the famous white letters, you'll have to be content with seeing them from afar. Good views of the sign can be found near Lake Hollywood, but you can also see those big block letters from most streets in Hollywood.

HOLLYWOOD WALK OF FAME

Hollywood Boulevard from Gower Street to La Brea Avenue; Vine Street, from Yucca Street to Sunset Boulevard, Hollywood, 323-469-8311; www.hollywoodchamber.net

Nothing marks the Entertainment Capital of the World better than the Hollywood Walk of Fame. Conceived in 1958, the Walk of Fame was designed to immortalize Hollywood's elite. While many enjoy seeing the stars engraved with the name of their favorite celebrities (Cameron Diaz, Anjelica Huston and Kyra Sedgwick are some recent inductees), many visit the Walk to pay homage to silver-screen greats like Charlie Chaplin, Marilyn Monroe, James Dean, Elvis Presley and Cary Grant—fans often decorate the stars with flowers, candles and photos. Keep an eye out for the more unconventional stars—Godzilla, Lassie, Big Bird and Bugs Bunny all have a plaque on the Walk as well.

HOLLYWOOD WAX MUSEUM

6767 Hollywood Blvd., Hollywood, 323-462-5991; www.hollywoodwax.com

It's not exactly Madame Tussauds, but if you have a yearning to see plastic celebrities immortalized in wax, then head to this museum. You'll see shoddy likenesses of tabloid favorites including Angelina Jolie and Tom Cruise, as well as efforts to celebrate such film icons as Marilyn Monroe and Clint Eastwood. While the waxwork isn't especially skillful, it's sort of interesting to see reproductions of clothing worn by celebrities like Hugh Hefner. Across the street at the Guinness World Records Museum, you can also see a display of Michael Jackson's gold records—the late star gave these to the museum in exchange for a wax figure of Roddy McDowell as Cornelius from the film *Planet of the Apes*. Purchase your tickets online and you'll pay less than you would at the box office. Also, combination tickets to both are available online.

Hollywood Wax Museum (box office): adults $15.95, seniors $13.95, children 5-12 $8.95, children 4 and under free. Hollywood Wax Museum (online): adults $12.95, seniors $10.95, children 5-12 $5.95, children 4 and under free. Hollywood Wax Museum and Guinness World Records Museum (box office): adults $17.95, seniors $15.95, children

WHAT ARE THE CITY'S CAN'T MISS SIGHTS?

Grauman's Chinese Theatre:
Since it opened in 1927, the theater has become one of the city's most iconic landmarks, and an essential stop on any tour of Los Angeles.

Hollywood Walk of Fame:
Admit it: you just can't resist putting your hands in your favorite movie stars' imprints. We don't blame you.

Rodeo Drive:
Rodeo is home to all the high-end shops, all of which have some of the best selections in the country.

Santa Monica Pier:
The popular Santa Monica Pier delivers good old-fashioned amusement park fun, along with great ocean views.

Venice Beach:
It might as well still be the 60s. Venice is still full of colorful characters, and is by far one of the country's most unique places.

5-12 $10.95, children 4 and under free. Hollywood Wax Museum and Guinness World Records Museum (online): adults $14.95, seniors $12.95, children 5-12 $7.95, children 4 and under free. Monday-Thursday 10 a.m.-midnight, Friday-Saturday 10 a.m.-1 a.m.

KODAK THEATRE
6801 Hollywood Blvd., Hollywood, 323-308-6300; www.kodaktheatre.com

If you've always dreamed of thanking the Academy, practice your acceptance speech at the Kodak Theatre. Every year, the 3,330-seat venue is flooded with thousands of Hollywood's best and brightest stars, and not just for the Academy Awards—the Daytime Emmys, BET Awards, ESPY Awards and the *American Idol* finals have all been hosted at the Kodak. If you don't have a chance to see the interior of the venue during a performance (artists Prince and the Dixie Chicks have played at the theater), take a guided tour. You can see a real statuette; find out who sat where at this year's awards; and take a peek at VIP areas, including the George Eastman VIP Room, a first-floor bar where stars order drinks to get them through the too-long awards ceremony. (Be sure to practice a short, sweet speech.)

Tours: adults $15, seniors and children 17 and under $10, children under 3 free. September-May, daily 10:30 a.m.-2:30 p.m. (every 30 minutes); June-August, daily 10:30 a.m.-4 p.m. (every 30 minutes).

THE LAUGH FACTORY
8001 Sunset Blvd., Hollywood, 323-656-1336; www.laughfactory.com

Legendary comedians such as Jerry Seinfeld, Jim Carrey, Chris Rock and Robin Williams have all performed here, making it L.A.'s go-to place for stand-up. Before you and your pals head to the club for some laughs, check out the garden party option, which allows groups to dine outside under a tent before seeing the comedians. If you think you can assemble your own Laugh Factory-worthy bit, test it out at the club's Tuesday open mic (sign-up is at 5 p.m.).

Daily; show times vary. See website for details.

LOS ANGELES COUNTY MUSEUM OF ART/BROAD CONTEMPORARY ART MUSEUM
5905 Wilshire Blvd., Midtown, 323-857-6000; www.lacma.org

Set aside a good chunk of time when you visit LACMA—with 100,000 art objects in its catalogue, LACMA is the biggest art museum in the West. The museum's collections span several continents and thousands of years, so you can see an Egyptian sarcophagus and photographs taken by Ansel Adams on the same day. LACMA's newest addition is the Broad Contemporary Art Museum, designed by architect Renzo Piano. On view at BCAM are works by artists including Richard Serra, John Baldessari, Ed Ruscha and Cindy Sherman. Along with having an impressive permanent collection, LACMA also manages to acquire top-notch exhibits. Past shows have included photographs from *Vanity Fair* from 1913 to 2008; portraits, frescoes, sculpture and decorative arts from the lost city of Pompeii; and paintings from Gustav Klimt. Every day, after 5 p.m., admission is "pay what you wish," and on the second Tuesday of each month, general admission to permanent exhibitions is free.

Admission: adults $12, seniors and students $8, children 17 and under free. Monday-Tuesday, Thursday noon-8 p.m., Friday noon-9 p.m., Saturday-Sunday 11 a.m.-8 p.m.

HIGHLIGHT

WHAT'S THE BEST WAY TO SEE THE STARS' HOMES?

Celebrity home tours (even if you are just driving past) are as impossible to resist as guilty-pleasure supermarket tabloids. So if you're going to see where the stars take up residence, do it right (you'll be sorry if you pick up one of those shoddy star maps on a Sunset Boulevard corner; they're useless). **Starline Tours** (800-959-3131; www.starline-tours.com) offers one of the most comprehensive tours out there. The company operates a "Movie Stars Homes Tour" that will shuttle you past the mansions of blockbuster stars like Tom Cruise and Angelina Jolie as well as the former estates of film icons like Elvis Presley, Marilyn Monroe, Frank Sinatra, Lucille Ball, Judy Garland and Humphrey Bogart. Be aware, however, that many of these homes are protected from peeping Toms by tall shrubberies and gates, so you might end up just seeing some roof shingles—but at least they're famous roof shingles.

In addition to spying celebrities' permanent homes, you'll also get to see some of their temporary ones. The tour bus swings by famous spots such as the Beverly Hills Hotel—which has housed the likes of Howard Hughes and Elizabeth Taylor—and the Chateau Marmont, which has seen more than its fair share of celebrity drama. At the Chateau, John Belushi died in a bungalow, Jim Morrison allegedly fell off one of the hotel's balconies, and Led Zeppelin band members rode through the lobby on their motorcycles.

Besides seeing celebrity digs, you'll also get a guided tour of the legendary Sunset Strip, where you'll be able to catch a glimpse of celeb-studded clubs like the Viper Room and the legendary Whisky A Go-Go, as well as Beverly Hill's shopping nexus, Rodeo Drive. The odds of seeing a real, live celebrity on Rodeo Drive are slim, but you can quickly scan all the designer boutiques including Gucci, Prada, Fendi and Dior.

The tour operates all year long and departs every half hour (from 9:30 a.m. to sundown) from Grauman's Chinese Theatre and various hotels in the area (call or check the website for a full list). The tour clocks in at about two hours, and tickets cost around $40 for adults and $30 for children—you'll save a few bucks if you get picked up at Grauman's Chinese Theatre.

PAGE MUSEUM AT THE LA BREA TAR PITS

5801 Wilshire Blvd., Midtown, 323-934-7243; www.tarpits.org

It's hard to imagine that saber-toothed cats and woolly mammoths once roamed the gridlocked streets of L.A., so to get a better idea of what prehistoric Southern California was like, take a trip to the La Brea Tar Pits. When you visit the tar pits, or Rancho La Brea, as it's often called, you'll still see (and smell) the bubbling pools of black asphalt that trapped hundreds of species thousands of years ago. Thanks to the tar, millions of Ice Age fossils were preserved and eventually recovered. After touring the tar pits (which feature life-size replicas of woolly mammoths), head inside the Page Museum, where you can see animal skeletons and watch scientists at work in the Page Museum Laboratory. *Admission: adults $7, seniors and students $4.50, children 5-12 $2, children under 5 free. Daily 9:30 a.m.-5 p.m. First Tuesday of the month free.*

WHICH FILM STUDIOS OFFER TOURS?

Paramount Film and Television Studios:
The only major movie studio still located in Hollywood offers a two-hour tour giving you a peek at the famous gates from the movie Sunset Boulevard, television sets such as Dr. Phil and props like the bench from *Forrest Gump*.

Sony Pictures Studio Tour:
See the Yellow Brick Road, and the sets from blockbusters such as *Spiderman* and television shows including Wheel of Fortune, at this busy lot.

Universal Studios Hollywood:
Tour a studio, jump aboard theme park rides, and then stay to dine and catch a movie at Universal CityWalk.

Warner Bros. Studios VIP Tour:
If you're really a movie buff, this studio begins with a deluxe five-hour tour that allows you to interact with crew members and crafts people for an up close look at how movies are made, and concludes with lunch in the commissary.

PANTAGES THEATER

6233 Hollywood Blvd., Hollywood, 323-468-1770; www.broadwayla.org

Southern California's version of Broadway is the Pantages, where musical theater is king. The historic Art Deco theater, which sits a few steps from the famous intersection of Hollywood Boulevard and Vine Street, opened in 1930. In 1949, billionaire Howard Hughes purchased the theater and turned it into an RKO movie house. Under Hughes' ownership, the Pantages became the venue for the Academy Awards—the awards show was held there for more than 10 years. Today, productions such as *Chicago*, *A Chorus Line*, *The Phantom of the Opera*, and *West Side Story* bring their razzle-dazzle to the Pantages.

Box office: Daily 10 a.m.-30 minutes after last show starts.

PARAMOUNT FILM AND TELEVISION STUDIOS

5555 Melrose Ave., Hollywood, 323-956-1777; www.paramount.com

Paramount's two-hour tour gives you a peek at the only major movie studio still located in Hollywood. When you enter the historic studio lot, you'll pass through the famous gates that made a cameo in the film *Sunset Boulevard*. Tour access depends on shooting schedules, so it's hard to say what you'll see, but what you can expect is a behind-the-scenes look at sound stages, wardrobe, production and sets, as well as props from popular films, including the bench from *Forrest Gump*. Advance reservations are required and tours occur only on weekdays, so plan your excursion ahead of time. Only children 12 and older are allowed on the tour.

Tours: $35. Monday-Friday 10 a.m., 11 a.m., 1 p.m. and 2 p.m.

PETERSEN AUTOMOTIVE MUSEUM

6060 Wilshire Blvd., Midtown, 323-930-2277; www.petersen.org

If you are a car fan, take a detour to the Petersen Automotive Museum. You can travel back in time with antique cars and steam engines, and then fast-forward into the future with forms of alternative power. If your eyes glaze over at the thought of fuel cells, then head to the Hollywood Gallery, where you can see Herbie from *The Love Bug*, a bright yellow Pantera driven by Elvis Presley, the Hannibal 8 driven by Jack Lemmon in *The Great Race* and much more. Check the website to see which exhibitions are on view—the museum has showcased everything from lowriders to Hot Wheels.

Admission: adults $10, seniors, students and active military $5, children 5-12 $3, children under 5 free. Tuesday-Saturday 10 a.m.-6 p.m.

RUNYON CANYON
2000 N. Fuller Ave., Hollywood, 213-485-5572; www.lamountains.com

To get a breather after inhaling the exhaust fumes of Hollywood Boulevard, head north of Hollywood's busy streets to Runyon Canyon Park. Runyon, whose rugged terrain sprawls across 130 acres, offers awesome views of the city (on a clear day you can see from Downtown to Santa Monica) and a network of trails that will tone your legs better than a StairMaster. Another reason why Runyon is packed almost every day of the week is because it serves as an off-leash dog park. Runyon Canyon can be accessed from the north via Mulholland Drive, or from the south at Fuller Avenue.

SUNSET RANCH
3400 N. Beachwood Drive, Hollywood, 323-469-5450; www.sunsetranchhollywood.com

If your trip out West is giving you the urge to saddle up, then head to Sunset Ranch, where you can rent a horse or take a riding lesson. What makes Sunset Ranch better than your average stable is its Dinner Ride. The ride starts off in Griffith Park and takes riders to Burbank, where they wine and dine at the Viva Fresh Mexican Restaurant. (If you would rather take a trip during the day, there are other trips to choose from. See website for details.) After dinner, you're treated to a moonlit ride back to Griffith Park. Be sure to wear comfortable clothes during your ride and sensible shoes (this means no flip-flops).
Dinner Ride: $105 for first person, $75 for every additional person. Daily 4 p.m., 4:30 p.m., 5 p.m. Office: Daily 9 a.m.-5 p.m.

UPRIGHT CITIZENS BRIGADE
5919 Franklin Ave., Hollywood, 323-908-8702; www.ucbtheatre.com

The Upright Citizens Brigade (or UCB) began in Chicago and is now in both L.A. and New York. The troupe's completely unpredictable sketch comedy, led by Matt Besser, Amy Poehler, Ian Roberts and Matt Walsh, is often sidesplittingly funny. Tickets can be hard to come by, so reserve yours early and take advantage of bargain shows like UCB's weekly $5 *Comedy Death Ray*, which features a lineup mixed with seasoned and novice stand-up comedians. The UCB also hosts *Not Too Shabby*, a free gig that offers the stage to the audience and which starts after midnight and goes into the wee hours.
Daily; show times vary. See website for details.

WHERE TO STAY

★★★ANDAZ WEST HOLLYWOOD
8401 Sunset Blvd., West Hollywood, 323-656-1234; www.andaz.com

The former Hyatt West Hollywood has had such a facelift, it is almost unrecognizable from before. Since the Hyatt's new trendy hotel brand ANdAZ is reaching for a younger audience, the hotel emerged transformed in early 2009. The new hotel attempts to wow with a dramatic glass garden pavilion with a Jacob Hashimoto sculpture and the intimate RH restaurant and bar (which features fresh, seasonal ingredients and a market to table approach), and a private wine room in charcoal and cream with mosaic tiles.
257 rooms. Restaurant, bar. Business center. Fitness center. Pool. $151-250

★★★CHAMBERLAIN WEST HOLLYWOOD

1000 Westmount Drive, West Hollywood, 310-657-7400;
www.chamberlainwesthollywood.com

People like the Chamberlain for its English-modern and neo-classical interior with striking and eclectic elements such as tropical jade and patina green tiles and lacquered Asian-style coffee tables. The location isn't shabby, either, as the intimate hotel is centrally set in West Hollywood, but in a less-traveled residential neighborhood. The dusty-blue and gray rooms have luxurious details such as gas log fireplaces, balconies, velvet chairs and modern conveniences such as iHome docks. Head down to the bistro (like a greenhouse with olive banquettes, plants line the patio outside the windows and the lush outdoor patio), where chef Mark Pierce puts a California twist on bistro fare

114 rooms. Restaurant, bar. Fitness center. Pool. $251-350

★★★CHATEAU MARMONT HOTEL AND BUNGALOWS

8221 Sunset Blvd., West Hollywood, 323-656-1010; www.chateaumarmont.com

If you can't take the scene (amid important Hollywood types and hangers-on lounging in heavy chairs, sipping wine and making demands), get out of the Chateau Marmont. Constant updates are not the thing at this elite hilltop retreat (although the rooms do have iPod docking stations and cashmere throws), where every celebrity you could conceive of lingers around the dimly lit lounge's couches. Outside, the pretty garden dining area is like another world: light, airy and peppered with flowers. Just above one of Hollywood's buzziest boulevards (a two-minute downhill walk), the hotel draws in crowds to the popular Bar Marmont restaurant and lounge. The restaurant's food wasn't anything special until the arrival in early 2008 of chef Carolynn Spence, formerly of New York's West Village hot spot, The Spotted Pig. Now diners come out to devour haute snacks like bacon-wrapped prunes and deviled eggs and entrées such as brown butter roasted halibut.

63 rooms. Restaurant, bar. Fitness center. Pool. $351 and up

★★★THE GRAFTON ON SUNSET

8462 W. Sunset Blvd., West Hollywood, 323-654-4600; www.graftononsunset.com

The Grafton is located right on the Sunset Strip, which offers endless bars and restaurants ranging from Asia de Cuba to kitchy but star-filled Ketchup. A rehab gave the hotel some pizzazz, including lively décor such as zebra-printed Italian bedding, oversized photographic prints and a heated saltwater pool (which means no need for toxic chlorine). If you're all about the pool, book a Deluxe Poolside room for immediate access to the pool party. The Grafton's long, enclosed pool area is a great place to lounge, especially late at night, when all the Sunset haunts have closed (usually by 2 a.m.).

108 rooms. Restaurant, bar. Business center. Fitness center. Pool. Pets accepted. $151-250

★★★HOLLYWOOD ROOSEVELT HOTEL

7000 Hollywood Blvd., Hollywood, 323-466-7000; www.hollywoodroosevelt.com

The Roosevelt is the perfect example of how inevitably L.A. life comes full circle. When the hotel opened in 1927, huge names of the time, from Marilyn Monroe to Clark Gable, set up residence at the swanky place, where the first Academy Awards ceremony was held. For a while it fell into disrepair, but then reemerged as a premium hot spot in 2005. Now, renovated but still retaining its original charm, the lavish Art Deco lobby hosts after-parties for premieres; refurbished old Hollywood celebrity suites are used by current A-listers for award show preparation; and tastemakers head to Dakota: restaurant for haute cuisine (where you might catch a sight of Brad and Angie) or to 25 Degrees for custom hamburgers and half bottles of wine. The Tropicana Bar—by the famous pool depicted by artist David Hockney—still draws scenesters and starlets, including Tom Hanks, Kate Hudson and the cast of *Entourage*. Teddy's—the elite bar out front—is one of L.A.'s most difficult doors to get through, though many a celebrity glides right on in (Leo DiCaprio is a regular there).

300 rooms. Restaurant, bar. Fitness center. Pool. Pets accepted. $351 and up

★★★LE MONTROSE SUITE HOTEL

900 Hammond St., West Hollywood, 310-855-1115; www.lemontrose.com

If you have a suite tooth, Le Montrose Hotel in West Hollywood may be the place for you. Only junior, executive and one-bedroom suites are available at this unassuming, recently refurbished boutique find. The apartment-style spot also offers laundry facilities, a heated saltwater pool and lighted tennis courts. Nestled on a quiet residential street, you'd never guess that frenetic Sunset Strip is just five minutes away. But the décor isn't quiet at all, and it borders on too-trendy, with wild elements such as oversized cylindrical lamps and mixed-pattern bedding. The private dining room is exclusively for guests, although many don't know about it, and it has plasma screens for your viewing pleasure. Santa Monica and Sunset boulevards are also both lined with tons of fabulous restaurants, so hop over to Café La Boheme for Wagyu beef sliders.

133 rooms. Restaurant, bar. Business center. Fitness center. Pool. Tennis. $251-350

★★★LE PARC SUITE HOTEL

733 N. West Knoll Drive, West Hollywood, 310-855-8888; www.leparcsuites.com

Hidden on a picturesque residential street right off Melrose that looks like it belongs in a small-town East Coast neighborhood, Le Parc Suite Hotel is worthwhile, if only for the easy underground parking. This particular part of Melrose offers

---

WHICH HOTELS HAVE BEEN FEATURED IN MOVIES?

Beverly Wilshire, A Four Seasons Hotel: Although most of the scenes were filmed in a studio, everyone knows this hotel was the setting for many of the scenes in the movie *Pretty Woman* starring Julia Roberts and Richard Gere.

Millennium Biltmore Hotel Los Angeles: Numerous movies have been filmed here, including scenes from *Wedding Crashers*, *Spiderman*, *Ocean's 11*, *Ghostbusters*, *Splash* and *Rumor Has It*. The hotel also hosted eight Oscar ceremonies in the 30s and 40s; in 1960, JFK turned the Music Room into his headquarters for the DNC; and in 1964, the Beatles landed on the rooftop in a helicopter and stayed in the presidential suite while on their first U.S. tour.

Hollywood Roosevelt Hotel: Many movies and television shows (including episodes of *Entourage*) have been filmed here. Movies include *Catch Me If You Can*, *Charlie's Angels* and *Beverly Hills Cop II*.

Chateau Marmont Hotel and Bungalows: Sophia Coppola just wrapped a movie that was filmed here, set for release sometime in 2010 and at press time titled *Somewhere*.

**The London West
Hollywood:**
The sibling of sister
property The London
NYC has been revamped
with Hollywood glamour
in mind. The spectacular
views are still there, but
now the rich brown-
and-cream rooms have
Waterworks jet and
raindrop shower heads,
docking stations and an
open floor plan.

**Thompson Beverly
Hills:**
Just as insiders know 60
Thompson as one of
Manhattan's hot spots,
this West Coast sibling
pulls in a hip crowd who
appreciate the mix of
late '70s and California
modernist design
with soft-hued leather
furniture and
wood décor.

**SLS Hotel at
Beverly Hills:**
This Beverly Hills
hotspot includes a private
guest lobby, hot restau-
rant, and guest rooms
and suites designed by
Philippe Starck, including
suites with personal gym
equipment and rooms
that are designed to be
hypoallergenic.

several lovely breakfast, brunch and lunch spots, from
Urth Caffé to Le Pain Quotidien (*8607 Melrose Ave.,
310-854-3700*) for delicious tartines, and the amazing
David Myers brasserie Comme Ça, located just across
La Cienega (try the crème brûlée French toast).
The hotel's own restaurant, Knoll, offers adequate
Mediterranean/French cuisine. Le Parc itself is low-key,
but offers a good value. All suite-style rooms are muted
in soft chocolates and purples and offer complimentary wireless Internet. Sporty types will want to volley
above West Hollywood—head up to the roof deck for
poolside chaises and a tennis court, a rarity in urban
hotels this small.

*154 rooms. Restaurant, bar. Business center. Fitness center. Pool.
Tennis. Pets accepted. $251-350*

★★★THE LONDON WEST HOLLYWOOD

1020 N. San Vicente Blvd., West Hollywood, 310-854-1111;
www.thelondonwesthollywood.com

The sibling of sister property The London NYC has
been revamped with Hollywood glamour in mind.
The spectacular views are still there, but now the rich
brown-and-cream rooms have Waterworks jet and
raindrop shower heads, multiple docking stations and
free phone calls for up to eight hours to the city of
London each day. Celebrity chef Gordon Ramsay adds
a California twist to the worldly cuisine at his namesake
restaurant, playing on seasonal local produce. The
spectacular pool/roof deck has been updated in the
vein of an English garden as well.

*200 rooms. Restaurant, bar. Fitness center. Pool. Pets accepted.
$351 and up*

★★★MONDRIAN

8440 Sunset Blvd., West Hollywood, 323-650-8999;
www.mondrianhotel.com

Once, Mondrian's Skybar was the most elite door in
all of L.A. Perhaps even more impressive in this ever-
changing city, the hip hotel and bar have managed to
maintain an A-list clientele even after the initial heat
diminished to a simmer. Still, it was time for a refresh
and, while excellent Asian-Latin fusion eatery Asia
de Cuba (the calamari salad is nothing but crunchy
goodness) has remained intact, designer Benjamin
Noriega Ortiz revised the rest of the original Philippe
Starck masterpiece (although the much-loved original
base stayed). The new aesthetic, often described as *Alice
in Wonderland* meets old Hollywood glamour, brings
a bit more color and eclectic touches to the famously

sleek, whitewashed space. You'll find high-tech gadgets, an updated Agua Spa and a new lobby lounge. Meanwhile, although Sunset Boulevard is one big chaotic party, some frat-boy havens have given way to impressive culinary ventures such as BLT Steak; so going out on Sunset is perhaps a bit more palatable than it used to be.

237 rooms. Restaurant, bar. Business center. Pool. Spa. $351 and up

★★★THE ORLANDO

8384 W. Third St., West Hollywood, 323-658-6600; www.theorlando.com

Those who claim that L.A. isn't a walking city may eat their words (and everything else in an eight-block radius) after visiting The Orlando. The simple hotel—with nice touches like a dimly lit lobby lounge with cushy armchairs and a 50-inch plasma TV—sits on Third Street, a blossoming stretch of trendy eateries (especially for brunch), including the newly expanded Joan's On Third (think Dean & Deluca, but with more celebrities and better cupcakes). On the downside, the pool is small, but overall it's a great value. Rooms have flat-screen TVs and warm, muted tones. Don't be surprised to bump into a famous musician or two, as—perhaps for privacy's sake—they tend to gravitate to this quiet, unpretentious best-kept-secret spot within walking distance to just about everything you need.

98 rooms. Restaurant, bar. Fitness center. Pool. Pets accepted. $151-250

★★★PALIHOUSE HOLLOWAY

8465 Holloway Drive, West Hollywood, 323-656-4100; www.palihouse.com

Hordes of actors and bicoastal types, who visit L.A. for productions and pilot season, are making their reservations now for Palihouse Holloway. The brand-new long-term-stay hotel, hearkening back to old Hollywood days when actors would hole up in hotels, is a welcome alternative to corporate options. As you traipse down the stairs at the hotel's entrance toward The Hall's beautiful brick-lined floors, it's almost like discovering a private club. To the right is an eclectic living-room-style lounge with distressed leather chairs and unusual *Indiana Jones*-type relics, and to the left is a French-style espresso bar and the indoor/outdoor eatery, The Hall courtyard brasserie. If you're planning on

WHICH HOTEL HAS THE MOST UNIQUE DÉCOR?

Palihouse Holloway: Entering this longer-term, lodge-style hotel is like discovering a private club. The décor is certainly unique with its eclectic living-room-style lounge with distressed leather chairs and unusual relics. Rooms have rain showers and hardwood floors, and amenities include a washer and dryer and a cleaning supply kit.

WHICH L.A. HOTELS ARE BEST FOR A LIVELY SCENE?

The Beverly Hills Hotel and Bungalows:
Make your way downstairs to the French-colonial inspired outdoor deck, or take in the scene at the famous Polo Lounge, which still buzzes with handshakes and business deals.

Chateau Marmont Hotel and Bungalows:
Just above one of Hollywood's buzziest boulevards, the hotel draws in crowds to the popular Bar Marmont restaurant and lounge, and has long been a hangout for scores of celebrities.

Hollywood Roosevelt Hotel:
The lavish Art Deco lobby hosts after-parties for premieres; refurbished old Hollywood celebrity suites are used by current A-listers for award show preparation; and The Tropicana Bar has seen the cast of *Entourage*.

SLS Hotel at Beverly Hills: Sam Nazarian (owner of hospitality giant SBE) has launched most of L.A.'s hottest restaurants and clubs. The SLS is his first hotel and it's the place to drink and eat in the city right now.

W Hollywood:
The new W Hollywood is practically a non-stop party, with places to sit and grab a cocktail practically everywhere you turn, from the glamourous lobby to the outdoor lounge with a movie screen to Drai's nightclub with panoramic views of the city.

staying a while (rates drop the longer you do stay), the studios and one-and two-bedroom suites upstairs have rain showers, C.O. Bigelow products, hardwood floors and Fili d'Oro Egyptian cotton linens. The roof deck is available for private parties.

36 rooms. Restaurant, bar. Pets accepted. $251-350

★★★RENAISSANCE HOLLYWOOD HOTEL & SPA
1755 N. Highland Ave., Hollywood, 323-856-1200; www.renaissancehollywood.com

There's no shortage of stimulation at the Renaissance Hollywood Hotel, housed inside L.A.'s elaborate Hollywood & Highland shopping complex, above frenetic visitors' destination Hollywood Boulevard and next door to the famous Grauman's Chinese Theatre. The hotel is also across from the Academy Awards' Kodak Theatre; many a starlet has primped in one of the hotel's Mid-Century modern rooms and then sneaked through secret passages to the red-carpet area. The lobby lounge, Caffé Fama, serves Italian Illy café espresso to give you that jolt to tackle all of the tourist attractions, and later, celebrity-designed signature cocktails are available to help you unwind after a tiring day of sightseeing. Spa Luce adds another layer of luxury (and another potential activity on your to-do list), with treatments that use upscale products from celebrity skincare experts such as Sonya Dakar, Red Flower and Somme Institute. It'll give you a nice break from the flurry of activity.

632 rooms. Restaurant, bar. Business center. Fitness center. Pool. Spa. $251-350

★★★SLS HOTEL AT BEVERLY HILLS
465 S. La Cienega Blvd., Midtown, 310-247-0400; www.luxurycollection.com

Visionary entrepreneur Sam Nazarian (owner of hospitality giant SBE) has launched most of L.A.'s hottest restaurant and nightlife destinations, from Katsuya to Hyde. In 2008, SBE launched its first hotel, SLS Hotel at Beverly Hills. In Le Meredien's former digs on La Cienega, the hotel aims to change the face of hospitality. Upon entering the Philippe Starck-designed hotel, you'll have the option of coming through two separate lobbies: Tres, the Private Guest Lobby (a serene space with an exclusive lounge), or The Bazaar (a constant party with culinary indulgences by Spanish chef José Andrés as well as cocktails and shopping). Guests are afforded preferential access to SBE's restaurants and nightclubs across the city. Continue the VIP treatment at Ciel Spa at SLS, use the fitness center with personal trainer in tow or rent one of the signature Lifestyle Suites, equipped with Technogym's Kinesis personal equipment series (which allows you to do hundreds of exercises on one machine). Each room's comprehensive pillow menu, from hypoallergenic to down, will ensure a good night's sleep, which you'll need after a night out on the town.

297 rooms. Restaurant, bar. Business center. Fitness center. Pool. Spa. Pets accepted. $351 and up

★★★SOFITEL LOS ANGELES

8555 Beverly Blvd., Midtown, 310-278-5444; www.sofitellosangeles.com

Renovated practically from top to bottom, the hotel has become a serious Hollywood hot spot thanks to the high-end, innovative comfort food at Simon L.A. restaurant (helmed by head chef Kerry Simon) and a sassy insider crowd at the adjoining Stone Rose cocktail lounge. LeSpa at Sofitel L.A. also draws bliss-seekers, and guestrooms include rain showers. Everyone mingles in the lobby, reveling in its futuristic parody of contemporary style—complete with a chair made from half dollars. The hotel's central location is a foodie's and shopper's paradise; it sits across from the city's most famed mall, The Beverly Center, and a couple of blocks from stretches of chic celebrity-filled eateries (from Toast to The Ivy) and boutiques on Third Street and Robertson Boulevard. The hotel is only minutes from Beverly Hills, West Hollywood and The Grove farmers' market, movie theaters and an outdoor mall. In this notoriously spread-out city, locations don't get more central than the Sofitel.

295 rooms. Restaurant, bar. Fitness center. Pool. Spa. $251-350

★★★SUNSET MARQUIS HOTEL & VILLAS

1200 Alta Loma Road, West Hollywood, 310-657-1333; www.sunsetmarquishotel.com

The intimate and refined Sunset Marquis Hotel & Villas—just off the Strip from famous music spot the Whisky A Go-Go—has long attracted music's biggest names, from Bette Midler to the Red Hot Chili Peppers to the Wu Tang Clan (and a few actors, including Brad Pitt, Uma Thurman and George Clooney). Having recently completed a $25 million renovation, the beautiful hotel renamed its notoriously elite lounge Bar 1200 (formerly Whisky Bar). Now exclusive Ross Halfin photographs of former hotel and onsite recording studio guests dot the bar's wall. Wander down lushly landscaped stone paths and over a bridge to 42 new villas with beautifully tiled bathrooms, butler service and 400-weave sheets; 12 original (but revamped) villas; and a two-story Presidential Suite, which comes with a Bentley or a chauffeured limo or SUV. The makeover also includes a new restaurant with illustrious executive chef Guillaume Burlion at the helm and a spa with exclusive Erbe products (from the longtime Vatican apothecary). Meanwhile, in case you rock stars need to stow your vehicles, Sunset Marquis also offers underground parking designed to hold (and wash) four tour buses.

153 rooms. Restaurant, bar. Fitness center. Pool. Spa. $351 and up

★★★SUNSET TOWER HOTEL

8358 Sunset Blvd., West Hollywood, 323-654-7100; www.sunsettowerhotel.com

You're in good company at the Sunset Tower Hotel (formerly The Argyle, but the hotel returned to its inaugural name), previously the stomping ground for

Marilyn Monroe, Frank Sinatra and Howard Hughes. Even now, heavy hitters like Tom Ford, Leonardo DiCaprio and Nicole Kidman are seen cavorting on the casual terrace or at the more upscale Tower Bar. While overlooking all of Los Angeles, you'll sip coffee from in-room cappuccino machines (in some suites), relax on Egyptian cotton sheets, slather yourself in Kiehl's products, park your iPod in docking stations, and let your pet indulge in services like mini-beds and an adjoining dog run. The lobby is nothing showy, but just beyond it is the updated Art Deco pool area that affords extraordinary views. Housed in Bugsy Siegel's old apartment, The Tower Bar and Restaurant is a welcome nostalgic throwback, as you'll sip martinis and sidecars amid fairly masculine, dark wood appointments (a gentlemen's library) and tap your foot to a jazz pianist's tunes. Downstairs, The Argyle Salon and Spa offers traditional men's shaves, private spa treatment rooms, med-spa offerings and some of the industry's most renowned hair stylists, such as stylist Mateo Herreros, whose clientele includes Uma Thurman and Helena Christenson, and colorist Steven Tapp, who works on big names such as Madonna.

74 rooms. Restaurant, bar. Fitness center. Pool. Spa. Pets accepted. $251-350

★★★W HOLLYWOOD

6250 Hollywood Blvd., Hollywood, 323-798-1300 ;
www.starwoodhotels.com

Like the other W hotels worldwide, the W Hollywood is a modern and lively space, but you're not likely to confuse this location with any of the others. First, there's the red carpet entrance. Then there's the bell cap who exclaims "Welcome to Hollywood!" The lobby is more like a big bar—you can sit back on white faux-crocodile banquettes and black tufted leather sofas to enjoy a cocktail. The social drinking extends out the floor-to-ceiling doors of the Living Room into Station Hollywood (a nod to the Metro red line train station just behind it), which has outdoor fireplaces and a movie screen. Stylish rooms are decorated in gray and white with black leather chaise lounges, window benches, fresh orchids, art books and rich fabrics. Marble bathrooms are stocked with Bliss products (there's a Bliss spa onsite) and have spacious standing showers. Delphine, the hotel's eatery and bar, serves classic French cuisine and features a soothing French Riviera-inspired decor. Other diversions include a rooftop pool, Drai's Lounge (which is members only) and Drai's nightclub (open to all), which offers great views of Hollywood—in case you were tempted for a moment to forget where you are.

305 rooms. Restaurant, bar. Business center. Fitness center. Pool. Spa. Pets accepted. $251-350

WHERE TO EAT

★★★XIV

8117 Sunset Blvd., West Hollywood, 323-656-1414; www.sbe.com/xiv

A powerful trio backs one of the city's most buzzed about restaurants—this is chef Michael Mina's first L.A. restaurant (and his 14th overall), the interior is designed by Philippe Starck, and nightlife powerhouse SBE is also part of the team. Needless to say, the place has been packed since it opened. The outdoor patio draws people who work nearby on Sunset, especially since they introduced 6IX, a happy hour where everything is $6 and includes a menu of champagne, wine and a collection of Mina classics such as black truffle popcorn and lobster corn dogs. Inside, you can order Mina's signature items such as the lobster pot pie and Kobe burger with a trio of French fries and "secret sauce," while taking in the interesting juxtaposition Starck is known for—lots of paintings and bookshelves and photos in frames, chandeliers and a sleek stainless-steel open kitchen. The wine list is substantial and this being an SBE venture, there are plenty of fun cocktails.

Contemporary American. Dinner. Reservations recommended. Bar. $36-85

★★★ANIMAL

435 N. Fairfax Ave., West Hollywood, 323-782-9225; www.animalrestaurant.com

Animal, a restaurant which aims to serve all the parts of a pig to its diners, has the audacity to do so in the heart of L.A.'s Jewish community. To be fair, Animal sacrifices its namesake in every variety: rabbit, duck, catfish, cow—the carnivorous list is neverending. Two guys are behind this popular restaurant: former Food Network stars Jon Shook and Vinny Dotolo, authors of *Two Dudes, One Pan*, and they've double-handedly succeeded in getting Angelenos to eat pig ear, marrow bone and crispy rabbit legs. The restaurant, decorated with off-white paint and not much else (the owners like to say it's about the food, not the design), keeps all of its 40 seats occupied consistently—but every night, the seven stools at the bar are available for spontaneous taking.

Contemporary American. Dinner. Reservations recommended. Bar. $16-35

★★★BLD

7450 Beverly Blvd., Midtown, 323-930-9744; www.bldrestaurant.com

Yes, BLD stands for "breakfast, lunch and dinner," but the offerings here are nothing so quotidian. The pancakes aren't just boring old buttermilk; they're blueberry-ricotta hotcakes with Berkshire maple syrup. Even better, they're served until 3 p.m. on the weekend, along with the rest of the still breakfasty brunch menu, which offers such options as grapefruit brûlée and eggs Florentine. Lunch features delicious salads, sandwiches, burgers and pastas. Try the eggless egg salad sandwich with tofu, celery, red onion, lemon tofu aioli and oven dried tomato spread on multi-grain bread, or the blackened

---

WHICH L.A. RESTAURANTS OFFER THE BEST OVERALL DINING EXPERIENCE?

Mélisse:
Chef Josiah Citrin opened this elegant but unpretentious eatery in 1999, where he offers his outstanding contemporary French cuisine paired with a superb wine list.

Patina:
Like the artists inside the Walt Disney Concert Hall (where Patina is located), the chefs here have created a bevy of classics—and continue to push the envelope with innovative dishes such as warm lobster salad with a tomato "air."

Ortolan:
Gourmands know executive chef Christophe Émé from his years at L'Orangerie. Named after a rare bird historically eaten as a delicacy in the south of France, Ortolan is the perfect backdrop for his mix of haute cuisine and playful irreverence.

The Belvedere:
The Belvedere at the Peninsula Beverly Hills has long catered to the city's most discerning crowd with its Modern American cuisine featuring well-executed dishes such as scallops in plum sauce and rack of lamb with Indian eggplant and Greek yogurt.

The Bazaar: This hotspot designed by Philippe Starck in the SLS Hotel Beverly Hills is part bar, part tapas restaurant and part patisserie.

Church and State: Angelenos have been flocking here for the delicious bistro fare served in a lively space with piazza lights and large windows overlooking Industrial Street.

Osteria Mozza: This Mario Batali-Linda Silverton venture has been packed since it opened in late 2006. Try to grab a seat at the mozzarella bar where you can watch all the action.

XIV: Michael Mina's first L.A. restaurant is filled with people nightly who pour onto the patio and linger over Mina classics like the lobster corn dog; it's as much of a scene inside at the long marble bar.

Koi: Perennial hot spot Koi has been consistently booked by A-list celebrities for years.

Mr. Chow: After four decades, Mr. Chow is still one of Los Angeles' go-to spots for high-powered Hollywood types who order champagne from the roving trolly while digging into hand-pulled noodles.

catfish sandwich with horseradish cole slaw, served with a side of Old Bay French fries. In the evening, get creative and go with the Self-Constructive Dinner; you choose a protein, like grilled flatiron steak; a side, like fresh polenta; and a sauce, such as arugula pesto—and voila. A meal as easy as the restaurant's name.

American. Breakfast, lunch (Monday-Friday), dinner, Saturday-Sunday brunch. Reservations recommended. Bar. $16-35

★★★BLT STEAK

8720 Sunset Blvd., West Hollywood, 310-360-1950; www.bltsteak.com

BLT Steak, part of the Laurent Tourondel restaurant empire, occupies a prime spot if ever there was one: the space formerly occupied by the swanky, star-studded Le Dôme on the Sunset Strip. And BLT lives up to the legendary digs, offering expertly prepared steakhouse fare such as the 22-ounce rib eye and the 40-ounce porterhouse for two. Although the steak is the main attraction, don't skip the generously sized popovers or the raw bar selections, such as the picture-perfect shrimp cocktail. And just order the onion rings, which come piled high in a golden-brown tower of deliciousness. If you can, save room for dessert: The lemon-cassis meringue pie is toothsome and fluffy.

Steak. Dinner. Reservations recommended. Bar. $36-85

★★★BOA STEAKHOUSE

9200 Sunset Blvd., West Hollywood, 310-278-2050; www.boasteak.com

Having recently moved from its old location in the Grafton Hotel on the Sunset Strip, BOA has settled into its new digs just a little west on Sunset Boulevard. This installation is a lot bigger—it now features 13,000 square feet of space, including a 4,000-square-foot outdoor patio. As you enter through the patio area to the interior, you'll note the bold colors of the bar, with sleek red leather couches and a red granite bar from India. The bold color carries over into the main dining room with its red felt walls which were hand-crafted in London. BOA offers an à la carte menu of your favorite surf-and-turf classics—think whole Maine lobster, 40-day dry-aged New York strip steak and premium Wagyu. Put yourself in your server's hands; despite its modern setting, the restaurant's staff is attentive, professional and down-to-earth, probably the best elements of an old-school steakhouse experience. Just be sure to try the Caesar salad, which is prepared tableside to your liking, and one of the specialty cocktails. Afterward, the lounge is a great spot for another drink—just flip over your cocktail table for a game of backgammon.

Steak. Lunch, dinner. Reservations recommended. Bar. $16-35

★★★CAFÉ LA BOHEME

8400 Santa Monica Blvd., West Hollywood, 323-848-2360; www.globaldiningca.com

A West Hollywood staple for nearly 20 years, Café La Boheme has long been known as the kind of over-the-top venue where yards and yards of red velvet upholstery go to die (or loom over diners). But at the end of 2007, it underwent a complete transformation. The velvet, the tablecloths and the elaborate trompe l'oeil and mosaic accents are all gone, and the dining room is more stripped down and casual. The red accents and signature chandeliers remain— they were too special to be discarded—but Café La Boheme is no longer just a special-occasion restaurant; it's now a great place for after-work dinner and drinks. The bar is much larger, and the dining room suggests a modern supper club, with lots of private booths, a roaring fireplace and handsome wood-beam ceilings. The menu, which reflects executive chef Christine Banta's classical French training and Japanese-American heritage, has been updated as well, offering comfort foods with an Asian touch, including Japanese pumpkin ravioli and miso glazed salmon.

International. Dinner. Bar. $16-35

★★★CAMPANILE

624 S. La Brea Ave., Midtown, 323-938-1447; www.campanilerestaurant.com

Joined to the famed La Brea Bakery, Campanile is something of a mid-city oasis: Housed in a unique, historic structure built by Charlie Chaplin in 1929, the atmosphere is airy and functional, with faded gray arched doorways, vaulted ceilings, concrete walls and plenty of natural light. But don't mistake an uncomplicated look for unsophisticated taste—in fact, this is an institution for people who are serious about good food. Owner and executive chef Mark Peel is a venerable name on the restaurant scene; he started out peeling vegetables for Wolfgang Puck and went on to open Spago with him in 1982. Peel still scours the local farmer's markets to make beautiful seasonal dishes, and you can taste his favorite finds in his special three-course Monday-night menus.

American, Mediterranean. Lunch (Monday-Friday), dinner (Monday-Saturday), Saturday-Sunday brunch. Reservations recommended. Bar. $16-35

★★★COMME ÇA

8479 Melrose Ave., West Hollywood, 323-782-1104; www.commecarestaurant.com

Foodies have been buzzing about Comme Ça, the busy Melrose Avenue bistro opened by chef-owner David Myers (who also created nearby Sona) in late 2007. If you're expecting classic bistro décor, however, you might be surprised by the quasi-minimalist design, which features stark white chairs, black wainscoting and a collage-like arrangement of mirrors adorning the walls. Plus, everyone on the waitstaff looks like a member of SAG, the tables (which you'll wait for in an elbow-to-elbow crowd for an infuriatingly long time) are placed a bit too close for comfort, and the noise level isn't conducive to intimate conversation. But you'll have plenty to talk about after your meal, which features well-prepared French-bistro fare such as a delightful duck confit with pommes Lyonnaise and cabbage slaw.

French. Breakfast, lunch (Monday-Friday), dinner, Saturday-Sunday brunch. Reservations recommended. Bar. $16-35

★★★DAKOTA

Hollywood Roosevelt Hotel, 7000 Hollywood Blvd., Hollywood, 323-769-8888; www.dakota-restaurant.com

With renowned chef Jason Johnston at the helm, this steakhouse in the storied Hollywood Roosevelt Hotel is nothing short of grand. There's the expansive dining room with its carved-beam ceilings; the prompt and professional service; and, most important, the food. In that department, Dakota puts other steakhouses to shame, dishing up some of the city's most flavorful cuts of beef (pair yours with the buttery black truffle cream sauce) and comfort-food sides, like mac and cheese and potato purée, as well as delectable seafood including succulent diver scallops. Appetizers are inventive and addictive, such as the crispy pork belly with fried quail egg and braised with apple cider—put the fork down or you'll be stuffed by the time the main course arrives. The wine list is long, but if you prefer cocktails, head outside to the Tropicana Bar: for a nightcap beside the pool and check out the underwater mural by David Hockney.

Steak. Dinner, Sunday brunch. Reservations recommended. Bar. $36-85

★★★GORDON RAMSAY AT THE LONDON

The London West Hollywood, 1020 N. San Vicente Blvd., West Hollywood, 310-358-7788; www.gordonramsay.com/gratthelondonwh

The inventive cuisine at one of the hottest restaurants in town does not come with a side of the celebrity chef's signature vitriol, so frequently dispensed during Fox's reality series *Hell's Kitchen* and *Kitchen Nightmares*. On the contrary, the environment here is a little slice of heaven, with serene pastel shades, lots of gold accents and a courteous staff that expertly explains the menu of delectable small plates. The restaurant's savory offerings, from seared Hudson Valley foie gras with pear and saffron chutney to grass fed pork loin with braised belly and crispy pig's head, pickled onion and apple gastrique, prove that Gordon Ramsay really can cook—not just shout at people who can't.

American. Breakfast, lunch, dinner. Reservations recommended. Bar. $36-85

★★★GRACE

7360 Beverly Blvd., Hollywood, 323-934-4400; www.gracerestaurant.com

With respected executive chef Neal Fraser at the helm, Grace has done what few high-profile restaurants manage to do: turn deafening early buzz into long-term success. Foodies from around town keep returning for the simple but divine roasted beet salad with feta, pistachios and goat cheese fondue—it's the perfect prelude to the grilled tenderloin of wild boar served with roasted Brussels sprouts, herbed Yukon gold potato spaetzle and violet mustard sauce. It's no wonder that even after six years, reservations at Grace are still essential.

American. Dinner. Closed Monday. Reservations recommended. Bar. $36-85

★★★HATFIELD'S

6703 Melrose Ave., Hollywood, 323-935-2977; www.hatfieldsrestaurant.com

Hatfield's, no longer the intimate little nook it used to be, is now a grown-up restaurant in a cushy space further east on Melrose. Frankly, they needed more room to cater to the droves of loyal fans. Husband-and-wife duo Quinn and Karen Hatfield, savory and pastry chefs, respectively, have developed a winning formula: a concise menu of local farmers' ingredients and surprising, yet comforting flavors. The menu fluctuates with the seasons, but a seasonal prix fixe of four courses is almost always available; there's also a nine-course tasting menu—pray that it includes the date and mint-crusted lamb.

Contemporary American. Lunch (Monday-Friday), dinner. Reservations recommended. Outdoor seating. $36-85

★★★JAR

8225 Beverly Blvd., West Hollywood, 323-655-6566; www.thejar.com

Jar might stand for "just another restaurant," but there's nothing derivative about this eatery from executive chef/owner Suzanne Tracht. It's a place that's just right when you can't handle another evening of small plates or you need some classic-but-high-end comfort food. With its excellent chophouse offerings—like the 16-ounce. Kansas City steak and the signature pot roast with carrots and caramelized onions—Jar is more like a distillation of everything a fine neighborhood restaurant ought to be: a place that offers reliably great food and service, and a warm atmosphere. The space is a little more sleek than your typical local bistro, but it's still functional. Designed as a 1940s supper club, the décor is simple yet stylish with warm shades of brown and hints of orange throughout, black and white photography hanging on wood-paneled walls and brown bucket chairs. Cheese lovers would do well to head here on Monday for the Mozzarella menu, which features a number of dishes that incorporate burrata and, of course, mozzarella, among other cheeses. And no matter which day you go, have a cocktail—all the mixed drinks, from martinis to Manhattans, are nonpareil, much like the restaurant itself.

American. Dinner, Sunday brunch. Reservations recommended. Bar. $16-35

★★★KATANA

8439 W. Sunset Blvd., West Hollywood, 323-650-8585; www.katanarobata.com

From the same folks who brought you BOA Steakhouse (right down the street), Katana sits above the Sunset Strip in the ornate Piazza del Sol. The place is always packed with scenesters who fill up the heated patio on any given night, but the sushi and robata (Japanese charcoal-grilled) styles are best enjoyed in the superbly lit Dodd Mitchell-designed interior. All the hard surfaces make it a bit loud, but once the food arrives, you'll forget that you're shouting to be heard. The ama ebi (sweet shrimp) sashimi is winsomely succulent and pairs well with one of Katana's numerous premium sakes.

Japanese. Dinner. Reservations recommended. Bar. $36-85

★★★KOI

730 N. La Cienega Blvd., West Hollywood, 310-659-9449; www.koirestaurant.com

Perennial hot spot Koi was recently remodeled, and the result is a predictably lovely, transporting space, with calming water elements, bamboo accents and twinkling glowing candles everywhere. It's a fitting backdrop for its equally beautiful clientele—which consists almost entirely of model types, industry bigwigs and their various entourages and, naturally, A-list actors—who have kept this Japanese restaurant and lounge consistently booked for years. An evening at Koi is more about seeing and being seen than about debating the subtle merits of a particular cut of mackerel or hamachi. The sushi here is fairly traditional, and signature dishes include yellowtail carpaccio with grape seed oil, ponzu and wasabi tobiko. For fans of the cooked stuff, there's a flavorful Kobe filet mignon toban-yaki, so tasty it may just have you drooling over dinner instead of the starlets around you.

Japanese. Dinner. Reservations recommended. Bar. $86 and up

★★★LUCQUES

8474 Melrose Ave., West Hollywood, 323-655-6277; www.lucques.com

Like so many buildings in Los Angeles, Lucques might look nondescript on the outside, but it boasts a storied past, having once been the carriage house of silent-film-era actor and producer Harold Lloyd. With an interior reimagined by designer Barbara Barry, Lucques retains its brick walls and its sense of history, even as a posh, minimalist space with warm, chocolate leather booths. Reservations are hard to come by, but when you finally score one, you'll be glad you waited for a taste of co-owner and chef Suzanne Goin's simple and absolutely delicious dishes, such as ricotta dumplings with fava beans, prosciutto, pecorino crema and mint; followed by braised beef short ribs with sautéed greens, cippolinis and horseradish cream.

American. Lunch (Tuesday-Saturday), dinner. Reservations recommended. Bar. $36-85

★★★OSTERIA MOZZA

6602 Melrose Ave., Hollywood, 323-297-0100; www.mozza-la.com

The "casual tavern" side of Mozza (the other portion of this trendy Italian eatery is Pizzeria Mozza), Osteria Mozza was hyped to death long before it even opened in mid-2007. It's still one of the hottest restaurants in town, and it's easy to see why: The restaurant is the brainchild of Nancy Silverton (of Campanile and La Brea Bakery fame), celebrity chef Mario Batali and winemaker Joseph Bastianich, who know a thing or two about the business. If you're a free-spirited sort, your best bet is to try to nab a seat at the central mozzarella bar; it's pretty much your only hope of eating here without a reservation. You'll end up sipping a glass of cabernet and nibbling on the crispy pig's trotter with cicoria and mustard, while watching Silverton herself dish up small bites of delectable mozzarella and burrata dishes. Try the pasta—the egg and ricotta raviolo is particularly good.

Italian. Dinner. Reservations recommended. Bar. $36-85

★★★PROVIDENCE

5955 Melrose Ave., Hollywood, 323-460-4170; www.providencela.com

Co-owner Donato Poto and partner-executive chef Michael Cimarusti know how to paint a pretty picture. Providence offers some of the most artful dishes we've seen; in fact, each is something of an edible sculpture. But, they're more than just nice to look at—they're also delicious. Choose from the market menu, which changes daily and acts as a canvas for creations by Cimarusti, who works with the freshest fish from around the world, or the à la carte menu, with raw and cold starters like Maine lobster with pink grapefruit, hearts of palm, avocado and coriander, hot ones such as "chowda" with smoky bacon, manila clams and a silky broth, and main courses including the wild king salmon with beets, Neuske's bacon and mustard emulsion. No wonder Providence is a favorite with Los Angeles gourmands.

Seafood. Lunch (Friday), dinner. Reservations recommended. Bar. $36-85

★★★RESTAURANT NISHIMURA

8684 Melrose Ave., West Hollywood, 310-659-4770

Los Angeles is a sushi town, and Nishimura, dipped in ivy and tucked into a tiny space across from the Pacific Design Center, has long commanded the respect of the town's critical sushi aficionados, for whom nothing will do but the freshest cuts and the most skilled preparation. (The toro here practically melts in your mouth.) Chef Hiro Nishimura oversees the offerings that arrive on your plate, which, coincidentally, are not just any plates, but one-of-a-kind pieces fashioned by acclaimed potter Mineo Mizuno. If you've got a fistful of cash to burn, relinquish all control and order the omakase, which starts at $100 a head.

Japanese. Lunch (Monday-Friday), dinner. Closed Sunday. Reservations recommended. Bar. $86 and up

SONA

401 N. La Cienega Blvd., West Hollywood, 310-659-7708; www.sonarestaurant.com

If you're looking for a familiar, been-there-done-that meal, then skip chef David Myers's Sona. Adventurous eaters, though, will be rewarded at this temple to culinary creativity, which clocks in as one of the most cutting-edge eateries in the city. Stark and minimalist with a six-ton granite wine bar at the center of the room, Sona is about both innovation and execution, offering two imaginative degustation menus: the six-course Découverte and the nine-course Spontanée. With either menu (which change frequently), your taste buds will fall in love with dishes such as Maine lobster with Vietnamese green curry and beef strip loin with fingerling potatoes and baby carrots. What will keep you coming back are the wild desserts, including the liquid chocolate with smoked foam, sassafras gel and tobacco ice cream or the fried lemon meringue pie with English peas and popcorn ice cream. *Note: At press time, the restaurant was closed and preparing to move to a new location.*

French. Dinner. Closed Sunday-Monday. Reservations recommended. Bar. $36-85

RECOMMENDED

AGO

8478 Melrose Ave., West Hollywood, 323-655-6333; www.agorestaurant.com

From the street, the façade of Ago is a blank wall of unassuming off-white, but a closer look at the fleet of luxury cars in the parking lot is a tip-off that this restaurant draws a Hollywood crowd—not a surprise considering that Ago is backed by some of the industry's heaviest hitters, including Bob and Harvey Weinstein, directors Tony and Ridley Scott, and Robert De Niro (who co-owns a number of restaurants, including Nobu). The cuisine, a combination of flavors from the Italian regions of Tuscany, Liguria and Emilia-Romagna, steals the spotlight here, with such dishes as rack of lamb cooked in a wood-burning oven, and spaghetti with clams.

Italian. Lunch (Monday-Friday), dinner. Reservations recommended. Bar. $16-35

ANGELINI OSTERIA

7313 Beverly Blvd., Midtown, 323-297-0070; www.angeliniosteria.com

Angelini Osteria is a restaurant in the tradition of the true osteria, the Italian version of a local cantina. Opened in 2001 by chef Gino Angelini, this is the type of place where friends gather for good wine, tasty food and lively conversation. (The service can be a bit snooty, which can be a real buzzkill.) For dinner, start with the grilled quail with guanciale, mixed baby greens and saba sauce, then move along to a pasta course of pumpkin tortellini with butter, sage and asparagus, and a second course of breaded veal chop alla Milanese with fritto zucchini and eggplant. For the perfect finish, save room for a little ice cream affogato, a scoop of gelato drowned in a shot of espresso.

Italian. Lunch (Tuesday-Friday), dinner. Closed Monday. Bar. $16-35

AOC

8022 W. Third St., Midtown, 323-653-6359; www.aocwinebar.com

Small plates remain en vogue in Los Angeles because of tapas eateries like AOC. The charcuterie selection is especially good, with savory offerings like the coppa, sopressata and cacciatorini, as well as the lomo and chorizos. In the fish department, you can't go wrong with the gulf shrimp with smoked tomato butter and cornbread. The staff will help you pair your choices with just the right wines (the list is vast, so let them). Getting a seat at the bustling wine bar itself isn't easy, so try the separate cheese and charcuterie bar instead. Just remember: It gets loud and crowded the later it gets, so follow another local trend—the early-to-bed movement—and make reservations for earlier in the night.

Tapas. Dinner. Reservations recommended. Bar. $16-35

LA POUBELLE

5907 Franklin Ave., Hollywood, 323-465-0807; www.lapoubellebistro.com

Resting on the same hipster-overrun stretch of Franklin Avenue as the long-standing Bourgeois Pig coffee house, La Poubelle, which means "the trash can," is aptly named, but not for the reasons you might think. The moniker actually refers to the menu—there's a little bit of everything here, from classic bistro fare such as pommes frites and escargot to a healthy array of pasta dishes and even tapas. It's always packed, and the cavernous acoustics make it a bit raucous, but if you can get a table, opt for a specialty of the house, such as the coq au vin, chicken stewed in burgundy with carrots, onions and mushrooms; or the bouillabaisse, a classic kitchen-sink Mediterranean fish stew with white fish, shrimp, mussels, clams and scallops.

French. Dinner, Friday-Sunday brunch. Reservations recommended. Bar. $16-35

LUNA PARK

672 S. La Brea Ave., Midtown, 323-934-2110; www.lunaparkla.com

With entertainment publications *Variety* and *The Hollywood Reporter* just down the street, you can bet that there's never a dull moment for eavesdropping on the lively media crowd, which congregates here for three-martini lunches and after-work cocktails. Like nearly every Los Angeles eatery, Luna Park has a nice selection of salads, but we think that some of the best items on the menu are about turn-a-blind-eye indulgence, so put away the calorie counter and order the warm goat cheese fondue appetizer, served with grilled bread and sliced apples. It pairs beautifully with the restaurant's award-winning mojito and the grilled cheezlitz, a grilled cheese sandwich served with mixed greens and tomato soup kept piping hot by a tiny tealight candle. The daily lunch specials are also hard to resist, especially the fried chicken with coleslaw and a buttermilk biscuit every Tuesday. Good food and drinks? Now there's something to talk about.

International. Lunch (Monday-Friday), dinner, Saturday-Sunday brunch. Reservations recommended. Bar. $16-35

MUSSO AND FRANK GRILL

6667 Hollywood Blvd., 323-467-5123; www.mussoandfrankgrill.com

Not much has changed since this historic institution opened in 1919 (the famed "Round Table" of Saroyan, Thurber, Faulkner and Fitzgerald met here). You can still order Welsh rarebit and enjoy what many swear is the most perfect martini on the planet. The dining room is as frozen in time as the menu, with lots of dark mahogany wood, lumpy booths and archival photos. Oak-beamed ceilings, chandeliers donned with tiny shades, and red-coated waiters, some of whom have been there since the 60s, add to the warm and cozy setting. Hollywood old-timers and up-and-comers alike meet here to do deals, or to simply get a taste of old Hollywood and enjoy a nice steak.

American. Lunch, dinner, late-night. Closed Sunday-Monday. $36-85

PIZZERIA MOZZA

641 N. Highland Ave., Hollywood, 323-297-0101; www.mozza-la.com

Getting a table at Pizzeria Mozza, the sister establishment of Osteria Mozza, remains a competitive sport among Los Angeles foodies, despite the fact that the place opened four years ago. The crowds just keep on coming—regardless of the noise level or the location, which has seen numerous eateries come and go—but you'll realize it's not all hype when you taste the rustic gourmet pies, which are handmade before your eyes in an open kitchen and baked in wood-burning ovens. The pizza topped with clams, bursting with the fresh flavors of garlic, oregano, Parmigiano and pecorino, is one of the best. Just remember to put the reservations line on speed dial, and sharpen those elbows before you show up.

Pizzeria. Lunch, dinner. Bar. $16-35

STREET

742 N. Highland Ave., Hollywood, 323-203-0500; www.eatatstreet.com

Go around the world at chef Susan Feniger's new restaurant. Feniger is one of the "Two Hot Tamales" (which ran on the Food Network for four years), co-founder of Border Grill in Santa Monica and, along with Mary Sue Milliken, fought her way into kitchens back in the 70s, when women weren't exactly welcome. Feniger's love of street food continues at her first solo venture with a menu that spans the globe and has a causal atmosphere to match. You know you've found the place when you see the neon sign out front on an otherwise near-empty block. Graffiti on the walls, a small outdoor area with a fire pit and staff dressed in black hoodies greet you inside. This is the place to be adventurous and try things. Servers describe dishes in detail and propel you forward by telling you how delicious everything is. The lunch menu is divided into tea cakes and dumplings, handhelds and more. The lamb tacos are one of the most popular items at lunch—crispy and spicy, and filled with refried white beans and cucumber mint sour cream. Dinner is the same sort of affair—with a variety of tea cakes and dumplings (lamb kafta meatballs, Kaya toast), noodles and curries and big plates such as Peking quail and Hawaiian barbecue pork.

International. Lunch, dinner, Sunday brunch. Reservations recommended. Bar. $16-35

URTH CAFFÉ

8565 Melrose Ave., West Hollywood, 310-659-0628; 267 S. Beverly Drive, Beverly Hills, 310-205-9311; 2327 Main St., Santa Monica, 310-314-7040; 451 S. Hewitt St., Downtown, 213-797-4534; www.urthcaffe.com

Long known for its organic teas and coffees, Urth Caffé is also famous for celeb sightings, especially at the original West Hollywood location. If you can stomach the overly hip crowd, you'll discover that the food here is excellent—in that healthy California way. The menu is chock-full of tempting lunchtime options, such as organic soups, hearty sandwiches with springtime-fresh mixed greens, and there is a pastry case full of gorgeous cakes and cookies. What's more, the place has charm, from the Spanish tile to the quaint jars of coffee beans and loose-leaf teas. Bring a few dollars for the valet, though, because parking is scarce.

American. Breakfast, lunch, dinner. $15 and under

WHERE TO SHOP

AMERICAN RAG

150 S. La Brea Ave., Midtown, 323-935-3154; www.amrag.com

You will easily find your perfect cocktail dress, heels and shades, courtesy of Cynthia Vincent, Casadei and Chloé, respectively, at this hip boutique. The shop provides a stellar vintage selection and World Denim Bar humbly dedicated to blue (and white, gray and black) jeans. Labels such as Ksubi, J Brand and Nudie are here to make sure every skinny leg in greater L.A. is clad in the best stretch.

Monday-Saturday 10 a.m.-9 p.m., Sunday noon-7 p.m.

DIAVOLINA

8741 W. Third Street, West Hollywood, 310-550-1341; www.shopdiavolina.com

Peppered with animal print, this bright and inviting shoe salon features footwear from all the brands you've heard of (Pour La Victoire and Chloé, for example)—but in funky, unique styles you've likely never seen. Every strap, heel and gem is kissed with eccentricity, so that you'll feel compelled to wear all-black attire to keep the attention pointed south. Collections of threads from 3.1 Phillip Lim and Alexander Wang are expertly curated, and the jewelry is so unique, people will assume you're wearing an inherited vintage piece.

Monday-Saturday 11 a.m.-7 p.m., Sunday noon-5 p.m.

HIGHLIGHT

WHAT ARE THE BEST L.A. STORES FOR VINTAGE CLOTHING?

L.A. denizens' best-kept dressing secret is buying vintage. If it weren't for the fashions of yesteryear, it's likely everyone would strut down Robertson Boulevard looking like clones (which is deliberate sometimes in L.A.).

The first stop for the stylists of, say, Anne Hathaway, Kiera Knightly and Gwen Stefani, would be **Decades** (*8214 Melrose Ave., West Hollywood, 323-655-0223; www.decadesinc. com*), a treasure trove filled with Chanel jewelry and Hermès handbags. With an upscale salon feel, complete with sleek white walls and a mix of animal-print and platinum furniture, Decades helps film stars take their period-movie wardrobe and recreate a wearable look for the street. The **Paper Bag Princess** (*8818 W. Olympic Blvd., Beverly Hills, 310-385-9036; www.thepaperbagprincess.com*), the interior of which takes after Kirsten Dunst's boudoir in Sofia Coppola's Marie Antoinette, is full of extravagant gowns. Stars such as Rachel Bilson, Ginnifer Goodwin and Katie Holmes shop at **The Way We Wore** (*334 S. La Brea Ave., Miracle Mile District, 323-937-0878; www.thewaywewore.com*), where they pick out Valentino gowns and Yves St. Laurent dresses.

For everyday wear, **Shareen's Vintage** (*350 N. Avenue 21, Downtown, 323-276-6226; www.shareenvintage.com*) is Downtown's biggest style weapon. Shareen herself has the ability to look at last era's trash and see true gems that she stashes into her warehouse and then sells, sometimes for dirt cheap. **Sielian's Vintage Apparel** (9013 Melrose Ave., West Hollywood, 310-246-9595; www.sieliansvintageapparel.com) is no less a vintage powerhouse, barely able to keep any Chloé-like frocks on the rack. **Lemon Frog Shop** (*1202 N. Alvarado St., 213-413-2143; www.lemonfrogshop.com*) is overflowing with goods and has a great selection of Gucci handbags. Certain boutiques like **Polkadots and Moonbeams** (*8381 W. Third St., West Hollywood, 323-655-3880; www.polkadotsandmoonbeams.com*), and **American Rag** let their vintagewear mingle with current pieces, so you can mix and match for that perfectly styled look.

HILLARY RUSH

8222 W. Third St., West Hollywood, 323-852-0088; www.hillaryrush.com

Her father hatched the preppy Le Tigre, and Hillary Rush went on to establish one of L.A.'s most reliable shopping stops. While it became widely known for having hard-to-find J Brand jeans and the popular Made T-shirts, the shop is much more than just a denim-and-cotton destination. It brings a New York-dressing sensibility to a fashion-lazy town. Ditch the flip-flops for a pair of platform pumps. Kate Moss, a Hillary Rush addict, would.

Monday-Saturday 11 a.m.-7 p.m., Sunday noon-6 p.m.

KITSON

115 S. Robertson Blvd., West Hollywood, 310-859-2652; www.shopkitson.com

It might as well be called: "As Seen in *Us Weekly*." This is the go-to casual wear boutique for the stars—even famously opening its doors in the middle of the night for the likes of Britney Spears. In addition to the large collection of slogan-slathered T-shirts, you'll also find party dresses, shoes, jewelry, beauty products and lots more. Afterward, with your Kitson bag in hand, make like a

HIGHLIGHT

WHERE DO CELEBRITIES SHOP?

Hillary Rush: Kate Moss has been seen coming in and out of this well-edited shop, which brings a New York-dressing sensibility to a laid-back town.

Jenni Kayne: The young designer's celebrity following includes Rachel Bilson and Jessica Alba. Her first store is an eco-friendly space in West Hollywood that also carries great gifts.

Kitson: Celebrities come here to buy everything from T-shirts to party dresses.

Lisa Kline: Known for discovering new designers and trends, Lisa Kline has a strong celebrity following, which includes Eva Longoria, Reese Witherspoon and other A-list stars.

WHAT IS THE BEST BOUTIQUE FOR ONE-OF-A-KIND PIECES?

Satine: The clothing—by the likes of Alexander Wang, Erin Fetherston and Thakoon—stocked at this boutique is quirky but unique.

WHICH STORE EPITOMIZES CALIFORNIA STYLE?

Planet Blue: This ever-popular boutique is always up on the latest trends and is stocked with luxurious T-shirts, party dresses and lots of designer den.

WHAT IS THE BEST PLACE TO BUY JEANS?

American Rag: The shop provides a superb vintage selection and denim bar with labels such as J Brand, Habitual, Ksubi, and Made in Heaven.

WHICH STORE HAS THE BEST SHOES?

Diavolina: This bright and inviting shoe salon features footwear from all the brands you've heard of (Chloé, Pour La Victoire) but in funky, unique styles you've likely never seen.

celebrity and have lunch at The Ivy: right down the street. Kitson Kids, Kitson Men and Kitson Studio are also right on Robertson.
Monday-Friday 10 a.m.-7:30 p.m., Saturday 10 a.m.-7:30 p.m., Sunday 11 a.m.-6 p.m.

LISA KLINE
138 S. Robertson Blvd., West Hollywood, 310-246-0907; www.lisakline.com
It's a little more elegant than the playful Kitson up the street, but it is still replete with expensive T-shirts and rhinestone-studded jeans. Lisa Kline is known for discovering new designers and spotlighting trends long before everyone else in Hollywood, and everyone from Eva Longoria to Tori Spelling shops here. Over

the years, Kline has branched out to include a men's and kid's store, which were also located on Robertson. Recently, she merged the women's store into the men's boutique for one-stop shopping.

Monday-Saturday 11 a.m.-7 p.m., Sunday 11-6 p.m.

JENNI KAYNE

614 N. Almont Drive, West Hollywood, 310-860-0123; www.jennikayne.com

She may only be 26, but designer Jenni Kayne has a huge celebrity following which includes Jennifer Gardner, Jessica Alba and Rachel Bilson. The L.A. native started working on her first line when she was only 19 and launched her first collection, which stores like Neiman Marcus and Intermix quickly scooped up, when she was just 21. Now, the designer, known for her refined yet edgy sportswear, has her first store, an eco-friendly space in West Hollywood with a bamboo ceiling and racks that hug the wall. In addition to the designer's current collection, the store exclusively stocks her line of footwear, plus many of Kayne's favorite things such as books, perfumes and vintage jewelry.

Monday-Saturday 11 a.m.-7 p.m., Sunday noon-5 p.m.

MAXFIELD

8825 Melrose Ave., West Hollywood, 310-274-8800

It brought the coveted duds of famed Japanese designer Yohji Yamamoto to Los Angeles, and the city's first power boutique still maintains a confident finger on the pulse of the avant-garde. In addition to couture staples such as Gucci, Prada and YSL, Maxfield offers the rarer fashion set, like Libertine and Rick Owens. It really comes as no surprise then that Mary-Kate Olsen has been spotted shopping here. Perhaps the most affordable items belong to James Perse, who happens to be the son of Maxfield owner Tommy Perse. The store's sister outlet, Maxfield Bleu, is located just over a mile south down Santa Monica Boulevard, and offers exceptional classics for friendlier prices *(301 N. Canon Drive, 310-275-7007)*.

Monday-Saturday 11 a.m.-7 p.m., Sunday noon-5 p.m.

MILK

8209 W. Third St., West Hollywood, 323-951-0330; www.shopatmilk.com

Milk claims it's inspired by literature, jazz and a jet-set lifestyle—and it shows. This sophisticated boutique presents Current/Elliot denim and European designers such as Sonia Rykiel and Derek Lam, plus a slew of names you've never heard of but will certainly want to be the first to unveil. Big Phaidon and Taschen books are stacked around the dark but sleek boutique, alongside the decorative vintage milk bottles that pay homage to the boutique's moniker.

Monday-Saturday 11 a.m.-7 p.m., Sunday noon-5 p.m.

OPENING CEREMONY

451 La Cienega Blvd., West Hollywood, 310-652-1120; www.openingceremony.us

Located in Charlie Chaplin's former dance studio, Opening Ceremony's L.A. location (there's also a store in New York, as well as one in Tokyo) boasts more than 10,000 square feet of space, which includes individual shops for designers such as Alexander Wang. Known as the United Nations of fashion, the concept behind this ultra-creative boutique/showroom/gallery is to shine the light on up and coming designers from around the world, highlighting the country's best and brightest along with vintage pieces and finds from open-air markets. The store also has its own line (and often enters into exclusive collaborations) and its racks are always full of the latest designs from Proenza Schouler, Topshop, Nom de Guerre and others.

Monday-Saturday 11 a.m.-7 p.m., Sunday noon-7 p.m.

SATINE

8134 W. Third St., West Hollywood, 323-655-2142; www.satineboutique.com

Satine is scattered with the kind of hipster couture celebrities live for (and pay beaucoup bucks to own). Offbeat clothing—by the likes of Alexander Wang, Jason Wu and Vanessa Bruno—is quirky and sexy. Shoes are often an unusual design and the jewelry is selected to transform a look. Despite their eccentricities, all of the items are romantic, unconventional and original, so you and others don't have to worry about showing up on a "who wore it best" list.

Monday-Saturday 11 a.m.-7 p.m., Sunday noon-6 p.m.

BEVERLY HILLS/BEL AIR

Looking for movie stars? You'll find them here, or at least see the imposing gates and security cameras outside their glamorous mansions. The maps of the stars' homes are centered on these neighborhoods west of Hollywood and east of the ocean. Los Angeles' toniest addresses are in Beverly Hills, a separately incorporated city with a famous zip code (90210)—you know you've crossed over when blue street signs give way to white ones. It is home to some of the world's most exclusive shopping areas like Rodeo Drive and the Beverly Center. Bel Air is just as posh with some of the most expensive homes in the country.

WHAT TO SEE

MUSEUM OF TOLERANCE

9786 W. Pico Blvd., Beverly Hills, 310-553-8403; www.museumoftolerance.com

When you go to the Museum of Tolerance, you get a passport featuring the name and picture of a Jewish child who was in the Holocaust. Only at the end of the tour will you discover the heart-wrenching truth about whether or not "your child" survived the horrific ordeal. It's the most eye-opening experience at the museum, which aims to eradicate intolerance thorough education. The Museum uses powerful interactive devices like the passport to illuminate the various ways intolerance has affected and continues to affect society. Special sections are dedicated to archiving the events of the Holocaust, including video and audio presentations as well as like the letters of Anne Frank. After traveling back in time to World War II, you'll be transported back to present day when you visit the museum's Tolerancenter, where you'll learn about modern-day human rights abuses and come face to face with your own prejudices.

Admission: adults $15, seniors $12, children 5-18 $11, children under 5 free. Monday-Friday 10 a.m.-5 p.m., Sunday 11 a.m.-5 p.m. November-March: Friday 10 a.m.-3:30 p.m.

THE PALEY CENTER FOR MEDIA

465 N. Beverly Drive, Beverly Hills, 310-786-1000; www.paleycenter.org

If you get the shakes from TiVo withdrawal while on vacation, the Paley Center for Media (formerly known as the Museum of Television and Radio) might help. At this Beverly Hills institution, you can watch thousands of television programs from around the world or rediscover the lost art of radio. But what the Paley Center does best is programming. The Paley Center's public programs allow visitors to poke the brains of all kinds of entertainment icons, from chef Giada De Laurentiis to actor Kenneth Branagh. To attend one of the Paley Center's events, make sure to get tickets well in advance. That'll give you a fix until you are reunited with your precious TiVo.

Suggested donation: adults $10, seniors and students $8, children under 14 $5. Wednesday-Sunday noon-5 p.m.

RODEO DRIVE

Rodeo Drive, between Wilshire and Santa Monica boulevards, Beverly Hills; www.rodeodrive-bh.com

If you've never strolled down Beverly Hills' most famous street, then get ready to see designer clothing and plenty of bling. A tour down Rodeo is like leafing through the pages of *Vogue*—Gucci, Prada, Fendi, Yves Saint Laurent, Dolce & Gabbana, Christian Dior, Valentino and Cartier are just a few of the names you'll see (and their selections are quite good—in fact, some stores house the brand's entire collection—so it's worth it to check here if you've been looking for, say, a certain bag for some time). Afterward, swing by the Beverly Wilshire, A Four Seasons Hotel on nearby Wilshire Boulevard, where you can sit at the hotel's street-side patio and drink the afternoon away while you try to spot celebrities.

WHERE TO STAY

★★★AVALON HOTEL BEVERLY HILLS

9400 W. Olympic Blvd., Beverly Hills, 310-277-5221; www.avalonbeverlyhills.com

Wandering into the Avalon Hotel is like taking a trip down Mid-Century modern memory lane, if Kelly Wearstler had been around back then for consultation. The famed interior designer's first hotel project is decked out in pieces by George Nelson, Isamu Noguchi and Charles Eames. Just around the corner from stellar shopping strip Beverly Drive (not to be confused with Beverly Boulevard) and staple lunch spot Urth Caffé, the Avalon combines retro-chic style with contemporary aesthetics. Hollywood A-listers and Beverly Hills execs seeking a bit of downtime sip sweet and savory martinis in cushy cabanas by the hourglass-shaped pool. Wearstler revised her original design in 2009 in everything from guest rooms to Oliverio (formerly Blue on Blue), the new restaurant featuring Italian cuisine from executive chef Mirko Paderno.

84 rooms. Restaurant, bar. Business center. Fitness center. Pool. Pets accepted. $251-350

★★★★★THE BEVERLY HILLS HOTEL AND BUNGALOWS

9641 Sunset Blvd., Beverly Hills, 310-276-2251; www.thebeverlyhillshotel.com

One of L.A.'s most enduring icons isn't some fame-starved ingenue or mysterious leading man—it's a stately, pale-pink-clad hotel on Sunset Boulevard. The Beverly Hills Hotel has been attracting guests (famous and not) since 1912, and its star power is by no means fading. While celebrities love the hotel for its private bungalows (perfect for canoodling and doing whatever else stars do),

WHICH HOTELS ARE MOST ICONIC?

The Beverly Hills Hotel and Bungalows:
One of L.A.'s most enduring icons isn't some fame-starved ingenue or mysterious leading man—it's a stately, pale-pink hotel on Sunset Boulevard. The Beverly Hills Hotel has been attracting guests (famous and not) since 1912, and its star power is by no means fading.

Beverly Wilshire, A Four Seasons Hotel:
When Warren Beatty was a swinging bachelor, he lived at the hotel for nearly 15 years during the '60s and '70s. Of course, it was also made famous when *Pretty Woman* premiered. This is still one of the top hotels in the city, with great restaurants and an unbeatable location at the mouth of Rodeo Drive.

Hotel Bel-Air:
A major renovation last year will no doubt make this fairytale hotel the place to stay for many years to come.

civilians love the tropical gardens (gorgeous) and the retro-style pool (movie-star chic). Guest rooms, which are bathed in soft hues, are kitted out in unique English furniture and marble baths. Once you've fully reveled in your good fortune (and the impeccable service and extra-comfortable beds), make your way downstairs to the French-colonial inspired outdoor deck. Or take in the scene at the famous Polo Lounge, which still buzzes with handshakes and business deals, or the new Bar Nineteen 12, which has turned into a place to party with the beautiful and affluent people.

204 rooms. Restaurant, bar. Business center. Fitness center. Pool. Spa. Tennis. $351 and up

★★★★THE BEVERLY HILTON

9876 Wilshire Blvd., Beverly Hills, 310-274-7777; www.beverlyhilton.com

The Beverly Hilton hosts the Golden Globes every January, but the hotel offers much more than a red carpet for stars to strut their stuff on. You'll be wowed by the lobby's mile-high ceiling, as well as its 1,400-gallon saltwater aquarium, but you'll be thankful for the hotel's pragmatism—you'll find ergonomic work-stations and wireless Internet, even by the enormous Aqua Star Pool, which is usually filled with sunning executives. Guest rooms (decked out in serene beige-and-brown tones) also boast that nice balance between luxe and practical: For every luxurious amenity (pillow-top mattresses, Penhaligon's bath products), there's a state-of-the-art one (Bose music systems, 42-inch HDTV plasma TVs). In case you want to groom and pamper yourself like the nominees, Aqua Star Spa and Bellezza Salon are on hand and stocked with Sonya Dakar treatments. You'll look award-worthy, even if you're only going to the poolside Trader Vic's Lounge.

570 rooms. Restaurant, bar. Business center. Fitness center. Pool. Spa. Pets accepted. $351 and up

★★★★BEVERLY WILSHIRE, A FOUR SEASONS HOTEL

9500 Wilshire Blvd., Beverly Hills, 310-275-5200; www.fourseasons.com

When Warren Beatty was a swinging bachelor, the Hollywood legend spent 15 years nesting in a palatial suite at the Beverly Wilshire (previously The Regent Beverly Wilshire). And thanks to a $35 million reno-vation and additions such as an ultra-sleek cocktail lounge and Wolfgang Puck's steakhouse CUT (designed by Richard Meier of Getty Center fame), the lavish 82-year-old historic grand hotel lures today's hottest celebrities, too. The rooms stay as hip as the clientele, with dark woods and moss-green accents. Make like a star and stroll just outside for a shopping spree at Chanel or Prada on Rodeo Drive, or nibble on a Dungeness crab cake by the pool.

395 rooms. Restaurant, bar. Business center. Fitness center. Pool. Spa. Pets accepted. $351 and up

★★★THE CRESCENT
403 N. Crescent Drive, Beverly Hills, 310-247-0505; www.crescentbh.com

Ladies who lunch dripping in diamonds troll Rodeo Drive, but just a few blocks away are some of Beverly Hills's more quaint and quiet tree-lined streets. The Crescent sits pretty on one such block. Once a residence for silent film stars such as John Barrymore, Clara Bow and Mary Pickford, the property feels more like a grandiose home. You'll stroll between two palm trees up some steps, and past a boisterous but refined cocktail crowd chatting and snacking on delicious small bites on the left veranda and upon white leather couches and a shag rug inside. Boé Restaurant stretches outdoors to the right and just indoors, and is popular with local executives and guests, as great outdoor dining spaces are surprisingly not always easy to find in L.A. Votives lead the way upstairs to minimal black-and-white guest rooms, where you can listen to the loaner iPod mini.

35 rooms. Restaurant, bar. $251-350

★★★★FOUR SEASONS HOTEL LOS ANGELES AT BEVERLY HILLS
300 S. Doheny Drive, Beverly Hills, 310-273-2222; www.fourseasons.com

Sitting pretty on quaint tree-lined Doheny, the famous hotel feels like a part of the posh Beverly Hills neighborhood. Chic locals make up half the clientele at the lauded spa thanks to excellent facials, like the exclusive Kerstin Florian Caviar treatment. After nourishing your skin, do the same for your body. Sit outside at Cabana Restaurant, where chef Ashley James puts out simply flavored Mediterranean-inflected treats such as mahi mahi tacos or the seafood salad. Then sabotage those healthy California-style eats with a cocktail at the must-see Windows Lounge, where celebrity sightings are practically inevitable. A parade of movie junkets at the hotel attracts all entertainment industry types from journalists to actors, who retreat after work to peachy rooms with iPod docking stations, French doors that open to balconies and bathrooms complete with cushy terrycloth robes. A new restaurant addition, Culina, Modern Italian, features a crudo bar, two lounges and a dazzling indoor-outdoor design.

285 rooms. Restaurant, bar. Fitness center. Pool. Spa. $351 and up

HOTEL BEL-AIR
701 Stone Canyon Road, Bel-Air, 310-472-1211; www.hotelbelair.com

This historic hotel closed in late 2009 for a major renovation and at press time, was expected to open sometime in April 2011. Look for completely refreshed décor, an expanded spa and updated dining options. Twelve hillside rooms and suites were also added, each consistent with the architecture and quality of the hotel, featuring lovely views, plunge pools and extensive outdoor living areas with dining areas and fireplaces. All existing interiors were also upgraded and new technologies and energy-efficient devices were added. La Prarie spa has a new fitness center, yoga studio and three additional suites.

★★★★★VICEROY L'ERMITAGE BEVERLY HILLS

9291 Burton Way, Beverly Hills, 310-278-3344; www.raffles.com

The high-profile set hides out at the Viceroy L'Ermitage Beverly Hills, a sanctuary that protects guests from prying eyes. This hotel sets itself apart by its intimate vibe and exclusivity (for one, the pool is for guests only, which isn't always the case at L.A. hotels). Each guest is given elegant, personal attention. The rooms are notoriously spacious, with cutting-edge technology, large walk-in closets and balconies overlooking lovely tree-lined Burton Way. Locals and guests alike enjoy California-French cuisine on the pretty patio. Expect enhancements to the property as the hotel completes the transition to become part of the Viceroy hotel group (at press time, this was scheduled to happen in early 2011, with renovations taking place without disruption to guests in late 2010), with the same level of excellent service.

119 rooms. Restaurant, bar. Business center. Fitness center. Pool. Spa. Pets accepted. $351 and up

★★★MAISON 140 BEVERLY HILLS

140 Lasky Drive, Beverly Hills, 310-281-4000; www.maison140beverlyhills.com

Originally the apartment of silent film star Lillian Gish in 1939, Maison 140 now mirrors a Left Bank Parisian motel, courtesy of designer Kelly Wearstler. But it still retains a homey, residential feel. Once past the exterior's brick façade, you'll see Bar Noir, where sweet cocktails such as Lady Godiva (as in the chocolate) are plentiful. The lobby lounge—dressed in sultry black and red—is a heady mix of contemporary and vintage, with touches that include Lucite bar stools and mirrored Chinoiserie to crystal chandeliers and Gallic antiques. All the guest rooms—divided by either Parisian or Mandarin designation—showcase Joshua Elias abstracts, but each space is a bit different thanks to eclectic wallpaper and décor in unorthodox patterns, colors and shapes, giving them a certain *je ne sais quoi*.

43 rooms. Bar. Fitness center. $151-250

★★★★★MONTAGE BEVERLY HILLS

225 N. Canon Drive, Beverly Hills, 310-860-7800; www.montagebeverlyhills.com

A newly constructed resort hotel tucked just steps from Rodeo Drive, this Spanish Colonial revival-style complex is a luxurious oasis set in one of the country's most high-end neighborhoods. Opened in November 2008, Montage Beverly Hills features 201 rooms and suites designed to bring to life the glamour of the glory days of early Hollywood—from the hand-painted and gilded stucco ceilings throughout the hotel to the lovely restaurant Parq and white glove service. Rooms are grown up and refined in décor, with flat-screen TVs and spacious mosaic-tiled marble bathrooms, and they're a fine place to escape to. But it's the common areas at this hotel that impress. The rooftop pool, with its mosaic-tiled surface, private cabanas and views of L.A., is relaxing and comfortable, while the sprawling spa, with its men's, women's and unisex lounges and 17 treatment rooms, is the place for personal retreats.

201 rooms. Restaurant, bar. Business center. Fitness center. Pool. Spa. Pets accepted. $351 and up

★★★★★THE PENINSULA BEVERLY HILLS

9882 S. Santa Monica Blvd., Beverly Hills, 310-551-2888; www.peninsula.com

While the luxe Peninsula is known for its old-school attention to service and swanky accommodations, it's all about the ultra-updated details, from electronic systems through which you control your room's lighting or temperature by pushing a bedside button to new Davi bath products, created by winemaker Robert Mondavi's grandson. On the re-hauled $4 million roof garden, poolside cabanas—surrounded by heated limestone tile flooring for year-round lounging—can be transformed into offices or massage treatment spaces. Opt for the latter, and the Precious Sapphire massage using gemstone oils and reflexology, will lull you into a state of absolute bliss. If you're famished afterward, ignite those taste buds at The Belvedere, where you will find fresh, farm-to-table delights such as spicy baked oysters with horse-radish-parsnip purée and spinach lemon cream. For those seeking immersion into the local customs, the hotel also offers Peninsula Academy, where you can take culturally specific high-end classes out and about in L.A. in everything from movie making to surfing.

248 rooms. Restaurant, bar. Fitness center. Pool. Spa. $351 and up

★★★THOMPSON BEVERLY HILLS

9360 Wilshire Blvd., Beverly Hills, 310-273-1400; www.thompsonbeverlyhills.com

Just as insiders know 60 Thompson as one of Manhattan's hot spots, this West Coast sibling pulls in throngs of beautiful people. Images by famed fashion photographer Steven Klein abound amid soft-hued

---

WHAT ARE THE MOST LUXURIOUS HOTELS?

The Beverly Hills Hotel and Bungalows: The bungalows are legendary for housing celebrities, the tropical gardens are gorgeous and the rooms are elegant and have extra comfortable beds. Add impeccable service and you have a place that's every bit as magical as you hope it to be.

Four Seasons Hotel Los Angeles at Beverly Hills: A parade of movie junkets at the hotel attracts entertainment industry types who retreat after work to peachy rooms with iPod docking stations and French doors that open to balconies.

Hotel Bel-Air: A major renovation to the hotel's rooms, restaurant and spa spells even more luxury at this legendary hotel.

Viceroy L'Ermitage Beverly Hills: In addition to the excellent service the hotel is known for, this year guests can expect enhancements to the property as the hotel makes the transition to become part of the Viceroy hotel group.

Montage Beverly Hills: This Spanish Colonial revival-style hotel is tucked just steps from Rodeo Drive and was designed to bring to life the glamour of the glory days of early Hollywood—from the hand-painted and gilded stucco ceilings to the lavish spa.

The Peninsula Beverly Hills: The Peninsula is a favorite with locals, celebrities and travelers for its great location, excellent service and high-tech rooms. The Belvedere is also one of the city's top restaurants.

leather and wood décor, mixing California modernism with eclectic elements from the late '80s and '90s. As you enter the lobby, you can't (and shouldn't) miss Japanese eatery BondSt. Upstairs, platform beds in rich wood are finished with highly contrasted black-and-white bedding and unusual pieces like jet-black leather and mirrored headboards that extend to the ceiling. But you want to go where the action is. Head to the roof deck, named ABH (for Above Beverly Hills), where wood and greenery intermingle to create a Zen vibe surrounding a Swarovski-embedded pool. There you can get on-demand spa treatments, snacks and exotic cocktails.

107 rooms. Restaurant, bar. Fitness center. Pool. Pets accepted. $351 and up

WHERE TO EAT

★★★THE BAZAAR

SLS Hotel at Beverly Hills, 465 South La Cienega Blvd., 310-246-5555; www.thebazaar.com

Bazaar, located in the SLS hotel, is perhaps the most exciting restaurant in L.A. right now. The restaurant is divided into four sections: tapas bar, restaurant, bar and patisserie (and you can transfer your check to any part). The menu is also divided into modern and traditional tapas, and while they're both excellent, the modern tapas are thrilling. Take the foie gras lollipops, for example, in which a piece of foie gras is wrapped in vanilla-scented cotton candy. At first you experience the sweetness and aroma of the cotton candy, and then your mouth is filled with the cold and creamy foie gras. The "not your everyday Caprese" salad is, indeed, unlike any Caprese salad you've ever had—it's in a cup and you drink it. The watermelon "nigiri," with hamachi, red wine, soy and jalapeno, is another taste sensation. After dinner, head over to the patisserie, decorated in a sugary pink as pretty as the confections lined up on the counter in front of the open kitchen, or to the sexy bar for a nightcap.

Tapas. Dinner. Reservations recommended. Bar. $36-85

★★★★THE BELVEDERE

The Peninsula Beverly Hills, 9882 S. Santa Monica Blvd., Beverly Hills, 310-975-2736; www.beverlyhills.peninsula.com

One of Los Angeles' most venerable fine-dining restaurants, the acclaimed Belvedere at the Peninsula Beverly Hills has long catered to the city's most discerning crowd and served as a deal-sealing destination in Beverly Hills serving exceptional modern American food. For a more laid-back experience, head there for Sunday brunch and grab a table on the cheerful patio, where you can sit amid flowers and trees and soak up the sun with a glass of Perrier Jouët and the special croque madame (a rich combination of truffled brioche with aged country ham, fontina cheese and organic eggs).

Contemporary American. Breakfast, lunch, dinner, Sunday brunch. Reservations recommended. Bar. $86 and up

★★★BONDST

Thompson Beverly Hills, 9360 Wilshire Blvd., Beverly Hills, 310-601-2255; www.thompsonhotels.com

Angelenos simply love their sushi restaurants. With BondSt they could finally taste the goods of one of Manhattan's favorite sushi dens, Jonathan Morr's trendy BondSt (so trendy, its name pays no mind to punctuation or space). While the restaurant is now managed by the hotel in which its located, not much as changed. It is still a scene—expect lots of black-clad people who look like they work in the industry. But the chef now offers a seasonal tasting menu each night, and all the menus change every day. After all, even scenesters have to eat sometime. The Japanese eatery also includes an outdoor terrace.

Japanese. Breakfast, lunch, dinner. No sushi served at lunch on weekends. Reservations recommended. Bar. $36-85

★★★BOUCHON BEVERLY HILLS

235 N. Canon Drive, Beverly Hills, 310-271-9910; www.bouchonbistro.com

Chef Thomas Keller's Buchon has finally arrived in Beverly Hills. Like the others, this third Bouchon (there's the one in Yountville as well as one in Las Vegas) offers the chef's wonderful bistro fare in a sprawling and lively space in the heart of Beverly Hills. A 16-seat bar offers full-dinner service plus close proximity to the seafood raw bar. The menu, an oversized fold-out of wax paper, is simple and unfussy—blood sausage, roasted chicken, even an $18-dollar Croque Madame. Splurge and get $135 worth of caviar, or settle for Keller's signature dish: the humble steak frites. Bar Bouchon is also open, and it serves small French plates meant for sharing and carafes of wine. A Buchon Bakery is expected in the near future.

Contemporary French. Lunch, dinner. Reservations recommended. Outdoor seating. $36-85

★★★CRUSTACEAN

9646 Little Santa Monica Blvd., Beverly Hills, 310-205-8990; www.anfamily.com

Distinguished Vietnamese restaurant Crustacean, in the heart of Beverly Hills, is perhaps best known for its winding aquarium walkway and famous garlic noodles, but this gorgeous French Colonial-style eatery offers far more. Book a romantic dinner for two (with sommelier service) in the exclusive Opium Cellar, or make merry in the remodeled, Hanoi-chic main dining room. Menu favorites include the grilled rack of lamb flambéed in chardon-nay, while the suit-and-tie crowd favors the healthful lunchtime "business express" menu, guaranteed to have you in and out in 45 minutes. Cocktails are a treat, too—we love the Beverly, made with fresh

---

WHAT ARE THE BEST PLACES FOR BRUNCH?

BLD:
The heavenly breakfast items like blueberry-ricotta hotcakes and grapefruit brûlée are all served until 3 p.m. on the weekend.

Jar:
Brunch at this modern chophouse is a great alternative to the always-busy dinner service. You'll find hearty choices such as corn pancakes, pot roast hash and steak and eggs.

Polo Lounge:
Listen to live jazz out on the patio as you bite into the sinfully rich French toast with cranberry bread, toasted pecans and banana cream—a Polo Lounge favorite.

WHAT ARE THE BEST STEAKHOUSES IN L.A?

BLT Steak:
BLT Steak, part of the Laurent Tourondel empire, offers expertly prepared steakhouse fare, addicting popovers and tempting raw bar selections.

CUT:
Wolfgang Puck's steakhouse is stark and sleek, and the cuisine is steakhouse fare with imagination, such as the starter of warm veal tongue, marinated artichokes, autumn shelling beans and salsa verde.

Dakota:
Renowned chef Jason Johnston dishes up some of the city's most flavorful cuts of beef and comfort-food sides, such as mac and cheese and potato purée.

Mastro's Steakhouse:
This consistently good steakhouse is equal parts food and scene. The central bar on the top floor is usually pretty lively, but the point of a meal at Mastro's is the perfectly-cooked steak.

Grill on the Alley:
Modeled after the great grills of New York and San Francisco, the focus is on classic and delicious American food.

Jar:
Chef Suzanne Tracht's retro chophouse offerings—like the 16-ounce Kansas City steak and the signature pot roast with carrots and caramelized onions—are wonderfully familiar and yet very contemporary.

orange and pomegranate juices, peach Cointreau and a squeeze of lime.

Vietnamese. Lunch (Monday-Friday), dinner. Reservations recommended. Bar. $36-85

★★★CUT

Beverly Wilshire, A Four Seasons Hotel, 9500 Wilshire Blvd., Beverly Hills, 310-276-8500; www.wolfgangpuck.com

Does Wolfgang Puck ever miss? Apparently not—the man's got another hit on his hands, this time with CUT, located in the posh Beverly Wilshire hotel across the street from the Rodeo Collection shopping center. Designed by celebrity architect Richard Meier of Getty Center fame, CUT is stark and sleek, with a skylight that plays up the moonlight glow after dark. The cuisine here is steakhouse fare with imagination, such as the starter of warm veal tongue, marinated artichokes, autumn shelling beans and salsa verde. Start with the Maryland blue crab and Maine lobster cocktail with spicy tomato horseradish, and follow it with the 14-ounce New York sirloin—it's Nebraska corn-fed and dry-aged for 35 days. Don't cut yourself off before dessert; the salted peanut butter and chocolate semifreddo (Italian for "half-cold" or chilled) with vanilla crème and dulce de leche is the perfect finish to a meal here.

Steak. Dinner. Closed Sunday. Bar. $86 and up

★★★GRILL ON THE ALLEY

9560 Dayton Way, Beverly Hills, 310-276-0615; www.thegrill.com

Although the Grill is in an alley near Wilshire Boulevard, you can simply follow the streams of fans filing in to find it. Modeled after the great grills of New York and San Francisco, the focus is on classic American food, including steaks and comfort foods like chicken pot pie, meatloaf and pasta dishes. The décor is also classic American, with mirrored walls, large chandeliers, dark wood flooring and semi-private booths.

Steak. Lunch, dinner. $36-85.

★★★IL CIELO

9018 Burton Way, Beverly Hills, 310-276-9990; www.ilcielo.com

It makes sense that countless weddings have taken place in this Beverly Hills institution, which opened in 1986. Arguably the most romantic restaurant in Los Angeles, Il Cielo is deserving of its name, which means "the sky," because patrons dine in the outdoor garden beneath a canopy of twinkling lights. Dining here will put you in the mood for love—it seems that every couple in the

place makes eyes at each other over plates of housemade pasta and focaccia—
so give in and order the antipasto Il Cielo, described as "good for two."

Italian. Lunch, dinner. Reservations recommended. Bar. $36-85

★★★MASTRO'S STEAKHOUSE

246 N. Canon Drive, Beverly Hills, 310-888-8782; www.mastrossteakhouse.com

Looking for good grub with a side of classic L.A. mayhem? Then head to
this reliable steakhouse, which is equal parts food and scene. Mastro's two
floors are dimly lit and on the noisy side; the first floor is decidedly old
school, but the upstairs is livelier, with a central bar packed with Hollywood
ingenues and the hangers-on who dote on them. Once you figure out
where you fit in, take a seat and start with the seafood tower; it's always
fresh and loaded with succulent oysters, shrimp, crab legs and the like.
The point of a meal at Mastro's, of course, is the steak, which arrives perfectly
cooked on a piping-hot plate, and goes beautifully with the gorgonzola mac
and cheese.

Steak. Dinner. Reservations recommended. Bar. $86 and up

★★★★ORTOLAN

8338 W. Third St., Beverly Hills, 323-653-3300; www.ortolanrestaurant.com

Executive chef Christophe Émé may be better known as the husband of sultry
blond actress Jeri Ryan, but gourmands know him from his years at L'Orangerie.
His wife's sex appeal may have rubbed off on the couple's restaurant Ortolan,
with its cream-colored tufted banquettes, cozy fireplace and bevy of sparkling
chandeliers, but it's Émé's haute cuisine (along with stellar service) that keeps
patrons coming back for more. Named after a rare bird historically eaten as a
delicacy in the south of France, Ortolan offers tempting à la carte options such
as the signature scrambled eggs with caviar and two prix fixe menus—appropriately dubbed Seduction and Plaisir, which is French for "pleasure."

French. Dinner. Closed Sunday-Monday. Bar. $86 and up

★★★POLO LOUNGE

The Beverly Hills Hotel and Bungalows, 9641 Sunset Blvd., Beverly Hills, 310-887-2777;
www.thebeverlyhillshotel.com

There are few more pleasant ways to spend a summer evening than by sitting in
the carefully tended garden on the patio of the Polo Lounge, cocktail in hand,
while live jazz plays in the background. Located at the Beverly Hills Hotel,
where Cary Grant's tuxedo collar still hangs on the wall, the Polo Lounge
remains a place for deal-making businessmen. The rest of the crowd—keen
on classics such as the roasted prime beef tenderloin, braised short rib and
pan-seared Nantucket Bay scallops—is more old-Hollywood than new, which
makes for a classy atmosphere befitting the historic digs, any time of the year.

American. Breakfast, lunch, dinner, Sunday brunch. Reservations recommended. $36-85

THE RESTAURANT AT THE HOTEL BEL-AIR

Hotel Bel-Air, 701 Stone Canyon Road, Bel Air, 310-472-5234; www.hotelbelair.com

This fine-dining restaurant within the Hotel Bel-Air was closed last year as part
of a major renovation. At press time, the dining room was scheduled to reopen
in April. The plan was for a refurbished dining room, bar area and terrace, plus

HIGHLIGHT

WHAT ARE THE BEST L.A. CELEBRITY CHEF RESTAURANTS?

XIV: Michael Mina does it again with his 14th restaurant, offering signature items such as the famed lobster pot pie, Kobe burger and trio of French fries, served in a rich and eclectic space designed by Philippe Starck.

Campanile: Owner and executive chef Mark Peel is a venerable name on the restaurant scene; he started out peeling vegetables for Wolfgang Puck and went on to open Spago with him in 1982. Peel still scours the local farmer's markets to make beautiful seasonal dishes, and you can taste his favorite finds in his special Monday night family dinners.

Gordon Ramsay at the London: You might see the chef spouting off on his two television shows, but the environment here is relaxed, the staff is courteous, and the savory offerings prove that this chef isn't all hot air.

Lucques: Suzanne Goin is a superstar in Los Angeles, with three restaurants (AOC, Tavern and Hungry Cat). Lucques, opened in 1998 to rave reviews, is her first and still draws foodies who come here for Sunday suppers, prix fixe lunches or the enjoyable bar menu.

Nobu: Reservations have been hard to come by at Nobu ever since the first one opened up in Malibu in 1999. These days sushi lovers can choose from more than one location for a mouthful of chef Nobuyuki Matsuhisa's new-style Japanese delights influenced by the chef's experiences in Peru.

Osteria Mozza: This super-hot restaurant is the brainchild of Nancy Silverton (of Campanile and La Brea Bakery fame), celebrity chef Mario Batali and winemaker Joseph Bastianich.

Spago Beverly Hills: Wolfgang Puck is perhaps the most recognizable name in and outside of the culinary world, and Spago Beverly Hills is the flagship of his empire. This Los Angeles institution continues to draw the biggest names in town for the blissful pizzas and fresh California cuisine.

Patina: He may not have his own television show, but Joachim Splichal is a star on the L.A. dining scene (and also has restaurants in Las Vegas and New York). His French-bistro style restaurants (which have a California twist) include Café Pinot.

new décor, concept and menu. Some things were left in tact—for example, the oak paneling in the bar. But guests can expect a better indoor/outdoor experience (which means additional outdoor seating) and the terrace was redesigned to better highlight the views and spectacular atmosphere surrounding Swan Lake. No doubt it will all be as lovely as ever.

★★★SPAGO BEVERLY HILLS

176 N. Canon Drive, Beverly Hills, 310-385-0880;
www.wolfgangpuck.com

Wolfgang Puck is perhaps the most recognizable name in and outside of the culinary world, and Spago Beverly Hills is the flagship of his empire. This Los Angeles institution continues to draw the biggest names in town, from Tom Cruise to Sidney Poitier. Celebrities pack the house nightly, looking to talk show business and indulge in the fine American cuisine from executive chef Lee Hefter, who uses only fresh (and often local) produce on the seasonal menu. Famous restaurateur and interior designer Barbara Lazaroff created the elegant and colorful dining room, where patrons enjoy the likes of iced Beau Soleil and Hama Hama oysters, grilled prime New York steak and, of course, Puck's signature pizzas.

American. Lunch (Monday-Saturday), dinner. Reservations recommended. Bar. $86 and up

ALSO RECOMMENDED

CHAYA BRASSERIE

8741 Alden Drive, Beverly Hills, 310-859-8833;
www.thechaya.com

After an especially long shopping session along nearby über-trendy Robertson Boulevard, Chaya feels like a comforting hug, with its welcoming, skylight-illuminated dining room and airy French-Japanese cuisine. The roomy bar is a neighborhood hot spot; locals gather here for the lively happy hour and delicious bar menu which includes such tasty nibbles as free range chicken liver mouse and jam, bacon wrapped organic mejool dates and crispy calamari with a jalapeno aioli. Lunch features salads, sushi, pasta, sandwiches and entrees such as free-range chicken dijon with pommes frites. The best pick-me-ups are the pastries, made from scratch every day in the bakery upstairs—the dessert sampler, for one, which includes a fallen chocolate cake, warm chocolate croissant bread pudding and a French apple tart.

French, Japanese. Lunch (Monday-Friday), dinner, Sunday brunch. Bar. $16-35

IL PASTAIO

400 N. Canon Drive, Beverly Hills, 310-205-5444;
www.giacominodrago.com

Master chef Celestino Drago and his brother, executive chef and partner Giacomino Drago, are dead serious about pasta. If it takes more than the

---

WHICH RESTAURANTS ARE SYNONYMOUS WITH LOS ANGELES?

Polo Lounge:
Located at the Beverly Hills Hotel, where Cary Grant's tuxedo collar still hangs on the wall, the Polo Lounge remains the go-to gathering place in Beverly Hills.

Spago Beverly Hills:
Celebrities still pack the house nightly, looking to talk show business and indulge in fine American cuisine.

Musso and Frank Grill:
Not much has changed since this historic institution opened in 1919, and that's just the way the loyal customers like it. You can still order Welsh rarebit and enjoy what many swear is the most perfect martini on the planet.

Campanile:
Joined to the famed La Brea Bakery, Campanile is an institution for people who are serious about good food. Owner and executive chef Mark Peel still scours the local farmers' markets to make beautiful seasonal dishes.

bottlenecking crowd engulfing the host to convince you, all you'll need is a bite of the mezzelune—a platter of housemade half-moon ravioli stuffed with lobster and topped with finely diced zucchini and yet more lobster—to turn you into a believer. So secure a reservation, get seated, and order from the à la carte menu or opt for the chef's six-course tasting menu, which comes with a little bit of everything: soup; salad; ravioli; your choice of pasta or risotto; meat or fish; and, of course, a housemade dessert or ice cream (selections change daily).

Italian. Lunch, dinner. Reservations recommended. Bar. $36-85

THE IVY

113 N. Robertson Blvd., Beverly Hills, 310-274-8303

The Ivy is a Los Angeles institution, and that's not just because celebrities are spotted here all the time. The restaurant is located on a strip of Robertson Boulevard that is home to some of the most unique boutiques in the city, which is why you'll often spot paparazzi trolling the sidewalk for a glimpse of the latest "it girls" as they power-lunch over salads and cocktails (and not much else). Despite the circus, the Ivy maintains a surprisingly laid-back ambiance, complete with a white picket fence surrounding the patio, which is adorned with flowers that the owners grow in their gardens at home. The reliable menu includes standbys such as the melt-in-your-mouth lobster ravioli, which co-owner and executive chef Richard Irving makes by hand every day.

American. Lunch, dinner. Reservations recommended. Bar. $36-85

LA PAELLA

476 S. San Vicente Blvd., Beverly Hills, 323-951-0745; www.usalapaella.com

La Paella is about as homey and charming an eatery as you could ask for, with quaint trinkets lining the walls and a staff that's sure to make you feel welcome. The terrific tapas menu—packed with tasty hot options like the patatas bravas (fried potatoes tossed with spicy tomato sauce) and cold ones like aceitunas rellenas (traditional Spanish olives stuffed with anchovies)—makes it difficult to save room for the main course. Exercise a little restraint nonetheless, because you don't want to miss the paella Valencia mixta, which tosses saffron, meat, vegetables, seafood, rosemary and red peppers into an aromatic, tasty dish. You'll probably be stuffed after that, but throw caution to the wind and order the light, orange-kissed, delicate flan de naranja.

Spanish, Mediterranean. Lunch (Monday-Friday), dinner. Closed Sunday. Bar. $16-35

MAKO

225 S. Beverly Drive, Beverly Hills, 310-288-8338; www.makorestaurant.com

For epicures craving a meal with more variety than that of your usual sushi restaurant, pay a visit to Mako. The simply designed restaurant—the space is bathed in soft lighting and outfitted with blond wood walls—offers a small-plates menu of ippin-ryouri, or individually sized portions; they allow diners to pick and choose from executive chef Makoto Tanaka's contemporary Asian dishes. Standouts include Mako's version of pad Thai and the bluefin tuna sashimi served with mixed greens, avocado and jalapeño with soy olive oil dressing. Mako also offers multiple-course bento boxes to go which make for a delightful picnic dinner.

Contemporary Asian. Lunch (Tuesday-Friday), dinner. Closed Sunday-Monday. Reservations recommended. Bar. $16-35

MR. CHOW

344 N. Camden Drive, Beverly Hills, 310-278-9911; www.mrchow.com

One of Michael Chow's six famed Mr. Chow locations, this 37-year-old Beverly Hills stalwart is kitted out in a stark black-and-white color scheme, complete with checkered floor and soaring vaulted ceilings, and remains one of the most striking (if not vaguely '80s) dining rooms in town. What's more, Mr. Chow is still one of Los Angeles' most notable see-and-be-seen restaurants for high-powered Hollywood types (hence the throngs of paparazzi outside), which means that often it's more about the people-watching than the food. If you drop in on an off night, shift your focus to solid signature dishes such as the green prawns sautéed with peppers and cashews, and lobster served fresh from a live tank.

Chinese. Lunch (Monday-Friday), dinner. Reservations recommended. Bar. $36-85

NATE 'N AL DELICATESSEN RESTAURANT

414 N. Beverly Drive, Beverly Hills, 310-274-0101; www.natenal.com

For more than half a century, Nate 'n Al has been one of the city's go-to spots for classic deli food, from reubens and melts to corned beef hash and smoked whitefish. The diner's Formica-heavy décor, deli counter and charismatic servers in kitschy uniforms have remained unapologetically the same all these years, and customers wouldn't have it any other way.

American. Breakfast, lunch, dinner. Bar. $16-35

PARQ

Montage Beverly Hills, 225 N. Canon Drive, Beverly Hills, 310-860-7800; www.montagebeverlyhills.com

Taking a cue from the hotel in which it is housed, Parq is a sunny spot located inside the Spanish Colonial-inspired Montage Beverly Hills, filled with mosaic tiles and large windows. You can dine outside on the patio overlooking the gardens or inside in one of the large half-moon booths. A mix of studio executives, creative types meeting over breakfast and a variety of guests come here to dine on the creative American cuisine, which runs the gamut from heavenly pancakes for breakfast to the juicy Parq burger at lunch and comfort foods like spiced short rib with buttered potato purée and onion jelly for dinner. Afterward, make time for a drink at the cozy bar, which specializes in classic cocktails. Service is crisp and professional. Note: At press time, this restaurant was being reconcepted.

American. Breakfast, lunch, dinner. Bar. $36-85

SPAS

★★★AQUA STAR SPA AT THE BEVERLY HILTON

The Beverly Hilton, 9876 Wilshire Blvd., Beverly Hills, 310-887-6048; www.beverlyhilton.com

The Aqua Star Spa at The Beverly Hilton (home to the Golden Globes every year) is all about California living. So it makes sense that the products they use are organic and that treatments include massages delivered outside by the hotel's famous pool. The menu includes everything from anti-aging facials to stretching massages to spray tanning (so you can safely get that California glow while you're in town). One of the standout treatments includes the Organic

Delight facial, which utilizes peach and apricot balm, and an herbal serum to rejuvinate skin. Follow that with the Organic Bliss body treatment, in which therapists use a warm fragrant organic sugar scrub to exfoliate and hydrate your skin, and you'll be ready to walk down the red carpet yourself.

★★★★THE BEVERLY HILLS HOTEL SPA BY LA PRAIRIE
The Beverly Hills Hotel and Bungalows, 9641 Sunset Blvd., Beverly Hills, 310-887-2505; www.thebeverlyhillshotel.com

In a town where face-lifts are as common as Louis Vuitton handbags, a spa like La Prairie, which focuses on anti-aging treatments, is an in-demand destination for those looking for a little pampering without the pain. The spacious spa caters to both the elegant old-money elite as well as young spa addicts who love to spoil themselves. You, too, can indulge in the high life with a luxe treatment such as the Caviar Intensive Eye Lift, which uses real roe to help reduce fine lines and dark circles. The rich proteins in the caviar are said to boost collagen production. To really fight Mother Nature (or crow's feet), the 60-minute Microdermabrasion Facial blasts away dead skin (and with it, fine lines) to reveal a super-smooth surface that makes you look younger. Seek relief in the Jet Lag Therapy package, which includes 30 minutes of aroma-therapy massage, 30 minutes of foot/hand reflexology and a 30-minute de-stressing facial.

★★★★THE PENINSULA SPA
The Peninsula Beverly Hills, 9882 S. Santa Monica Blvd., Beverly Hills, 310-975-2854; www.beverlyhills.peninsula.com

Diamonds may be a girl's best friend, but at the Peninsula, ladies (and gents) can get their fill of rubies, emeralds and sapphires, too. The spacious indoor/outdoor spa is the first in North America to use Shiffa precious gem oils, which contain micro-fine fragments of the aforementioned sparklers. The Shiffa services on the menu—massages and body scrubs—can be customized with your gem of choice, each of which comes with its own special healing powers: Diamond is for balance and harmony, emerald for stability and strength, ruby for stimulation and vitality, and sapphire for peace and tranquility. Whether or not the gems actually work wonders on your skin, a scrub-down with diamond dust definitely feels luxurious

★★★★THE SPA AT BEVERLY WILSHIRE

Beverly Wilshire, A Four Seasons Hotel, 9500 Wilshire Blvd., Beverly Hills, 310-385-7023; www.fourseasons.com

A lot of spas deal in luxury for the sake of luxury. This retreat specializes in treatments most of us really need. In addition to a range of massages, facials and body treatments, the spa offers a special rub-down for stiletto-worshippers (the High Heel Appeal)—a massage designed to soothe heel-addicted feet and legs. There's also the Techie Neck, a stretching massage that goes to work on the place where most of us hold our tension.For the super stressed, there's the Mind Unwind, a pressure-points-targeted scalp massage along with a neck and shoulder rub that aims to relieve the sinuses and help you focus. Facials feature Kate Somerville products, and there's even one for men that focuses on calming the irritation caused by daily shaving. Kids can also enjoy treatments such as the Sticky Hands, a flavored hand scrub followed by a hand massage, wrap and a dusting of shimmer. The spa itself is a beautiful space with a curved water wall and amethyst crystal geode.

★★★★THE SPA AT FOUR SEASONS HOTEL LOS ANGELES

Four Seasons Hotel Los Angeles at Beverly Hills, 300 S. Doheny Drive, Beverly Hills, 310-786-2229; www.fourseasons.com/losangeles

The Four Seasons in Beverly Hills is the place for celebrities and industry business (someone is always taping an interview somewhere in the hotel). The concierge service will cater to your every whim, not only letting you choose the type of massage you'd like but where you'd like to have it. In your suite? In one of the outdoor cabanas? Word is that celebrities love the all-over body polishes. The Traditional Turkish Scrub is applied in two steps: For the first, a mix of thermal salts and minerals are rubbed into clean skin. Then comes the loofah, which leaves no dead skin cell behind. Exclusive to the spa is the Four Seasons Swe-Thai, a combination of Swedish and Thai massage that invovles yogic stretching, pressure point stimulation and deep tissue massage—it's the perfect massage after a workout.

★★★★SPA MONTAGE

Montage Beverly Hills, 225 N. Canon Drive, Beverly Hills, 310-860-7840; www.montagebeverlyhills.com

This sprawling spa housed in the luxury Spanish-style Montage Beverly Hills offers a variety of

WHAT ARE THE BEST L.A. HOTEL SPAS?

The Beverly Hills Hotel Spa by La Prairie:
Not only are the products top-notch—it's La Prairie, after all—but the estheticians and therapists do a stellar job. (Best of all, you can head to the pool for a drink afterward.)

The Peninsula Spa:
This attractive spa has a wonderful tranquility room, loads of amenities in the super-clean locker room and decadent treatments.

The Spa at Beverly Wilshire:
This retreat specializes in treatments most of us really need, such as a foot massage for stiletto-worshippers, a stretching massage for your neck, and a shoulder rub that aims to relieve sinuses.

The Spa at Four Seasons Los Angeles at Beverly HIlls:
Visiting this spa is like having your own private staff; a concierge will arrange everything for your perfect day.

Spa Montage:
Treatment rooms here are decorated like lavish suites in a private house, and treatments are truly customized to meet your needs.

HIGHLIGHT

WHAT'S THE BEST WAY TO SHOP AROUND BEVERLY HILLS?

Even if people don't chase you down for an autograph, spending a day in Beverly Hills can make you feel like a star (and, by the end of the day, you'll certainly be dressed like one). To get the most out of your time in this most famous of zip codes, you'll need a game plan. First, fuel up at **Nate 'n Al Delicatessen** in the form of pancakes or any of the classic deli items on the menu. Next, go south from the deli to hit up the enclave's smaller, independent boutiques first, including **Planet Blue.**

Keep heading south from Planet Blue to **Taschen** *(354 N. Beverly Drive, 310-274-4300; www.taschen.com)*, an upscale bookstore, then go across the street to **Gearys Beverly Hills** *(351 N. Beverly Drive, 310-273-4741; www.gearys.com)* where you'll find a well-edited selection of baubles that attracts jewelry-loving customers.

Take a break for some pampering at **The Spa at Beverly Wilshire**. Just keep trekking south until you get to Wilshire Boulevard, then hang a right. The spa's High Heel Appeal massage relieves tired legs with a 20-minute treatment that includes a foot soak, exfoliation and massage (a great treatment for women and men). Afterward, you don't have to walk far (or even out of the building) for lunch. Sit down at Wolfgang Puck's **CUT**, whose skylight allows you to enjoy your 14-ounce dry-aged, corn-fed New York sirloin beneath sunny rays.

Now it's time to walk over to the stores that are a must-stop for all serious shoppers. Head west on Wilshire and scour the racks of **Saks Fifth Avenue** *(9600 Wilshire Blvd., 310-275-4211; www.saksfifthavenue.com)* and **Neiman Marcus** *(9700 Wilshire Blvd., 310-550-5900; www.neimanmarcus.com)*.

After your warm-up at the department stores, it's time to let loose on California's shopping mecca: **Rodeo Drive**. Make your way back toward the Beverly Wilshire, head north on Rodeo and start gawking at the gorgeous garb in the shop windows. Start at **Tiffany & Co.** *(210 N. Rodeo Drive, 310-273-8880; www.tiffany.com)* to take home a sparkly souvenir in one of those trademark blue boxes. You can opt to go on a detour through **Via Rodeo**, a little European-inspired cobblestone street lined with haute shops such as **Versace**.

Otherwise, keep going north on Rodeo, stopping at big-name shops such as **Dolce & Gabbana** and **Prada**. Keep going north and spend the rest of the afternoon and early evening buying more beautiful new things at **Chanel**, **Hermès** and **Ralph Lauren**.

Right along the Drive among all the shops, you'll find the **Rodeo Collection** *(421 N. Rodeo Drive, 310-276-9600; www.rodeocollection.net)*. Enter the mini-mall, one of the few in Beverly Hills, and check out **BCBG Max Azria**, **La Perla** and **Stuart Weitzman**.

When you're all shopped out, enjoy some bistro food at **Bouchon Beverly Hills**, located across from **Montage Beverly Hills**. The restaurant from chef Thomas Keller also includes Bar Bouchon, a nice place for drinks and snacks.

relaxing—and effective—treatments in a peaceful and glamorous environment. The 17 individual treatment rooms are decorated like lavish suites in a private house, with mosaic tiles, plush, padded treatment tables and deep club chairs for relaxing post-treatment. Massages and facials can be tailored to your needs, and the water therapies can be added on to any treatment. Before a massage, try a hydrotherapy bath with essential oils and underwater massage to loosen you up. Afterward, put your locks in the very capable hands of the stylists at the onsite Kim Vo salon (he's famous for coloring the tresses of Goldie Hawn, Britney Spears and scores of other stars). The fitness center is brimming with cutting-edge machines, freeweights and more, and private or group pilates and yoga classes are also available.

CENTURY CITY/WESTWOOD/CULVER CITY

Century City is a corridor of office buildings, apartments and hotels. Westwood is the home of UCLA, while Culver City, south of the 10 Highway, is L.A.'s newest dining scene. A revitalization plan has brought live theater, cineplexes and dozens of exciting new restaurants to Culver's city center.

WHAT TO SEE

HAMMER MUSEUM

10899 Wilshire Blvd., Westwood, 310-443-7000; www.hammer.ucla.edu

While it's technically not on the UCLA Campus, the Hammer Museum is under the jurisdiction of the university, so if you're taking a tour around the campus, be sure to include the Hammer in your itinerary. The museum's permanent art collection features heavyweights like Paul Gauguin, Camille Pissarro, Vincent van Gogh and Rembrandt. Otherwise, the Hammer is very much dedicated to featuring revolutionary contemporary art—the museum's ongoing "Hammer Projects" exhibitions highlight the work of up-and-coming artists. But what makes the Hammer unique is its eclectic free programming. The museum attracts literary minds such as Joan Didion and James Ellroy, as well as creative powerhouses such as Oliver Stone, Miranda July and Brian Grazer. As if that weren't enough, you can watch cinematic treasures from the UCLA Film & Television Archive in the Billy Wilder Theater, and hear everything from progressive jazz to indie rock in the museum's courtyard.

Admission: adults $7, seniors $5, children under 17 and students free. Tuesday-Wednesday, Friday-Saturday 11 a.m.-7 p.m., Thursday 11 a.m.- 9 p.m., Sunday 11 a.m.-5 p.m. Free Thursday.

MILDRED E. MATHIAS BOTANICAL GARDEN

UCLA Campus, Hilgard and Le Conte avenues, Westwood, 310-825-1260; www.botgard.ucla.edu

Smack-dab in the middle of the bustle of Westwood is a real oasis: the Mildred E. Mathias Botanical Garden. This seven-acre garden is a good choice for those who don't want to make the long trek to the L.A. Arboretum. The garden was started in 1929, around the same time that UCLA began classes in Westwood, and is still used for some botanical experiments, although today the garden mostly serves as a peaceful place for visitors to enjoy. Walk among 5,000 different species, including tropical and sub-tropical plants, and be sure to stroll the garden's Metasequoia (the tallest dawn redwoods in North America) and its Eucalyptus grandis trees, planted here more than 40 years ago, long before the trees popped up all over the region.

Admission: free. Monday-Friday 8 a.m.-5 p.m. (in winter months, until 4 p.m.), Saturday 8 a.m.-4 p.m.

SONY PICTURES STUDIO TOUR

10202 W. Washington Blvd., Culver City, 310-244-8687; www.sonypicturesstudiostours.com

Sony Pictures Studios will show you behind-the-scenes Hollywood. But don't expect to spy any movie stars strolling around the lot. Instead, you may see the sets of *Jeopardy!* and *Wheel of Fortune*, sans Alex Trebek and Vanna White, that is. You'll also get a chance to look at Academy Awards earned by films like *Lawrence of Arabia*. Be prepared: This is a two-hour walking tour. If you're looking to sit back and relax on a tram ride, you're better off going to Universal Studios.

Tours: $28. Monday-Friday 9:30 a.m., 10:30 a.m., 1:30 p.m. and 2:30 p.m.

WHERE TO STAY

★★★HOTEL PALOMAR LOS ANGELES-WESTWOOD

10740 Wilshire Blvd., Westwood, 310-475-8711; www.hotelpalomar-lawestwood.com

They say that art imitates life, but at the new Hotel Palomar Los Angeles-Westwood, hospitality imitates film. Event spaces have been named for festivals, ranging from Sundance to Cannes, while casting couches in each room and planned movie breaks with popcorn go all but overboard with the theme. Guest rooms ignite neutral tones like charcoal and chocolate with pops of turquoise and patterns evoking everything from peacock feathers to French bordello-chic florals. Accents include black faux fur throws, iHome docking stations, in-room Kerstin Florian spa treatments and, in the bathroom, spa tubs and L'Occitane products. Head to buzzed-about restaurant BLVD 16, where chef Simon Dolinky serves seasonal specials such as white corn ravioli stuffed with Maine lobster and roasted mushrooms, using sustainable, organic produce from local farms.

268 rooms. Restaurant, bar. Business center. Fitness center. Pool. Pets accepted. $351 and up

★★★HYATT REGENCY CENTURY PLAZA

2025 Avenue of the Stars, Century City, 310-228-1234; www.hyatt.com

When presidents come to town, they check into the enormous Hyatt Regency Century Plaza. After just completing a significant renovation, the swanky spot now features brand-new suites, which include the use of the Regency Club, a private lounge with complimentary refreshments as well as a new pool and pool deck with posh cabanas. You can hang out in the new Lobby Court and Patio for afternoon coffee or evening cocktails, or hit the new X bar to nibble on tapas amid outdoor fire pits and greenery. The best perk is the adjoining multi-tiered Equinox Fitness Club + Spa, the company's West Coast flagship gym (there is a $20 fee to access the club, unless you have a spa treatment booked). The cutting-edge classes and some of the city's best aestheticians offering almost a dozen different massage techniques draw high-level executives from surrounding offices, but it's also fit for a commander-in-chief.

726 rooms. Restaurant, bar. Business center. Fitness center. Pool. Spa. $351 and up

★★★INTERCONTINENTAL LOS ANGELES CENTURY CITY

2151 Avenue of the Stars, Century City, 310-284-6500; www.intercontinental.com

The InterContinental sits among Century City's high-rises, housing major agencies such as CAA and ICM and entertainment bigwigs like 20th Century Fox. Executives often powwow at the Park Grill over organic California cuisine and at Park Grill Lounge, where cocktails are named for Fox characters and programs, including the American Idoltini and the Jack Bauer and Coke (after 24, if you've been living under a rock). Another reason to visit the hotel is the Spa InterContinental. Treatment rooms lie within three villas, each of which include an Infiniti Kohler jet tub, shower, flat-screen TV, lounging area and outdoor patio; guests are greeted with a signature aromatherapy ritual in order to de-stress before their treatment. If you don't feel like fighting for swimming space in the new pool, plunge into your oversized in-room tub instead.

364 rooms. Restaurant, bar. Business center. Fitness center. Pool. Spa. $351 and up

★★★W LOS ANGELES – WESTWOOD

930 Hilgard Ave., Westwood, 310-208-8765; www.starwoodhotels.com

Adrift in Westwood's sea of UCLA students, chain restaurants and nondescript luncheonettes, the W is incongruously trendy. You'll wander from the sleek lobby, past the outdoor Backyard café to the retro-chic pool area, and wonder how this scene landed amid so many sub shops. Stroll over to the nearby weekly Thursday Farmers' Market for fresh fruit and tamales and to snag finds such as ridiculously inexpensive and good Diddy Riese cookies (grab an ice-cream cookie sandwich), but the W is mostly a self-contained experience, complete with summer poolside film screenings, lobby art openings, Bliss Spa treatments and Whiskey Blue cocktail hours. Thom Filicia of *Queer Eye for the Straight Guy* helmed a recent redesign of bungalow rooms and poolside cabanas (hooked up with "Intellichaise" technology, so sun worshippers can order refreshments and peruse local offerings without effort). New executive chef Monique King elevates food at eateries NINETHIRTY and The Backyard—the latter is a perfect outdoor spot to sip a cocktail.

258 rooms. Restaurant, bar. Fitness center. Pool. Spa. Pets accepted. $351 and up

WHERE TO EAT

RECOMMENEDED
TENGU

10853 Lindbrook Drive, Westwood, 310-209-0071; www.tengu.com

Being a college town—Westwood is home to plenty of inexpensive California roll sushi joints. But for something hip and upscale (and not exactly fit for a college-student budget), Tengu is the place. With bamboo accents, mood lighting, shoji screen partitions and DJs spinning mellow but uptempo tunes, the vibe here is equal parts Zen and lounge. For libations, opt for the signature house sake, which is infused with fresh Maui pineapples; it makes for the ideal counterbalance to the standout sashimi picante, a tuna, yellowtail and salmon trio with jalapeño and ginger-garlic ponzu sauce.

Japanese. Lunch (Monday-Friday), dinner. Bar. $36-85

VERSAILLES

10319 Venice Blvd., Culver City, 310-558-3168; 1415 S. La Cienega Blvd., Midtown, 310-289-0392; 17410 Ventura Blvd., Encino, 818-906-0756; 1000 N. Sepulveda Blvd., Manhattan Beach, 310-937-6829; Universal CityWalk Hollywood, 100 Universal City Plaza, Universal City, 818-505-0093; www.versaillescuban.com

One of Los Angeles' most popular eateries, Versailles offers generous portions of savory Cuban dishes, such as fried fish and roasted garlic chicken, and nearly everything comes with sweet plantains, white rice and black beans. Regulars know to order the addictive Cuban-style roasted pork; it's arguably one of the most flavorful dishes in the city, and people talk about it with reverence. On your way out, pick up a bottle of Versailles' famous garlic-citrus mojo sauce. It's what makes the roasted pork so special, and it lends a delightfully garlicky and savory flavor to just about anything.

Cuban. Lunch, dinner. Bar. $16-35

SPAS

★★★THE SPA AT EQUINOX CENTURY CITY

Hyatt Regency Century Plaza, 10220 Constellation Blvd., Century City, 310-286-2900; www.equinoxfitness.com

If you've been to an Equinox gym, you know it's a great place to get in a workout. At this location, you can also head to the attached spa afterward to relax. For a great post-workout treatment, try the Lemon Sugar Body Polish, a body scrub, which uses raw cane crystals and lemon to give you baby soft and glowing skin. Or try the Body Melt, a customized wrap/massage/detox treatment that's supposed to shed inches from flab-prone areas: you choose to focus on your abs, glutes, arms, chest or thighs. We've never taken out a tape measure afterward to see if it actually works, but 80 minutes of targeted treatment does have a way of making you feel "lighter."

SANTA MONICA/BRENTWOOD/BEACH TOWNS

Here is Los Angeles at its finest: beautiful ocean beaches at the fringe of one of the worlds largest metropolises. Despite some new high-end condo buildings, Venice is still funky by most people's definition, with buskers and street performers lining the Boardwalk every weekend, hawking anything from incense and pipes to crass T-shirts and self-published rap CDs. Malibu is a surfer's paradise. Multi-million-dollar homes line the oceanfront, but visitors without their own screenplay are welcome on dozens of public beaches up and down the coast. Santa Monica is literally and figuratively halfway between the two. Its recreation path along the beach welcomes bikers, skaters and runners by day, while its amusement park on the pier lights up the area after dark. For a peerless view of it all, Brentwood's mansion-packed hills are just the spot.

As its name suggests, Marina Del Ray, located next to Venice and only four miles from LAX, attracts many boating and sport fishing enthusiasts. The dominant feature is the largest man-made harbor in the world, with more than 5,000 slips. Sail and power boat rentals, ocean cruises and fishing expeditions are available. Besides boating, there's biking and jogging in front of the marina, numerous restaurants, shops and beaches. The once-quiet Manhattan Beach enclave has become a vibrant neighborhood. Just blocks from the beach, rolling hills are dotted with quaint homes and mini-mansions. Still, a mellow beach atmosphere prevails. You'll see groups of surfers walking down the street or families in flip-flops from the beach shopping in the local markets. The main zone of activity is Manhattan Beach Boulevard and the Pier, which are crammed with trendy nightclubs, surf shops and restaurants. Along the strand, in-line skaters, beach volleyball players, bikers and dog lovers make for an active scene.

WHAT TO SEE

FISHERMAN'S VILLAGE

13755 Fiji Way, Marina del Rey, 310-823-5411; www.visitthemarina.com

Modeled after a turn-of-the-century New England fishing town and located on the main channel of the largest man-made small craft harbor in the country, this area and its well-known lighthouse have appeared in many television and movie productions. Cobblestone walks complement the nautical atmosphere and provide a panoramic view of the marina. You can find boat rentals, fishing charters and harbor cruises here, as well as shops, boutiques and restaurants. Entertainment is provided throughout the year, including free jazz concerts on Saturday and Sunday.

THE GETTY CENTER

1200 Getty Center Drive, Brentwood, 310-440-7300; www.getty.edu

Home to the J. Paul Getty Museum and a beacon for Los Angeles' art and cultural sensibility, the Getty Center contains some of the U.S.'s finest and most valuable European art. Designed by architect Richard Meier, the Center is a real beauty that sits high atop the Santa Monica Mountains; its slabs of pale stone perfectly reflect the rosy light of the rising and setting sun. In addition to browsing the art inside, take a walk along the charming Central Garden, part of which is designed like a maze with flower-fringed pathways. Beauty aside, the Center isn't without its share of intrigue. In 2005, accusations surfaced that several pieces of its antiquity collection, largely handled by former Getty curator Marion True, were illegally obtained from Italy. The Getty Trust has since worked with Italian officials in returning 40 artworks, including a highly coveted 2,400-year-old limestone statue of Aphrodite. So head to the free museum quickly, before the rest of the collection gets shipped back to the boot. *Admission: free. Tuesday-Friday 10 a.m.-5:30 p.m., Saturday 10 a.m.-9 p.m., Sunday 10 a.m.-5:30 p.m.*

THE GETTY VILLA

17985 Pacific Coast Highway, Pacific Palisades, 310-440-7300; www.getty.edu

West of the Getty Center, the free Getty Villa is an additional treat for art-hungry eyes. J. Paul Getty purchased 64 acres of seaside property in Pacific Palisades to house his collection of Greek and Roman antiquities. Using a first-century Roman country house (specifically, the Villa dei Papiri in Herculaneum, Italy) as his inspiration, construction of the Getty Villa began in the 1970s. Now you can see the villa's hundreds of Greek, Roman and Etruscan antiquities, including statues, terra cotta urns, gold jewelry and bronze armor. Among those on display is *Statue of a Victorious Youth*, a treasured bronze sculpture that dates back to 300 to 100 B.C. Make sure to leave enough time to tour the villa's magnificent gardens—the Outer Peristyle is the largest and the

HIGHLIGHT

WHAT ARE THE BEST PLACES FOR FAMILY FUN?

California Science Center: This free, hands-on museum makes science fun and accessible with special exhibits and an IMAX Theater, where you can take 3D tours of exotic places.

Disney's California Adventure Park: California Adventure's rides let you explore the Golden State with rides such as Soarin' Over California, which makes you feel as if you're hang gliding over the Golden Gate Bridge and other places.

Disneyland Park: Scream your lungs out Space Mountain, spin around at the Mad Tea Party and say hello to Mickey at the original Disney park.

Griffith Observatory: Find out how much you weigh on other planets, see real meteorites and explore the Milky Way without leaving the comfort of planet Earth, all for free.

Los Angeles Zoo: The resident primates, including apes, gorillas and chimpanzees make this zoo fun for the whole family.

Natural History Museum of Los Angeles County: Confront a Tyrannosaurus rex; look Megamouth, one of world's rarest sharks, in the eye; and discover more than 300 pounds of gold at the third-largest natural history museum in the United States.

Santa Monica Pier Aquarium: See species native to the Santa Monica Bay at this popular aquarium, which houses octopuses, eels and sharks, and which regularly puts on fun activities for kids such as "A Fishy Fest Celebrating Halloween and Dia De Los Meurtos."

Travel Town: Travel Town has an impressive collection of locomotives and motorcars; kids will be all about Thomas the Tank Engine and the miniature train that circles the premise.

most impressive. Modeled after an ancient Roman garden, the Outer Peristyle features plants native to the Mediterranean, pools of aqua water, vibrant murals and replicas of bronze statues found at the Villa dei Papiri.

Admission: free. Wednesday-Monday 10 a.m.-5 p.m.

SANTA MONICA MOUNTAINS NATIONAL RECREATION AREA

West of Griffith Park in Los Angeles County and east of the Oxnard Plain in Ventura County, 805-370-2301; www.nps.gov

When the luster of Hollywood begins to fade, get back to basics for free at the Santa Monica Mountains. This mountain range is home to some of L.A.'s most beautiful hiking, biking and horseback riding trails (try Malibu Lake Riders—818-510-2245; www.malibulakeriders.com—for the latter). The Santa Monica Mountains can be accessed from a number of locations throughout Los Angeles, and since it's the biggest urban park in the United States, there are plenty of trails from which to choose. You'll probably want to pick a trail close to where you're staying, but here are some popular trails and where to find them: Runyon Canyon (Hollywood), Fryman Canyon (Studio City), Temescal Canyon Park (Pacific Palisades), Topanga State Park (Topanga), Malibu Creek State Park (Calabasas) and Point Mugu State Park (Malibu).

Admission: free. Daily 9 a.m.-5 p.m.

SANTA MONICA PIER

380 Santa Monica Pier, Santa Monica, 310-260-8744; www.pacpark.com

Sometimes there's nothing like some good old-fashioned fun. The Santa Monica Pier delivers that—along with great ocean views—with Pacific Park, a pint-size amusement park. Hop aboard the world's only solar-powered Ferris wheel, feel your stomach drop on the West Coaster (the West Coast's only oceanfront steel roller coaster) and spin in circles on Inkie's Scrambler. If you've forgotten to pack Dramamine, make a beeline for the park's games section, where classic amusements like Wac-A-Mole, ring toss and skeeball await. To make your theme park experience authentic, hit up the vendors selling hot dogs, popcorn, cotton candy and funnel cake.

Admission (unlimited rides): children 8 years and older $21.95, children 7 and under $15.95. Memorial Day-Labor Day, Sunday-Thursday 11 a.m.-11 p.m., Friday-Saturday 11 a.m.-12:30 a.m.; January-May, Labor Day-Memorial Day, Monday-Thursday noon-7 p.m., Friday noon-midnight, Saturday 11 a.m.-midnight, Sunday 11 a.m.-9 p.m.; Memorial Day-Labor Day, Sunday-Thursday 11 a.m.-11 p.m., Friday-Saturday 11 a.m.-12:30 a.m.

SANTA MONICA PIER AQUARIUM

1600 Ocean Front Walk, Santa Monica, 310-393-6149; www.healthebay.org

You won't see any exotic fish at the Santa Monica Pier Aquarium, but you will see species native to the Santa Monica Bay. Get up close with a number of ocean dwellers in the touch tanks and tide pools, which feature resident sea stars, crabs, sea urchins, snails and sea cucumbers. Also on view (but not available for touching), are octopuses, eels, lobsters and sharks. If you can swing it, go to the aquarium on the popular Shark Sunday, when you can watch the aquarium staff feed the resident sharks.

Admission: adults $5 suggested donation, children 12 and under free. Tuesday-Friday 2-6 p.m., Saturday-Sunday 12:30 p.m.-6 p.m.

WHAT ARE SOME
OF L.A.'S BEST
FREE ACTIVITIES?

**The Getty Center/
Getty Villa:**
For the price of parking,
you can see some of the
U.S.'s finest and most
valuable European art
as well as J. Paul Getty's
collection of Greek and
Roman antiquities.

South Bay Bicycle Trail:
The South Bay Bicycle
Trail provides a beautiful
scenic tour of L.A.,
starting out at Will
Rogers State Beach in
Pacific Palisades and
winding 22 miles down
the coast to Torrance
County Beach
in Torrance.

SOUTH BAY BICYCLE TRAIL

17700 Pacific Coast Highway, Pacific Palisades; www.scc.ca.gov

There's nothing like exploring a city on a bike. The South Bay Bicycle Trail provides a beautiful scenic tour, as it starts out at Will Rogers State Beach in Pacific Palisades and winds 22 miles down the coast to Torrance County Beach in Torrance. Most of the path is along the beach (except for a few spots where the trail ends and you have to take the streets), so it makes for a nice, low-key ride (especially since you don't have to worry about getting run over). There are many places along the bike path to stop and grab a drink or a bite to eat, so you can turn your biking adventure into a leisurely trek instead of an arduous workout. The path does get crowded near the Santa Monica Pier and Venice Beach, where you'll have to weave around the pedestrians and rollerbladers.

THIRD STREET PROMENADE

Third Street, between Wilshire Boulevard and Broadway, Santa Monica, 310-393-8355; www.thirdstreetpromenade.org

Just a few blocks from the beach, Third Street Promenade is an outdoor, pedestrian-friendly mall where you can peruse hundreds of shops while enjoying the Santa Monica sun. If you're looking for a specific store, chances are it's on the Promenade—Gap, Anthropologie, Urban Outfitters, Barnes & Noble, Banana Republic, Old Navy and Abercrombie & Fitch are just a few of the many shops here. As far as dining options go, there are restaurants and bars as well as the usual food court staples. After you've bought one too many basics, stroll the Promenade and watch the impromptu street performances, in which you'll see people of all ages singing, dancing and playing musical instruments.

VENICE BEACH AND BOARDWALK

1800 Ocean Front Walk, Venice; www.laparks.org

Venice Beach probably hasn't changed much since the swinging '60s and '70s, when skateboarders and hippies ruled the boardwalk. Although many of the area's homes are now owned by wealthy yuppie types, Venice is as zany as ever. Skateboarders still flood the Venice Skatepark, artists still make their mark on the Venice Beach graffiti wall, and bodybuilders still pump iron at Muscle Beach's legendary outdoor gym. The Venice Boardwalk is inundated with shopkeepers peddling all kinds of wares, from cheap sunglasses to snarky T-shirts. The area also attracts a variety of street performers, everything from human statues to jugglers who favor chainsaws over clubs. With this cast of characters, it's a great spot for people-watching.

WILL ROGERS STATE HISTORIC PARK

1501 Will Rogers Park Road, Pacific Palisades, 310-454-8212; www.parks.ca.gov

In the 1920s, cowboy entertainer Will Rogers bought more than 100 acres in Pacific Palisades. Eventually, Rogers' purchase became the site of a 31-room ranch house, stable, corrals, riding ring, roping arena, polo field, golf course and hiking trails. When Rogers' widow died in the 1940s, the ranch was turned into a state park, where the public could be one with nature and learn about the life and career of Rogers. You can tour the ranch house, take horseback riding lessons and hike on one of the many trails surrounding the park. If you're visiting on a weekend during the spring, summer or fall, you'll be able to see the Will Rogers Polo Club in action. Aside from being a movie star, humorist, rope-trick expert and cowboy, Rogers also was an accomplished polo player.

Daily 8 a.m.-sunset. Tours: Thursday-Friday 11 a.m., 1 p.m. and 2 p.m., Saturday-Sunday 10 a.m.-4 p.m.

WHERE TO STAY

★★★THE FAIRMONT MIRAMAR HOTEL & BUNGALOWS

101 Wilshire Blvd., Santa Monica, 310-576-7777; www.fairmont.com

Although the Fairmont Miramar Hotel & Bungalows sits a block from the beach and from overcrowded and touristy Third Street Promenade, it's a secluded oasis reminiscent of a great estate, separated from the street performers and harried shoppers by waterfalls, lush greenery and 32 new private bungalows. The addition of Exhale Spa (a Santa Monica mainstay) ensures relaxation. The acclaimed spa is known not only for great treatments, but also for signature Core Fusion and Core Energy Flow fitness classes (tough, but definitely effective). The longtime celebrity fitness secret uses Qigong techniques to tone and strengthen. Once you've worked up an appetite, head to the new Fig restaurant for organic and sustainable seasonable California cuisine and then to the Lobby Lounge, which overlooks the koi fish pond, for cocktails.

300 rooms. Restaurant, bar. Business center. Fitness center. Pool. Spa. $351 and up

★★★THE GEORGIAN HOTEL

1415 Ocean Ave., Santa Monica, 310-395-9945; www.georgianhotel.com

If The Georgian Hotel was good enough for the Kennedy family matriarch (Rose Kennedy summered here for years), then it's good enough for all. Marking its 75th anniversary in 2008, the beachside (and Santa Monica Pier-adjacent) hotel opened in 1933—when Prohibition speakeasies lined Pacific Coast Highway—and was dubbed "Lady" for its infamously successful owner, Mrs. Rosamond Borde. Rich Hollywood history pervades the Art Deco details, from archways to ornate bathroom tiles. Although the hotel recently underwent a $2 million makeover to include modern amenities including complimentary wireless Internet, flat-screen TVs and MP3 alarm clocks, the historic land-mark's deep character and charm have been meticulously preserved. The rooms' décor is both modern and reflective of the hotel's original aesthetic, while The Veranda restaurant draws a buzz for both its food and California wines. Though there's no pool to lounge around, activities ranging from surfing lessons to Santa Monica Pier visits are easily arranged. Plus, the big blue expanse of the Pacific Ocean is just a minute away.

84 rooms. Restaurant, bar. Business center. Fitness center. Pets accepted. $251-350

★★★HOTEL CASA DEL MAR

1910 Ocean Way, Santa Monica, 310-581-5533; www.hotelcasadelmar.com

Casa Del Mar originally opened its Renaissance Revival doors and became the place to be seen in 1926, but it reemerged on the contemporary hospitality radar in 1999 after the classic beachside hotel underwent a $50 million renovation. Now, the original sophisticated digs have been rejuvenated. The sparkling new décor is fresh and romantic, revolving around vintage-style four-poster walnut beds à la 1920s chic, with ivory sateen drapes and sea-blue walls. The rooms also boast modern amenities, including 42-inch plasma TVs and iPod docking stations. Though executive chef Michael Reardon—a La Bernardin vet—offers innovative and delicious seafood and sushi at new restaurant Catch, it may be the incredible view overlooking the beach that stays with you after enjoying a meal at the upscale but mellow addition. Be sure to grab a cocktail at the bar around sunset.

129 rooms. Restaurant, bar. Fitness center. Pool. Spa. $351 and up

★★★HOTEL OCEANA SANTA MONICA

849 Ocean Ave., Santa Monica, 310-393-0486; www.hoteloceanasantamonica.com

After a $16 million renovation, Hotel Oceana is like a home away from home (if your house happens to sit directly across from the Pacific Ocean and embody a refreshingly eclectic slant on Cape Cod chic). Formerly the residence of Stan Laurel of comedy duo Laurel and Hardy, Oceana now is one of L.A.'s most amazing finds. The mellow enclave with apartment-style rooms makes you feel like nesting for the long haul. Rejecting the long-enduring trend of cool minimalism, Oceana has an accessible, breezy freshness with warm, feel-good colors and playful patterns that don't overwhelm. Spacious suites surrounding the courtyard offer practical oversized wooden desks, while chess tables and other thoughtful touches give rooms a distinct personality. In-room amenities such as two HDTVs in several suites, Aveda toiletries, iPod docking stations and Egyptian cotton sheets further elevate this luxe boutique hotel. Electric-blue chaises line the courtyard pool, as do tables spilling out from the casual yet high-end Ocean Lounge helmed by chef Joseph Feldman. There's no place like (this) home.

70 rooms. Restaurant, bar. Fitness center. Pool. $351 and up

★★★THE HUNTLEY

1111 Second St., Santa Monica, 310-394-5454; www.thehuntleyhotel.com

Location, location, location—that's the secret to The Huntley's popularity amidst sun-seekers. The boutique hotel is not just unmistakable due to its location inside a tall, 18-floor building just one block away from the beach, but also for its striking, art-gallery-like lobby, which is outfitted in the cool whites and warm chocolate-and-beige browns of California-contemporary design. The guest rooms feature 42-inch plasma TVs, pillow-top beds and Egyptian cotton linens, and Gilchrist & Soames bath products. When you've had enough of your room's gorgeous bird's-eye ocean views, keep taking advantage of the location and head to the beach or to Third Street Promenade, which is also just steps outside the door. If you want to stay on your high, head to the top of the building for gorgeous vistas, dinner and drinks at The Penthouse restaurant—you won't be the only one to recognize a well-situated stomping ground, so expect a packed dining room on weekends.

209 rooms. Restaurant, bar. Business center. Fitness center. $251-350

★★★LE MERIGOT

1740 Ocean Ave., Santa Monica, 310-395-9700; www.lemerigothotel.com

Just down from Ivy at the Shore (one of several chic Westside eateries), Le Merigot sits in a slightly busier section of beach-adjacent Ocean Avenue. It's worth upgrading to a deluxe or at least an ocean-view room at this pet-friendly hotel, so that you're ensured a patio with water in sight. If the soundtrack of the ocean's lapping doesn't untangle your nerves (driving in this city knots them right up), the signature Italian linens and goose-down pillows will coax you to a mellow state. If you're still wound up, head over to The Spa for globally inspired treatments, from Epicuren's Chai Soy Mud Wrap to soothe post-sun exposure, to aromatic Moroccan Rassoul Wraps, where you get slathered in mud and seep in all the good enzymes. Then, once you're lulled into a relaxed stupor, let executive chef Desi Szonntagh at Cézanne ply you with French fare that includes black truffle mac and cheese with lobster, roasted pear salad with fennel, spiced pecans, pomegranate, Point Reyes blue cheese and balsamic vinaigrette, and seafood cocktail served with red and green chili sauce.

175 rooms. Restaurant, bar. Business center. Fitness center. Pool. Spa. Pets accepted. $351 and up

★★★LOEWS SANTA MONICA BEACH HOTEL

1700 Ocean Ave., Santa Monica, 310-458-6700; www.santamonicaloewshotel.com

One of the bigger hotels in the area, Loews Santa Monica Beach Hotel stands tall along the ocean. From your room, look out onto white sand and blue water, sparkling cityscape or even, from the Presidential Suite, the entire Santa Monica Pier, complete with nostalgia-inducing Ferris wheel and

WHAT ARE THE BEST PLACES TO STAY NEAR THE BEACH?

Loews Santa Monica Beach Hotel:
One of the bigger hotels in the area, Loews Santa Monica Beach Hotel stands tall along the ocean. From your room, look out onto white sand and blue water, sparkling cityscape or even, from the Presidential Suite, the entire Santa Monica Pier.

Shade Hotel:
Before Manhattan Beach visitors could take refuge in the Shade, the beach town didn't have a luxury hipster hotel. Now, lobby bar Zinc Lounge has become the place to party in Manhattan Beach, and rooms book up fast.

Shutters Hotel on the Beach:
Shutters is Santa Monica's most beloved spot for everything from seaside brunches and cocktails to poolside basking, especially since fine dining restaurant One Pico and the pool deck both received a makeover.

Viceroy Santa Monica:
Located a block off the beach, this hotel is done up in a tongue-in-cheek, slightly Mad Hatter-ish décor and is always buzzing.

all (even if you can't remember a time when Ferris wheels were all the rage). In your room you'll find many tactile treats: 300-thread-count cotton sheets, 100 percent combed and ring-spun cotton terry towels, and the hotel's signature amenity, the sinfully soft "Ultimate Doeskin" robe by Chadsworth & Haig. The bathroom is filled with natural Lather products, made from plant and herb extracts—great for the environment, but note they don't foam as much because they're chemical-free. Dining options, in addition to the many lining Ocean Avenue, include Papillon lounge for tapas, fireplaces and ocean views; Ocean & Vine for farmers'-market-fresh cuisine (Santa Monica's Wednesday farmers' market is highly esteemed by chefs throughout the country); and a poolside menu for a bite while soaking up the sun. Speaking of relaxing, Ocean Spa's Beachcomber massage uses tiger clam shells from the ocean, heating them with kelp and sea water for a heated massage in the spa's eco-friendly treatment rooms.

342 rooms. Restaurant, bar. Fitness center. Pool. Spa. Pets accepted. $351 and up

★★★MALIBU BEACH INN – CARBON BEACH

22878 Pacific Coast Highway, Malibu, 310-456-6444; www.malibubeachinn.com

Before its 2007 overhaul, the Malibu Beach Inn was as bland as any chain. After David Geffen's $10 million renovation, the "Billionaire's Beach"—which sits on the ocean—is worth the excursion (even for east siders looking to get away from it all and see how the other half lives). The hotel doesn't look showy from the outside, but upon entering the lobby, you'll see the ocean through a windowed back wall and restaurant deck (where later you'll sip limited-run California wines). In rooms upstairs (well-appointed, but sometimes small), you'll find treats such as Trina Turk robes, entertainment centers with on-demand sports, Nintendo games and 400 pre-loaded CDs, 350-thread-count linens and a refreshment center filled with snacks. Swanky options for food and shopping at Malibu Country Mart are worth a peruse (for star sightings as well), but you can also enjoy less touristy activities ranging from seafood shack fare at the once endangered Reel Inn (kept open thanks to local protest) to waterfall hikes near where Sunset Boulevard and Pacific Coast Highway meet.

47 rooms. Restaurant, bar. Spa. $351 and up

★★★MALIBU COUNTRY INN

6506 Westward Beach Road, Malibu, 310-457-9622; www.malibucountryinn.com

Despite Malibu's major draws—from sandy beaches to upscale restaurants and shops at Malibu Country Mart (including Nobu and L.A. favorite Ron Herman)—there are few hotels in the area. So although it's not fancy, Malibu Country Inn is a bed-and-breakfast-style abode just off Zuma Beach that fills that need. You'll forget that Hollywood is in the vicinity while you're tucked away in this oceanside residence that's a far cry from too-cool hotels on the east side. The mellow, beachy Collection Restaurant & Bar—which technically isn't part of the hotel but is undeniably linked by close proximity—offers standard American fare for breakfast, lunch and dinner as well as views of the ocean from its rooftop. Surf's up all the time here.

16 rooms. Restaurant, bar. Pool. $151-250

★★★MARINA DEL REY MARRIOTT

4100 Admiralty Way, Marina Del Rey, 310-301-3000; www.marriott.com

The Marina del Rey Marriott pioneers a new trend of dispensing signature fragrances throughout the hotel by emitting floral "Zanzibar Mist" aromatherapy in lobbies, hallways and anywhere else your nose may wander. Don't worry: It's not as overpowering as it sounds. Neither is the interior, though it offers big personality in the form of oversized cartoonish lime-green love seats and a high ceiling held up by large red pillars. Stones Restaurant and The Lobby Bar are serviceable, but the property's pride and joy is Glow Bar. The outdoor lounge—with plush banquettes, fireplaces and a large illuminated archway—regularly hosts a parade of DJs spinning house and dance remixes, not to mention a young crowd sipping light cocktails that taste more like fresh fruit, such as the Cucumber Collins and Summer Lemonade. Nearby is Venice's Main Street and Abbot Kinney, the best blocks for strolling among bohemian bookstores and shops.

370 rooms. Restaurant, bar. Business center. Fitness center. Pool. $251-350

★★★RENAISSANCE LOS ANGELES AIRPORT HOTEL

9620 Airport Blvd., Playa Del Rey, 310-337-2800; www.marriott.com

Airport hotels are usually drab places whose only draw is their convenient location. But LAX's neighboring Renaissance proves you can't paint in broad brushstrokes. While the hotel's brightly colored modern décor brings the space to life, its unusual and extensive art collection is the main aesthetic draw. Traditional and contemporary works dot the hotel, including a piece by postmodern painter David Bierk. Take your own self-guided tour; ask the concierge for a copy of the hotel's art pamphlet, which identifies and explains every piece.

499 rooms. Restaurant, bar. Business center. Fitness center. Pool. $61-150

★★★THE RITZ-CARLTON, MARINA DEL REY

4375 Admiralty Way, Marina Del Rey, 310-823-1700; www.ritzcarlton.com

The Ritz-Carlton, Marina Del Rey is constantly putting on the ritz. Now, the stylish hotel—with L.A.'s only waterside palm-tree-lined pool—has added more. The new Spa Chakra and fitness center includes high-end beauty products from Guerlain and a new treatment menu featuring facials, body treatments, massages, manicures, pedicures and more. Signature afternoon tea service (at Jer-Ne Restaurant + Bar) is bumped up a contemporary notch with new artisan hand-blown glass Sontu teapots and flavorful brews from Tea Forte (made from rough-cut herbs). You can also hop over to Chaya Venice, if you want to mix with the local Westside scenester set. If you're more into rescue than ritziness, you can opt to spend an afternoon helping to restore the salt marshes and dunes of nearby Ballona Wetlands.

304 rooms. Restaurant, bar. Business center. Fitness center. Pool. Spa. Pets accepted. Tennis. $251-350

★★★SHADE HOTEL

1221 N. Valley Drive, Manhattan Beach, 310-546-4995; www.shadehotel.com

Before Manhattan Beach visitors could take refuge in the Shade, the beach town didn't have an upscale hotel (for shame). Half a block from the area's main drag—littered with quaint old-fashioned ice cream shops, beach stores, independent boutiques and ethnic restaurants such as Greek destination Petros—Shade is like a bastion of trendy in a universe of cozy. And the combination is ideal. In deep amber woods and white leather upholstery, lobby bar Zinc Lounge has become the place to party in Manhattan Beach. You could stay busy for days in the rooms, too: Cuddle up on an idyllic Tempur-Pedic bed, turn on the Heat & Glo Cyclone fireplace (basically, a cool-looking electric version), brew some java with an in-room Lavazza espresso machine, then soak in the tub with connected chromatherapy lights that throw off different colors depending on your mood (which will inevitably be good). A complimentary breakfast—a step above most—seals the deal.

38 rooms. Restaurant, bar. Complimentary breakfast. Pool. $351 and up

★★★SHERATON GATEWAY HOTEL LOS ANGELES

6101 W. Century Blvd., Playa Del Rey, 310-642-1111; www.sheratonlosangeles.com

Sheraton Gateway touts itself as a boutique hotel, and though it's just another link in a megachain, you might agree. Since a 2005 makeover, the décor has gotten more intimate and au courant. Deep charcoals and blacks and playful in-room design elements such as red faux ostrich feathers and Lucite lamps elevate the style, while the signature plush beds make it comfy. Enjoy Californian cuisine for breakfast and lunch at the casual Brasserie and then for dinner, go to the restaurant, Paparazzi, for some contemporary Italian cuisine. If you're headed out of town and would like to make it easy on yourself, take advantage of Gateway's valet parking package, which includes overnight accommodations the night before or after your trip, 14 days of valet parking (so your car is waiting at the hotel when you get back) and a 24-hour shuttle to and from LAX.

802 rooms. Restaurant, bar. Business center. Fitness center. Pool. $151-250

★★★SHUTTERS HOTEL ON THE BEACH

1 Pico Blvd., Santa Monica, 310-458-0030; www.shuttersonthebeach.com

For in-the-know locals (including major names whom the hotel prefers to keep hush-hush), Shutters is a frequent destination. It is Santa Monica's most beloved spot for everything from seaside brunches and cocktails to poolside basking, especially since it received a makeover by designer, Michael S. Smith, who did Obama's White House no less. As you enter the lobby, you're embraced by the sea air and a nautical vibe; you'll see cozy spaces near fireplaces and art from beloved California greats like David Hockney and Claes Oldenburg. Charmingly bleached-out and airy guest rooms are adorned in pure whites, sea blues and deep woods and outfitted with everything from an LCD TV in the bathroom to beachfront patios with light wicker furniture. At One Pico, below lofted ceilings decorated with antique boat hulls and art nouveau lanterns casting warm light, you'll sample chef Michael Reardon's new seasonally driven menu—upscale, but never stuffy. Casual sand-side eatery Coast beach café and bar is another option, as are refreshments at the Lobby Lounge. As celebrity-spa guru Ole Henriksen is steering the ship, One the Spa is a treat for out-of-towners who might not be accustomed to L.A.'s excessive spa services. Make like a local and get a Moon Glow facial and a cucumber-rich Nature Baby signature body treatment. Afterward, head to the pool deck for futher relaxation.

198 rooms. Restaurant, bar. Fitness center. Pool. Spa. $351 and up

★★★TERRANEA RESORT
100 Terranea Way, Rancho Palos Verdes, 310-265-2800; www.terranea.com

Just 20 miles south of LAX in Rancho Palos Verdes you'll find this beautiful and secluded oceanfront property. Discover the height of luxury in the form of bungalows, casitas and villas (most of which offer a view of the Pacific), a nine-hole golf course, a luxurious 50,000 square-foot spa, and a beachfront walking path. Spend leisurely days relaxing on the sand—the infamous Bat Cave featured in the original *Batman* movie is on the beach—or by one of the resort's three pool. A pool for kids includes a fun water slide, while an adults-only pool features a full-service bar and DJ. A third pool is reserved exclusively for spa guests and offers poolside treatments. If you're feeling more active, you can arrange for an afternoon of kayaking, mountain biking or horseback riding. For dining, Terranea's mar'sel is sustainable cooking at its finest. Chef Michael Fiorelli uses locally produced, organic ingredients, many of which are homegrown in the onsite herb garden. Rooms have a relaxing Mediterranean style décor with soft blues and supremely comfortable beds; some rooms have telescopes. This is not the property to go to if you're looking to spend a lot of time in L.A., though the staff will arrange trips for you. The resort is perfect for romantic getaways, family retreats and weekends away with friends.

582 rooms. Restaurant, bar. Business center. Fitness center. Pool. Spa. Pets accepted. Beach. Golf. $251-350

★★★VICEROY SANTA MONICA
1819 Ocean Ave., Santa Monica, 310-260-7500; www.viceroysantamonica.com

As luxurious as Santa Monica is, it never quite had a handle on hip until Viceroy exploded onto the scene. Located a block off the beach, this ultra-sleek, modern yet romantic hotel—where there's always music and mingling—attracts the Westside's young beautiful set. The lobby is done up in tongue-in-cheek, slightly Mad Hatter-ish décor, with old-fashioned embellishments like candelabras updated in kitschy sleek white. You'll find the same eclectic details in the rooms, along with custom-designed beds with linens so pretty you won't want to ruffle them. By the pool, you can savor some snacks and drinks, but Viceroy takes poolside activities to another level: There are three dining cabanas which can be reserved for private dinners and the hotel can even turn the spaces into mini movie theaters complete with popcorn and cocktails for a respite from the sun or manicure/pedicure stations, if you'd like some extra pampering.

162 rooms. Restaurant, bar. Business center. Fitness center. Pool. Pets accepted. $251-350

RECOMMENDED

HOLIDAY INN SANTA MONICA BEACH – AT THE PIER
120 Colorado Ave., Santa Monica, 310-451-0676; www.ichotelsgroup.com

The newly renovated Holiday Inn Santa Monica Beach rests at the entrance to Santa Monica Pier, the famous boardwalk that juts out into the Pacific Ocean and is lined with carnival games, fairway food and several rides (take a spin on the famous Ferris wheel, which was recently replaced with a state-of-the-art, partially solar powered one). The Holiday Inn's guest rooms are well kept, with blue-and-brown bedding and upholstered furniture accented with white ribbing. While Windows Restaurant and Lounge is the hotel's onsite dining spot (where kids eat free), there are plenty more exciting culinary and scenic experiences just steps away, ranging from Latin fusion destination Border Grille to star-studded Ivy at the Shore to good old junk food galore on the Pier. *132 rooms. Restaurant, bar. Business center. Fitness center. Pool. $151-250*

WHERE TO EAT

★★★CAPO

1810 Ocean Ave., Santa Monica, 310-394-5550; www.caporestaurant.com

Keep your eyes peeled or you'll easily speed right past this tiny, hospitable eatery. Capo means "boss" or "chief," which is aspirationally fitting, as the cuisine is upscale Italian and the atmosphere is elegant in that old-school sort of way, with a blazing fireplace, gentle candlelight and a crowd that comprises both wealthy Westside gourmands and real-deal industry types who'd rather not shout to be heard. The wine list is comprehensive, and the risottos—made with either porcini, Dungeness crab or lobster—are creamy perfection. Finish up with the vassoio da formaggio. Don't speak Italian? Then practice fast, because this place is authentic all the way.
Italian. Dinner. Closed Sunday-Monday. Reservations recommended. Bar. $36-85

★★★CATCH RESTAURANT & WINE BAR

Hotel Casa del Mar, 1910 Ocean Way, Santa Monica, 310-581-7714; www.catchsantamonica.com

Catch captures the best aspects of Santa Monica. The restaurant, located at the recently renovated Hotel Casa del Mar, features enviable ocean views that have inspired many to enjoy more than leisurely meals here, happily relaxing amid the beachfront-chic décor with its hints of seafoam green and its central bar inlaid with mother-of-pearl and accented by gnarled driftwood branches. The service, too, is classy but welcoming—a refreshing change from the over-wrought minimalism of so many Los Angeles restaurants. What will really nab your attention, however, is the restaurant's simple and delicious seasonal food, particularly the seafood. The menu is packed with fresh offerings including simple grilled fish and pan roasted scallops, as well as a variety of sushi. You'll also find items such as skirt steak with truffle-cheese fries and roasted farm chicken with market vegetables and thyme.
American. Lunch, dinner. Bar. $36-85

★★★CHINOIS ON MAIN

2709 Main St., Santa Monica, 310-392-9025; www.wolfgangpuck.com

A longtime Wolfgang Puck mainstay, Chinois on Main has been serving up delectable Asian-fusion cuisine—executed with French technique and California flair—since 1983. Pull up a chair at the counter and watch the magic happen in the open kitchen while you sip on a vintage from the extensive wine list. As fitting as this spot is for private tête-à-têtes, it's even better for big groups, since the offerings—such as the whole sizzling catfish with ponzu dipping sauce and the pork shoulder with mustard and Chinese eggplant—are served family-style and at communal tables. Once you take a bite, you'll see that sharing is actually a very selfish motive.
Asian, French. Dinner. Reservations recommended. Bar. $36-85

★★★DRAGO CENTRO

525 S. Flower St., Downtown, 213-228-8998; www.dragocentro.com

One of L.A.'s Italian forefathers has gone modern. With a $7 million budget, Celestino Drago (who has restaurants all over the city, including the flagship Drago Ristorante in Santa Monica) has erected a masterfully sleek dining room complete with a 15-foot floor-to-ceiling glass wine cellar in the middle of it. The cellar holds more than 2,000 wines (and those are just the Italian varietals; the rest are stored elsewhere), all waiting to be paired with Drago's heavenly pastas. (Main dishes are good but the pastas are excellent.) The pasta menu is divided into fresh egg, hard duram wheat, and filled and baked pastas. You'll find dishes here that you don't see on every menu, including the *pizzocherri*, a wonderfully wintery dish from the mountains of Italy that's made with buckwheat pasta, cabbage and potatoes, fontina and sage cream. The pappardelle with roasted pheasant and morel mushrooms is another standout. Many of the dishes are offered at lunch in half portions. You might be too stuffed from eating so much pasta, but if you're not, the Italian doughnuts are a nice choice for dessert. Another surprise is the wonderful cocktail menu.

Italian. Lunch (Monday-Friday), dinner. Reservations recommended. Outdoor seating. Bar. $36-85

★★★INN OF THE SEVENTH RAY

128 Old Topanga Canyon Road, Topanga, 310-455-1311; www.innoftheseventhray.com

Topanga Canyon is one of the last remaining flower-child enclaves of Los Angeles; its residents love its proximity to the beach and its woody natural beauty, and many of them have lived in the neighborhood since the '60s. The canyon's single fine-dining establishment, the Inn of the Seventh Ray, fits perfectly into its serene atmosphere, with tables overlooking a gentle creek and a menu of healthy and almost entirely organic fare. The restaurant goes the extra mile for the latter, baking its own organic-grain bread daily and using only naturally raised, range-fed chickens and natural meats from animals that were never fed hormones or antibiotics. The kitchen, presided over by chef Bradley Miller, also uses many local ingredients in dishes such as lamb chops with fresh vegetables, fennel purée and homemade blackberry jam.

American. Lunch (Monday-Saturday), dinner, Sunday brunch. Bar. $36-85

★★★JOSIE

2424 Pico Blvd., Santa Monica, 310-581-9888; www.josierestaurant.com

Located on the unprepossessing corner of Pico Boulevard and 24th Street in Santa Monica, Josie is the creation of chef Josie Le Balch, who's done time in the kitchens of Remi and the Saddle Peak Lodge. Le Balch is known for combing the city's farmers' markets for fresh seasonal ingredients, and the daily specials change based on what's been inspiring her lately. Still, there's a slew of reliable favorites on the cards, such as the buffalo burger with truffle fries or the whole boneless trout with corn, green beans and asparagus in a lemongrass nage.

American. Dinner. Reservations recommended. Bar. $36-85

★★★★MÉLISSE

1104 Wilshire Blvd., Santa Monica, 310-395-0881; www.melisse.com

Named after an aromatic, calming Mediterranean herb also known as lemon balm, Mèlisse is a favorite spot for Westside gourmands. Chef Josiah Citrin opened this elegant but unpretentious eatery in 1999, creating contemporary American dishes with French influences, like the tasting menu's 48-hour short rib with celery confit, dijonnais and herbed bordelaise sauce. The dishes here are artfully presented and innovative but not overly intellectual, and ingredients are always fresh, as Citrin takes advantage of southern California's year-round growing season and frequents local farmers' markets to find the best produce to soothe those Westside foodies' ravenous appetites.

French. Dinner. Closed Sunday-Monday. Reservations recommended. Bar. $86 and up

★★★MICHAEL'S

1147 Third St., Santa Monica, 310-451-0843; www.michaelssantamonica.com

Many Los Angeles restaurants claim a celebrity clientele, but Michael's in Santa Monica (there's also one in New York that's a media favorite for lunch), arguably the birthplace of California cuisine, is the real deal. Under the direction of Michael McCarty, Michael's keeps a database of its famous clients, right down to what they do for a living, how many times they've been in and what they've ordered. (Mel Brooks is among the many regulars.) Indeed, the 30-year-old Michael's has seating arrangements down to a science; they're tweaked multiple times a day (to accommodate dueling agents, of course). Like many loyal (and not necessarily famous) Michael's patrons, however, we prefer to dine in the lovely garden with a retractable ceiling; it's just the place to seal a deal while enjoying a juicy Michael's burger with applewood-smoked bacon.

American. Lunch (Monday-Friday), dinner. Closed Sunday. Reservations recommended. Bar. $36-85

★★★NOBU

3835 Cross Creek Road, Malibu, 310-317-9140; 903 N. La Cienega Blvd., West Hollywood, 310-657-5711; Matsuhisa, 129 N. La Cienega Blvd., Beverly Hills, 310-659-9639; www.noburestaurants.com

In 1999, Nobu Malibu opened its doors in the Malibu Country Mart shopping center at Cross Creek Road and the Pacific Coast Highway, and reservations have been hard to come by ever since. But, Nobu Los Angeles has finally taken over the space formerly occupied by L'Orangerie—not to mention Matsuhisa Beverly Hills has opened as well—so sushi lovers can choose from more than one location for a mouthful of chef Nobuyuki Matsuhisa's signature yellowtail sashimi with jalapeño. Nobu's acclaimed new-style Japanese cuisine shows the influence of Matsuhisa's experiences in Peru (in dishes like tiradito and ceviche), and fans and foodies have ensured that all locations are booked up.

Japanese, sushi. Dinner. Reservations recommended. Bar. $36-85

★★★ONE PICO

Shutters on the Beach, 1 Pico Blvd., Santa Monica, 310-587-1717; www.shuttersonthebeach.com

Located on a spot of Los Angeles's priciest beachfront real estate, One Pico, the acclaimed eatery inside Shutters Hotel on the Beach, actually sits on the sand, with the psychedelic colors of the Santa Monica Pier's Ferris wheel spinning in the distance. The restaurant was recently renovated, but the fare remains reliably delicious. One Pico is helmed by chef Michael Reardon, who also heads up nearby Catch at the Casa del Mar. Reardon's menu hinges on what's fresh and in season; the dishes boast a light touch with an Italian sensibility incorporating an array of spit-roasted meats and whole fish, as well as mouth-watering starters like the roasted market beets with black truffle goat cheese and lemon. The view can't be beat, and the décor has been redone in perfect beachy-chic fashion by in-demand designer Michael S. Smith, who has created interiors for everyone from Cindy Crawford and Dustin Hoffman to most recently, President Obama at the White House.

American. Lunch (Monday-Saturday), dinner, Sunday brunch. Bar. $36-85

★★★THE PENTHOUSE
The Huntley Hotel, 1111 Second St., Santa Monica, 310-393-8080; www.thehuntleyhotel.com

Poised high atop the stylish Huntley Hotel on Santa Monica Beach, the Penthouse is a tasteful jewel box rendered life-sized. The curvy white chandeliers, paper-thin white curtains and pale-blue upholstered chairs with backs shaped like ocean waves will inspire a trip to your interior decorator. The restaurant is accessible through the hotel's interior elevator, or you can take the glass-encased exterior lift. The restaurant provides stunning views of the Pacific through a wall of windows, while executive chef Seth Greenburg's creations draw inspiration from France, Spain and beyond. Try a black truffle omelet with goat cheese and wild mushrooms for breakfast; a grilled chicken panini with roasted peppers, arugula, goat cheese and pesto aioli for lunch; or the spicy seafood stew with clams, black sable, calamari, crab, chorizo and white wine broth for dinner.

American. Breakfast, lunch, dinner, Sunday brunch. Bar. Reservations recommended. Bar. $36-85

★★★TAVERN
11648 San Vicente Boulevard, Brentwood, 310-806-6464; www.tavernla.com

You can't go wrong at any of Suzanne Goin's restaurants (Lucques and Hungry Cat are among her other L.A. places). Her latest, Tavern, serves the same outstanding seasonal cuisine in a manor-like setting with wingbacked chairs and a sun-drenched atrium filled with olive trees. Lunch includes salads, sandwiches, burgers and main courses, while dinner features entrées such as the Niman ranch rib-eye alongside a baked potato topped with market vegetables or orecchiette carbonara with English peas, green garlic and pea tendrils. You'll also find a nice list of desserts and cocktails. Or simply pop into the larder, a storefront café where you can pick up sandwiches with housemade chips, salads, fresh-baked bread, cupcakes and other sweet treats.

American. Breakfast (Monday-Friday), lunch, dinner, Saturday-Sunday brunch. $36-85

★★★WHIST
Viceroy Santa Monica, 1819 Ocean Ave., Santa Monica, 310-260-7500; wwwviceroysantamonica.com

Whist is quirky and cool. What else could you expect from a restaurant named after an old-school card game? Inside, it's like the Mad Hatter decorated for a grown-up tea party: lime-green walls, row after row of English china and accents of silver damask wallpaper. But as charming as the dining room is, it may not compare with the Santa Monica sun for some, which is why you can also take it outside to one of the luxe poolside tables or cabanas. Ditch the tea party altogether and have a coffee klatch by pairing one of the sinful desserts—such as the ricotta cheesecake with huckleberry, lemon and basil—with Whist's broad selection of coffees. The menu is simple—there are just seven choices for dinner—but well executed under the direction of acclaimed chef Tony DiSalvo. Try to visit on Monday or Tuesday evening for the widly popular wine nights, when all of the more than 100 bottles of wine on the menu are available for only $25.

American. Breakfast, lunch (Monday-Saturday), dinner, Sunday brunch. Reservations recommended. Bar. $36-85

RECOMMENDED

ANISETTE BRASSERIE

225 Santa Monica Blvd., 310-395-3200; www.anisettebrasserie.com

Less than two breaths away from the shopping scurry that is Third Street Promenade lies Anisette, a little slice of Paris just three blocks away from the Pacific Ocean. Even if you've never stepped foot in France, you know that this is what it's like: moody Parisian lighting, old-world tiled floors, bottles of wine stacked to the ceiling, a full bar of patrons tossing back oysters. Its menu only enhances the effect—think duck confit, primesteak tartare and an out-of-this-world French onion soup with cave-aged gruyere.

Contemporary French. Lunch (Monday-Friday), Saturday-Sunday brunch, dinner. Reservations recommended. $16-35

GEOFFREY'S MALIBU

27400 Pacific Coast Highway, Malibu, 310-457-1519;
www.geoffreysmalibu.com

Geoffrey's is as classic Malibu as it gets—it began as the Holiday House, a Richard Neutra-designed resort and restaurant that opened in 1948 and catered to the era's biggest Hollywood stars, including Frank Sinatra, Lana Turner and Marilyn Monroe. The restaurant became Geoffrey's in 1983 and didn't miss a beat. Perhaps its success has something to do with its enviable location atop a bluff overlooking the Pacific—or perhaps it's the deliciously classic fare. We especially love this spot for its Sunday brunch; the stunning ocean views make for the perfect accompaniment to favorites like eggs Benedict topped with prosciutto, housemade hollandaise sauce and rosemary potatoes, and chicken picatta with sautéed vegetables, mashed potatoes and a lemon-caper butter sauce.

American. Lunch (Monday-Friday), dinner, Saturday-Sunday brunch. Reservations recommended. Bar. $36-85

GJELINA

1429 Abbot Kinney Boulevard, Venice, 310-450-1429; www.gjelina.com

In pronunciation, the "g" in Gjelina is nonexistent, but its presence on Venice's main drag is anything but. Venice masses and even those who live east and beyond the 405 freeway (now that's rare) are enamored with the rustic yet polished Gjelina. Chef Travis Lett, a budding young force who quite literally appeared out of nowhere, possesses an ability to make you feel as if a simple margherita pizza tastes as it *should*. With a slight Mediterranean influence, Lett goes to great lengths to source seasonal and sustainable ingredients, and then let's them shine in perfect pizzas and in dishes such as braised rabbit tortellini with pea tendrils, mint and pecorino. The food and space—brick floors, a few large communal tables, an outdoor space with a firepit—fits perfectly on Abbott Kinney Boulevard.

Contemporary American, eclectic. Lunch (Monday-Friday), Saturday-Sunday brunch, dinner. Reservations recommended. $16-35

LA CACHETTE BISTRO

1733 Ocean Ave., Santa Monica, 310-434-9509; www.lacachettebistro.com

L.A. staple La Cachette, beloved for its fine French cuisine, recently relocated to Santa Monica and is now a more casual bistro than a fine-dining spot. You'll find hardwood floors, booths, French posters and an outdoor patio. The setting may have changed but chef-owner Jean Francois Meteigner's wonderful French cooking and wines haven't. Start with the creamy foie gras terrine with rhubarb and brioche, and follow up with the coq au vin. Or stop in for happy hour (Monday-Friday 5-7 p.m. and 8:30-10 p.m.) and have a croque monsieur or grass-fed beef slider with horseradish dijon mustard, grilled onions and blue cheeses (both are just $6 during happy hour), with a Mexican or Italian beer. The regular menu incluces favorites such as steak frites and mussels in a saffron broth.

French. Lunch (Monday-Friday), dinner, Sunday brunch. Reservations recommended. Bar. $36-85

MOONSHADOWS

20356 Pacific Coast Highway, Malibu, 310-456-3010; www.moonshadowsmalibu.com

Despite its gorgeous, ridiculously perfect vistas—schools of dolphins cruising the horizon, beautiful sunsets—Malibu suffers from a strange dearth of ocean-view restaurants, which makes Moonshadows and its trendy Blue Lounge an oasis right off the Pacific Coast Highway. Diners swarm the outdoor patio at sunset, sucking down cocktail after cocktail, while nibbling on oysters on the half shell and the Snake River Farm Kobe beef burgers. The scene really heats up after dark, when DJs, including local favorite Raul Campos of KCRW, spin an eclectic mix for a hip crowd.

Contemporary American. Lunch, dinner, Saturday-Sunday brunch. Reservations recommended. Bar. $36-85

PECORINO

11604 San Vicente Blvd., Brentwood, 310-571-3800; www.pecorinorestaurant.com

Pecorino, in the space formerly occupied by Zax, is a triple threat: There's the friendly, doting service; the warm but elegant dining room, complete with beam ceilings and an exposed brick wall; and, last but not least, the food. There are plenty of hearty classics on offer, from lasagna and ravioli to spaghetti and fettuccine alla Bolognese, and the agnello cacio e uovo—a de-boned New Zealand rack of lamb casserole with artichokes, eggs and pecorino—is tender and savory. For the finale, indulge in the tiramisu with amaretto liqueur; it's deliciously creamy. Or try the delightful cheese platter for dessert—with a variety of pecorinos, of course.

Italian. Lunch (Monday-Saturday), dinner. Bar. $36-85

LOS FELIZ/SILVER LAKE/ECHO PARK

These largely residential neighborhoods still retain their bohemian character, though rising real estate prices are always a threat to the funky coffee shops, eccentric art galleries, offbeat restaurants and gritty music clubs. The area is home to Griffith Park, an expanse so large and wild that mountain lions have been spotted nearby, and not just in the Los Angeles Zoo.

WHAT TO SEE

AUTRY NATIONAL CENTER

4700 Western Heritage Way, Los Feliz, 323-667-2000; www.autrynationalcenter.org

Co-founded by "America's Favorite Singing Cowboy," actor-singer Gene Autry, the Autry National Center is composed of the Museum of the American West, the Southwest Museum of the Native American and the Institute for the Study of the American West. The Autry isn't dedicated to exhibiting how the West was won, but rather to telling the stories of how the diverse peoples of the American West influenced the rest of the country and the world. Expect to see an impressive collection of art and artifacts, including textiles created by Navajo and Pueblo Indians, movie paraphernalia from Western films and television shows, and one of the largest collections of arms and armor in the western United States. Not into guns and knives? The museum also offers a wide range of more family-friendly activities. You can pan for gold like an original 49er; watch old Gene Autry flicks during the summertime series, Dinner and a Movie; and buy works from Native American artists at the annual Intertribal Arts Marketplace.

Admission: adults $9, students and seniors $5, children 3-12 $3, children under 3 free. Tuesday-Friday 10 a.m.-4 p.m., Saturday-Sunday 11 a.m.-5 p.m.

GRIFFITH OBSERVATORY

2800 E. Observatory Road, Los Feliz, 213-473-0800; www.griffithobservatory.org

The Griffith Observatory came into being in 1935 after "Colonel" Griffith J. Griffith (he wasn't a military man; he probably thought "Colonel" was a better alternative to Griffith Griffith) donated $100,000 to the city to build a public observatory on Mount Hollywood. And $93 million worth of renovations later, the observatory now combines Art Deco charm with superior technology. While the exterior's neo-classical architecture and the foyer's Foucault pendulum (which was one of the observatory's original exhibits) are testaments to the structure's history, the state-of-the-art planetarium and interactive exhibits are evidence of its foray into the future. You can find out how much you weigh on other planets, see real meteorites and explore the Milky Way without leaving the comfort of planet Earth, all for free.

Admission: free. Tuesday-Friday noon-10 p.m., Saturday-Sunday 10 a.m.-10 p.m.

GRIFFITH PARK

4730 Crystal Springs Drive, Los Feliz, 323-913-4688; www.laparks.org

Don't come to this park (which happens to be the largest municipal park with an urban wilderness area in the United States) expecting to see a larger version of Central Park. Griffith Park is real wilderness—lots of dirt, naturally occurring fauna and some dangerous wildlife, including coyotes and rattlesnakes. At more than 4,000 acres, Griffith also has tamer offerings, including

miles of trails for both hikers and horseback riders, picnic areas, tennis courts, a swimming pool, and athletic fields for soccer, rugby, baseball and badminton. The area, which was once inhabited by Native Americans, was purchased in the 19th century by Welsh immigrant "Colonel" Griffith J. Griffith. In 1896, Griffith gave the city 3,015 acres of the park that now bears his name.
Admission: free. Daily 5 a.m.-10:30 p.m.

LOS ANGELES ZOO
5333 Zoo Drive, Los Feliz, 323-644-4200; www.lazoo.org

The L.A. Zoo is home to animal species originating from all around the world, but the special habitats are what make the zoo stand out. The best of these belong to the resident primates, so make sure to swing by the Red Ape Rain Forest, Campo Gorilla Reserve and the Chimpanzees of Mahale Mountains. The Winnick Family Children's Zoo gives kids the opportunity to pet and groom barnyard animals, including goats and sheep.
Admission: adults $13, seniors $10, children 2-12 $8, children under 2 free. Daily 10 a.m.-5 p.m.

TRAVEL TOWN
5200 Zoo Drive, Los Feliz, 323-662-5874; www.lacity.org

This outdoor transportation museum is on the northeast corner of Griffith Park, so take that into consideration if you're planning on visiting the park or the L.A. Zoo. Travel Town lives up to its name with an impressive collection of locomotives, freight cars, passenger cars and motorcars dating all the way back to the 19th century. While the museum is for people of all ages, it shouldn't come as a big surprise that Travel Town is highly trafficked by kids who want to see trains or who are big fans of Thomas the Tank Engine. Admission is free, but if you want to ride the miniature train that circles the premises, you'll have to fork over $2.50.
Monday-Friday 10 a.m.-4 p.m., Saturday-Sunday 10 a.m.-6 p.m.

WHERE TO EAT

★★★EDENDALE GRILL
2838 Rowena Ave., Silver Lake, 323-666-2000; www.edendalegrill.com

Located in trendy Silver Lake, the Edendale Grill occupies what was once Los Angeles Fire Station Number 56. Though the owners retained the brick façade and cavernous feel, along with a pressed-tin ceiling and beautiful wood floors, the space has been lovingly updated with a classy dining room, expansive bar and cozy heated patio. The food is equally warm; try the Edendale meatloaf wrapped in applewood-smoked bacon with a tomato-brown sugar glaze and mashed Yukon gold potatoes. While this might not be NYC, the bartenders here make a mean Cosmo. Sadly, it's not all good news: Service can be spotty, but that's nothing the decadent blue cheese-tarragon French fries can't fix.
American. Dinner, Sunday brunch. Bar. $16-35

RECOMMENDED

EL CHAVO
4441 Sunset Blvd., Los Feliz, 323-664-0871; www.elchavorestaurant.com

A longtime Los Feliz favorite for its tangy margaritas, authentic Mexican cuisine and quirky décor, El Chavo was recently remodeled, but breathe easy—the glow-in-the-dark portrait of Dolly Parton still hangs in the corner, and the ceiling of the bar is still festooned with Day-Glo sombreros. It's a little louder now due to the expanded dining room, but menu favorites—such as the enchiladas rancheras and chiles rellenos—remain the same.

Mexican. Dinner. Bar. $16-35

FIGARO BISTRO
1802 N. Vermont Ave., Los Feliz, 323-662-1587; www.figarobistrot.com

You can expect a slice of the City of Light at this Los Feliz restaurant, where local hipsters head for classic bistro fare and true turn-of-the-century Parisian décor. (Think long banquettes and ornate iron overhead lamps.) If you can't find a spot at the tightly packed sidewalk tables (just as if you really were in Europe), grab a stool at the zinc bar and spend a happy hour (or two) with a chilled glass of rosé and some escargot, then indulge in the sole meunière with green beans and lemon sauce. Breakfast at Figaro is also a special Gallic treat; the croissants, baguettes and an array of pastries—baked fresh daily in the adjoining bakery—will have you ooh-la-laing in no time.

French. Breakfast, lunch, dinner. Bar. $16-35

FRED62
1850 N. Vermont Ave., Los Feliz, 323-667-0062; www.fred62.com

In a city where most restaurants stop serving by 10 p.m., this 24-hour eatery is a godsend. Decked out like a retro diner, with bulbous midcentury light fixtures and chrome toasters everywhere, this trendy Los Feliz outpost has an appropriately hip-and-happenin' (and tasty) menu, with nouveau-diner offerings such the Mrs. Loaf sandwich (housemade turkey meatloaf served on a toasted roll with mozzarella and housemade marinara), the Mac Daddy and Cheese (a spicy version of the comfort dish) and the Super Rico sandwich (a beer-battered tuna patty stuffed with pasilla chiles, onion and cheddar cheese). Whether you're here seeking alcohol-sopping grub or a hearty breakfast, make sure to order the onion rings; they're fluffy, golden and the best in the neighborhood.

American. Breakfast, lunch, dinner. Bar. $16-35

SURROUNDING AREAS

ARCADIA
Located just 13 miles from downtown Los Angeles at the base of the San Gabriel mountains, Arcadia is home to the Santa Anita Park Racetrack, a world-class thoroughbred racing facility.

WHAT TO SEE

LOS ANGELES COUNTY ARBORETUM & BOTANIC GARDEN
301 N. Baldwin Ave., Arcadia, 626-821-3222; www.arboretum.org

At the Los Angeles County Arboretum & Botanic Garden, you'll find 127 acres of lush plant life originating from the four corners of the world. If you're determined to see the arboretum's five botanical sections (Africa, Australia, The Americas, The Asiatic and the Historic Circle) in one day, you might want to take the tram. The tram travels from the Madagascar Spiny Forest to Tallac Knoll, showing you thousands of species on the way. Besides seeing plants, you'll also be able to see various types of wildlife, including ducks, geese, herons, hawks and peafowl. It's not all plants here; you can tour several structures on the property, including Native American huts (a.k.a. kiys), an adobe and a 19th century Victorian cottage.

Admission: adults $8, students and seniors $6, children 5-12 $3, children under 5 free. Daily 9 a.m.-5 p.m.

SANTA ANITA PARK
285 W. Huntington Drive, Arcadia, 626-574-7223; www.santaanita.com

Santa Anita Park offers all the excitement of the Kentucky Derby—without the enormous hats—just outside Los Angeles. The park opens annually on December 26, with races occurring daily until April 18; from late September to early November, the Oak Tree Racing Association holds races at the park. The 320-acre park has a 1,100-foot-long Art Deco grandstand, a historic landmark that seats 26,000 people. Casual dining options (hot dogs and burgers) are available around the Grandstand, but for a more refined racing experience, put on your Sunday best and head for The Turf Club, where the dress code of daytime suits or dresses for the ladies and suits for the gents are strictly enforced. Popular days to attend the park include Opening Day, Sunshine Millions Day, Santa Anita Handicap, and Santa Anita Derby, or come in hopes of catching a glimpse of singer Mark McGrath, quizmaster Alex Trebek or music impresario Burt Bacharach, all of whom race their horses here.

Admission: $5.

LONG BEACH

Located between Los Angeles and Orange County, a multibillion dollar redevelopment program has finally helped Long Beach become one of Southern California's most diverse waterfront destinations, recapturing the charm it first attained as a premier seaside resort in the early 1900s. A 21½-mile light rail system, the Metro Blue Line, connects Long Beach and Los Angeles.

WHAT TO SEE

AQUARIUM OF THE PACIFIC
100 Aquarium Way, Long Beach, 562-590-3100; www.aquariumofpacific.org

This enormous aquarium houses more than 12,000 animals in 50 exhibits, including a hands-on shark lagoon where you can touch the sharks. Other exhibits feature sea lions and Australian birds. Take a behind-the-scenes tour to learn about the daily operations of the aquarium, see a movie in 3D exploring the deep ocean, take a harbor cruise, and much more.

Admission: adults $23.95, seniors $20.95, children 3-11 $11.95. Daily 9 a.m.-6 p.m.

CATALINA EXPRESS
95 Berth, San Pedro, 800-481-3470; www.catalinaexpress.com

Board one of eight state-of-the-art catamarans and cruise over to Catalina Island in about an hour. The boats include airline-style seating, panoramic viewing windows and on-deck seating.

SPECIAL EVENTS

LONG BEACH JAZZ FESTIVAL

562-424-0013
Held every year on a grassy knoll, this annual event features top artists, delicious food and fabulous art.
Mid-August.

NAPLES CHRISTMAS BOAT PARADE

562-570-5333; www.longbeach.gov
Festively decorated boats wind through the canals of Naples Island and along the water by Shoreline Village each year.
December.

TOYOTA GRAND PRIX

3000 Pacific Ave., Long Beach, 562-981-2600; www.longbeachgp.com
This international race takes place on downtown streets.
April.

Admission: adults $66.50, seniors $60, children 2-11 $51, children under 3 $4. Schedules vary, check the website for more information.

LONG BEACH MUSEUM OF ART

2300 E. Ocean Blvd., Long Beach, 562-439-2119; www.lbma.org
The permanent collection features American art, German expressionists and video art. It also includes a contemporary sculpture garden and an education gallery. The café and gift shop are housed in a 1912 mansion overlooking the Pacific Ocean.
Admission: adults $7, students and seniors $6, children under 13 free. Free Friday. Tuesday-Sunday 11 a.m.-5 p.m.

QUEEN MARY SEAPORT

1126 Queens Highway, Long Beach, 562-435-3511, 800-437-2934; www.queenmary.com
For 25 years, the rich and famous boarded this 12-deck luxury ocean liner to cross the Atlantic in grand style. Since 1967, the ship has been docked in Long Beach and now people board it for tours, special events, shipboard dining or an overnight hotel stay in one of its 365 staterooms. The price of admission includes a ghosts and legends tour (some say the vessel is haunted), but for $5 extra, a World War II tour is offered, giving insight into the role the ship played in transporting American military personnel from 1940 to 1946. You can also board a Foxtrot submarine Russians used to track enemy forces in the

Pacific during the Cold War. Self-guided and Ghosts and Legends tours included with admission.

Admission: adults $24.95, seniors $21.95, children 5-11 $12.95. Daily 10 a.m.-6 p.m.

SHORELINE VILLAGE

429 Shoreline Village Drive, Long Beach, 562-435-2668; www.shorelinevillage.com

This seven-acre shopping, dining and entertainment complex recaptures the look and charm of a turn-of-the-century California seacoast village. It includes a collection of unique shops and galleries, plus a historic carousel and a complete marine center with daily harbor cruises and seasonal whale-watching excursions. Transportation to Shoreline Village is available via the free Promenade Tram from downtown Long Beach, the Runabout Shuttle (also from downtown Long Beach) and the water taxi that transports passengers between Shoreline Village and the downtown marina.

Daily.

WHERE TO STAY

★★★HILTON LONG BEACH

701 W. Ocean Blvd., Long Beach, 562-983-3400, 800-345-6565; www.hilton.com

Conveniently located in downtown Long Beach, this hotel is within walking distance of theaters and shopping, and within four blocks of the convention center and beach. The comfortable guest rooms feature a gray and gold motif, interesting artwork of historic Long Beach, large showers and Crabtree & Evelyn bath amenities.

393 rooms. Restaurant, bar. Business center. Fitness center. Pool. Pets accepted. $251-350

★★★HYATT REGENCY LONG BEACH

200 S. Pine Ave., Long Beach, 562-491-1234; www.hyatt.com

Located next to the convention center and within walking distance of the Pier and the downtown area, this California-style Hyatt is a good choice for both business and leisure travelers. The spacious guest rooms provide plush bedding, work areas and views of the harbor.

528 rooms. Restaurant, bar. Business center. Pool. $151-250

★★★RENAISSANCE LONG BEACH HOTEL

111 E. Ocean Blvd., Long Beach, 562-437-5900, 888-236-2427; www.renaissancehotels.com

This downtown Long Beach property features is within walking distance to shops, restaurants and sights and includes guest rooms with comfy beds with white linens and marble bathrooms. The new restaurant, Tracht's, serves steaks and seafood in a sleek dining space.

374 rooms. Restaurant, bar. Fitness center. Pool. Pets accepted. $251-250

WHERE TO EAT

★★★L'OPERA RISTORANTE

101 Pine Ave., Long Beach, 562-491-0066; www.lopera.com

This local favorite serves up modern Northern Italian cuisine. Sample dishes include ravioli stuffed with duck, and mint pasta filled with fava beans and ricotta cheese. Massive marble columns grace the lovely dining room and the service is warm and attentive.

Italian. Lunch (Monday-Friday), dinner. Bar. $36-85

REDONDO BEACH

This recreation and vacation center just south of LAX features a two-mile beach and the popular King Harbor, which houses hundreds of watercraft. Once a commercial port, the historic beach town's pier now features shops, restaurants and marinas. Biking, fishing, surfing and all sorts of water sports are popular here.

WHAT TO SEE

GALLERIA AT SOUTH BAY
1815 Hawthorne Blvd., Redondo Beach, 310-371-7546; www.southbaygalleria.com

The Galleria at South Bay includes Nordstrom and Robinsons-May department stores, as well as perennial favorites such as Banana Republic and Gap. Restaurants include California Pizza Kitchen.

Monday-Friday 10 a.m.-9 p.m., Saturday 10 a.m.-8 p.m., Sunday 11 a.m.-7 p.m.

REDONDO BEACH PIER
Torrance Blvd., Redondo Beach, 310-318-0631, 800-280-0333; www.redondopier.com

With its laid-back atmosphere and white sandy beaches, Redondo is a beach bum's paradise. Surfing and volleyball are popular and there are many funky beach restaurants and bars.

WHERE TO STAY

★★★CROWNE PLAZA
300 N. Harbor Drive, Redondo Beach, 310-318-8888, 800-368-9760; www.crowneplaza.com

This oceanfront Crowne Plaza is seven miles from LAX and close to attractions and activities. Many restaurants are within walking distance and a free shuttle is offered to area shopping malls. Guests also get access to the adjacent Gold's Gym. Comfortable guest rooms feature a separate living room, work desks and refrigerators. Some guest rooms offer balconies with a water view.

339 rooms. Restaurant, bar. Fitness center. Pool. Pets accepted $61-150

WHERE TO EAT

★★★CHEZ MELANGE
1611 S. Catalina Ave., Redondo Beach, 310-540-1222; www.chezmelange.com

Chez Melange raised the bar for fine California cuisine in the beach cities years ago, and the upscale clientele is still fiercely loyal. The décor may scream 1985 with its peach walls, but the menu is up-to-the-minute, offering a full sushi list as well as modern twists on classics like rabbit three ways, spicy fried oysters and steak tartare.

American. Lunch (Monday-Friday), dinner, Sunday brunch. $36-86

WESTLAKE VILLAGE

This affluent neighborhood in the western edge of Los Angeles County is close enough to the city but far enough away to escape the hustle and bustle (about 20 miles from Malibu). Many celebrities call it home, and you'll find some nice accommodations.

WHERE TO STAY

★★★★FOUR SEASONS HOTEL WESTLAKE VILLAGE

2 Dole Drive, Westlake Village, 818-575-3000, 800-819-5053; www.fourseasons.com

Set on expansive, landscaped grounds, this hotel in suburban Los Angeles offers a tranquil escape from the city. Connected to the California Longevity and Health Institute, a premier medical spa, the hotel provides serenity-seeking Angelenos a place to rest up and rejuvenate themselves in style. Rooms are traditionally decorated with classic touches like mahogany furniture, chintz-covered sofas and marble bathrooms. The onsite Onyx restaurant serves light, healthful Asian cuisine.

269 rooms. Restaurant, bar. Pool. Spa. $351 and up

★★★HYATT WESTLAKE PLAZA

880 S. Westlake Blvd., Westlake Village, 805-557-1234, 800-633-7313; www.hyattwestlake.com

Spanish mission-style architecture can be found at this comfortable hotel. Rooms include flat-screen televisions, iHome stereos with iPod docks and large work desks. Many rooms also have a balcony or patio.

262 rooms. Restaurant, bar. Business center. Fitness center. Pool. $151-250

★★★WESTLAKE VILLAGE INN

31943 Agoura Road, Westlake Village, 818-889-0230, 800-535-9978;
www.westlakevillageinn.com

Relax by the Mediterranean-style pool or hit the links. For practice at night, try the area's only lighted driving range. Enjoy live entertainment at Bogies, the hotel's nightclub, or dine at Le Café, the bistro and wine bar onsite. Guest rooms at this charming inn include Italian bedding and flat-screen televisions, among other things.

144 rooms. Restaurant, bar. Complimentary breakfast. Pool. $151-250

SPA

★★★★THE SPA AT FOUR SEASONS WESTLAKE VILLAGE

2 Dole Drive, Westlake Village, 818-575-3000; www.fourseasons.com

A 40,000-square-foot space with Asian-influenced décor, this spa in the Four Seasons Los Angeles, Westlake Village is a peaceful spot for top-notch pampering. Treatments also take their cue from Asian traditions, with everything from shiatsu to reiki making an appearance on the spa menu. Couples can opt for a traditional massage in the outdoor spa cabanas, which include a private plunge pool. Or book a spa suite for your treatment, which features a fireplace and plunge pool.

SIDE TRIPS FROM LOS ANGELES

BIG BEAR LAKE

Angelenos head to Big Bear in the San Bernardino Mountains in the winter to ski and enjoy the Alpine setting (the average annual snow fall is 100 inches). There are two excellent ski resorts less than five minutes from the quaint village. Big Bear is also a nice place to visit in warmer months for fishing, boating, canoeing, hiking and other outdoor activities.

WHAT TO SEE

ALPINE SLIDE AT MAGIC MOUNTAIN

800 Wildrose Lane, Big Bear Lake, 909-866-4626; www.alpineslidebigbear.com

Check out the bobsled-style Alpine Slide in winter and the double waterslide in summer. The site is a popular year-round attraction. Other activities include tubing, miniature golf and go-carts.

Alpine slide: single ride $4, five-ride book $18. Waterslide: single ride $1, 10-ride book $8. Daily.

BIG BEAR MARINA

Big Bear Marina, 500 Paine Road, Big Bear Lake, 909-866-3218; www.bigbearmarina.com

Big Bear Marina offers a variety of boat rentals including fishing boats that can hold four to five people ($45 for two hours) and large pontoons that can accommodate up to 12 people ($140 for two hours). You can also rent wave runners ($85 per hour for a two-seater), kayaks/canoes ($20 per hour) and boats with waterskiing ($150 per hour). (Note: All rentals require a security deposit and fuel charges are extra; additional fees may apply.) If you'd rather join an organized ride, you can board the Big Bear Queen, a small Mississippi-style paddle wheeler, for a 90-minute narrated tour of Big Bear Lake.

Adults $15, children $9. April-November.

BIG BEAR MOUNTAIN RESORTS

880 Summit Blvd., Big Bear Lake, 909-866-5766; www.bearmountain.com

Big Bear Mountain Resorts is made up of Bear Mountain and Snow Summit ski areas, which together offer 438 skiable acres, 26 lifts and 55 runs. Snow Summit includes plenty of wide-open groomed runs, a family park with low-intermediate terrain and three double black-diamond runs. Big Bear has the longest advanced run (nearly a mile) and includes a park with 150 jumps. You'll also find six full-service ski and snowboard rental facilities, 14 food outlets and four full-service bars between the two areas. One lift ticket is good for both resorts; a free shuttle will take you back and forth from both resorts. When the weather warms up, you can ride the sky chair at Snow Summit for an incredible view, then hike back down or go mountain biking on the web of trails at 8,000 feet. There's also a nine-hole golf course at the base of the mountain that's open from April through November.

Admission: Ski pass: Adult $66 during peak season (January 10-March 15, Saturday-Sunday)/$53 during regular season; young adults 13-21 $56 during peak season/$43 during regular season; children 7-12 $29 during peak season/$20 regular season; Children under 7 free. Green Fees: Monday-Friday $25, weekends and holidays $30. Sky Chair (roundtrip): Adults $10, children $5.

WHERE TO STAY

★★★NORTHWOODS RESORT AND CONFERENCE CENTER

40650 Village Drive, Big Bear Lake, 909-866-3121, 800-866-3121;
www.northwoodsresort.com

This rustic mountain resort and conference center offers rooms and suites filled with handcrafted wood furniture and is located just minutes from the lake and ski resorts. Many rooms feature fireplaces, and suites have spa tubs and wet bars.

147 rooms. Restaurant, bar. Fitness center. Pool. Spa. $61-$150.

LAKE ARROWHEAD

People are drawn to this mountainous lake region in the San Bernardino National Forest for the outdoor recreation. Although the lake itself is private (visitors can tour it on the Arrowhead Queen, take waterskiing lessons or use the beach as guests of the Lake Arrowhead Resort), everyone can enjoy hiking, biking, horseback riding and camping. There are also plenty of shops, restaurants and other attractions, including the ice-skating rink where Michelle Kwan trained. In winter, skiers and snowboarders take to the powdery slopes.

WHAT TO SEE

ARROWHEAD QUEEN & LEROY'S SPORTS

28200 Highway 189, Lake Arrowhead, 909-336-6992

Enjoy a 50-minute narrated boat cruise on Lake Arrowhead, past architectural points of interest and historical sites.

WHERE TO STAY

★★★LAKE ARROWHEAD RESORT AND SPA

27984 Highway 189, Lake Arrowhead, 909-336-1511, 800-800-6792;
www.lakearrowheadresort.com

There's much to do around Lake Arrowhead, but this lakefront resort nestled in the San Bernardino forest is so warm and luxurious, visitors may never want to leave. Guest rooms feature plush goose-down comforters, granite bathrooms and private balconies or patios. Guests have access to the private beach as well as golf and tennis privileges at Lake Arrowhead Country Club. The resort's fine dining restaurant Bin 189 offers a menu of contemporary American fare for breakfast, lunch and dinner. Weekly movies featuring films made in Arrowhead are also shown.

173 rooms. Restaurant, bar. Pool. Tennis. Spa. $151-250

PASADENA

The calm, quiet city of Pasadena is, of course, the spot for the Tournament of Roses Parade every New Year's Day and football at the Rose Bowl. But there are things to enjoy year-round. The Rose Bowl, for example, has a great flea market on Sundays during the off-season. You can also view some historical architecture, including the American Craftsman Gamble House and sniff the roses at the botanical gardens. Old Town Pasadena looks the same as it did 70 years ago, lending it antique charm.

SPECIAL EVENT

ROSE PARADE

391 S. Orange Grove Blvd., Pasadena, 626-449-4100; www.tournamentofroses.com
Millions turn out each New Year's Day to watch the gorgeous floral floats, high-stepping marching bands and beautiful equestrian units. The first parade was held in 1890. It was put on by members of the Valley Hunt Club, who had moved here from the East and Midwest and who were eager to celebrate their new home's warm winter weather. The parade grew so large that in 1895, the Tournament or Roses parade was formed to oversee the festival. Today, elaborate floats are constructed by professional float building companies. The football game was added in 1902, the first game taking place between Stanford University and the University of Michigan, with U-M crushing West Coast Stanford 49-0, leading Stanford to simply give up in the third quarter. The loss was so embarrassing, the Tournament decided to give up football for chariot racing. They brought back the football game in 1916 and by 1920, a large stadium had to be built to accommodate the spectators.

WHAT TO SEE

GAMBLE HOUSE
4 Westmoreland Place, Pasadena, 626-793-3334; www.gamblehouse.org
Designed by brothers Charles and Henry Greene in 1908 for David and Mary Gamble of the Procter and Gamble Company, The Gamble House is a national landmark. The two architects heralded the American Craftsman movement, which is characterized by buildings with natural materials and was a stepping-stone for Art Deco designs.
Guided tours take place every 30 minutes beginning at noon to 3:00 p.m. on Thursday through Sunday (closed Monday to Wednesday). Adults $10, children under 12 free.

HUNTINGTON LIBRARY AND GARDENS
1151 Oxford Road, San Marino, 626-405-2100; www.huntington.org
The Huntington is home to one of the country's largest research libraries, but get your nose out of those books and instead check out the art collection and gardens. The Huntington Art Gallery once was the estate of Henry E. Huntington and his wife, but today it is home to impressive collections of 18th century British paintings and 18th century French decorative art. Must-sees in the Huntington Gallery include Thomas Gainsborough's *Blue Boy*, Thomas Lawrence's *Pinkie*, John Constable's *View on the Stour near Dedham*, and Joshua Reynold's *Sarah Siddons as the Tragic Muse*. If you still want to see more art after wandering around the Huntington Gallery, the Scott, Erburu and Boone Galleries are at your disposal; otherwise, head out to the botanical gardens. Huntington started planting the gardens in 1903, and today 14,000 kinds of plants span the area's 120 acres. You'll see gardens dedicated to everything from desert plants to roses, as well as plant species from China, Japan and Australia. If you love to read while you're on vacation, there's no prettier place to do so than here.
Admission: Monday-Friday: adults $15, seniors $12, students $10, children 5-11 $6, children

under 5 free. Saturday-Sunday: adults $20, seniors $15, students $10, children 5-11 $6, children under 5 free. Monday, Wednesday-Friday noon-4:30 p.m., Saturday-Sunday 10:30 a.m.-4:30 p.m. First Thursday of the month free (with advance tickets).

KIDSPACE CHILDREN'S MUSEUM

480 N. Arroyo Blvd., Pasadena, 626-449-9144; www.kidspacemuseum.org

Kids can climb aboard raindrops as they travel through the water cycle or dig up fossils and dinosaur eggs at this interactive museum.

Admission: adults and children $10. September-May, Tuesday-Friday 9:30 a.m.-5 p.m., Saturday-Sunday 10 a.m.-5 p.m.; June-August, Monday-Friday 9:30 a.m.-5 p.m., Saturday-Sunday 10 a.m.-5 p.m.

NORTON SIMON MUSEUM

411 W. Colorado Blvd., Pasadena, 626-449-6840; www.nortonsimon.org

The Norton Simon may not be as large as Los Angeles County Museum of Art, but it boasts an impressive collection that's worth seeing. The museum opened to the public in the mid-1970s, and Frank Gehry updated the interior in the late 1990s, adding skylights and limestone floors to create a sense of light. The Norton Simon houses sculpture and paintings originating from all over Asia, and showcases works by Picasso, Rembrandt, Goya, Degas, Van Gogh and Kandinsky. Stop by the museum's garden, which features a number of sculptures by Henry Moore and is reminiscent of Monet's garden in Giverny, France.

Admission: adults $8, seniors $4, students and children 18 and under free. Monday, Wednesday-Thursday, Saturday-Sunday noon-6 p.m., Friday noon-9 p.m. Free first Friday 6-9 p.m. of every month.

PACIFIC ASIA MUSEUM

46 N. Los Robles Ave., Pasadena, 626-449-2742; www.pacificasiamuseum.org

Inside this Chinese Imperial Palace-style building, you'll see changing exhibits of traditional and contemporary Asian and Pacific Basin art. The grounds also include a Chinese courtyard garden, a research library and a bookstore. Docent tours are available.

Admission: adults $9, seniors and students $7, children under 11 free. Wednesday-Sunday 10 a.m.-6 p.m.

PASADENA MUSEUM OF HISTORY

470 W. Walnut St., Pasadena, 626-577-1660; www.pasadenahistory.org

Housed in the 18-room Fenyes Estate since 1970,the museum includes original furnishings, antiques, paintings and accessories, giving a glimpse of the elegant lifestyle that existed on Orange Grove Boulevard at the turn of the century.

Mansion tours: Wednesday-Friday 1 p.m., Saturday-Sunday 1:30 p.m. and 3 p.m. Exhibit hours: Wednesday-Sunday noon-5 p.m.

ROSE BOWL

1001 Rose Bowl Drive, Pasadena, 626-577-3101; www.rosebowlstadium.com

Although no longer the home of the annual big game between the winners of the Pac-10 and the Big Ten conferences, the Rose Bowl still hosts the Bowl Championship Series games every year. During the regular season, UCLA's Bruins football team plays at the venue.

WHERE TO STAY

★★★HILTON PASADENA

168 S. Los Robles Ave., Pasadena, 626-577-1000, 800-445-8667; www.hilton.com

Located just steps from the Pasadena Convention Center and Old Town Pasadena and its hundreds of dining, shopping and entertainment options, the spacious guest rooms at this hotel are equipped with data ports, wireless Internet access and comfortable ergonomic chairs for business travelers. The lively bar has a pool table and multiple video screens.

296 rooms. Restaurant, bar. Business center. Fitness center. Pool. Pets accepted. $151-250

★★★THE LANGHAM, HUNTINGTON HOTEL & SPA, PASADENA

1401 S. Oak Knoll Ave., Pasadena, 626-568-3900; www.langhamhotels.com

People have been escaping to the quiet beauty of Pasadena for decades and, since 1907, they've often been heading straight for The Huntington Hotel & Spa. This landmark hotel, set on 23 acres at the foothills of the San Gabriel Mountains, is a destination unto itself. The 11,000-square-foot award-winning spa is reason alone to visit, as are the elegant European-style rooms fitted with Italian marble baths and Frette linens.

380 rooms. Restaurant, bar. Business center. Fitness center. Pool. Spa. $251-350

★★★SHERATON PASADENA HOTEL

303 E. Cordova St., Pasadena, 626-449-4000, 800-457-7940; www.starwoodhotels.com

Within walking distance of many of the city's attractions, this hotel is a nice spot for business and leisure travelers. Guest rooms include pillow-top mattresses and large desks. A complimentary shuttle will take you to places within a three-mile radius.

317 rooms. Restaurant, bar. Business center. Fitness center. Pool. $151-250

★★★WESTIN PASADENA

191 N. Los Robles Ave., Pasadena, 626-792-2727; www.westin.com/pasadena

This beautifully appointed hotel in the heart of downtown appeals to families and those traveling on business. An in-house kids' club supplies coloring books, bath toys and a phone line dedicated to bedtime stories. Office rooms come with a fax and printer, and all accommodations feature signature Heavenly Beds with pillow-top mattresses.

350 rooms. Restaurant, bar. Business center. Fitness center. Pool. $151-250

WHERE TO EAT

★★★BISTRO 45

45 S. Mentor Ave., Pasadena, 626-795-2478; www.bistro45.com

Located in an Art Deco building on a quiet Old Pasadena street, this top-ranked restaurant features a French-influenced California menu focused on fresh ingredients. Notable specialties include pan seared bluefin crab cake, roasted wild brook trout with caramelized shallot and marble potatoes, and beef tenderloin with sautéed mushrooms.. All dishes are presented with refined service and a wine list that should impress even the most discerning connoisseur.

California. Lunch (Tuesday-Thursday), dinner. Closed Monday. Bar. $36-86

★★★THE DINING ROOM

1401 S. Oak Knoll Ave., Pasadena, 626-568-3900; www.langhamhotels.com

Dine on perfectly prepared grilled meats and seafood at this clubby dining room located within the elegant Langham hotel. The service is top-notch, and the waitstaff and kitchen will gladly accommodate any special request. The dimly lit dining room surrounds guests with warm, neutral tones and tables topped with crisp white linens and candles. It's a perfect spot for either a romantic dinner or for entertaining clients.

American. Dinner. Closed Sunday-Monday. $36-85

THE CENTRAL COAST

The Central Coast area spans from Santa Barbara to Monterey and includes sandy beaches, rocky coastline, charming villages and wonderful wineries. Ever since Miles Raymond stumbled around this wide-open, folksy wine country in the movie *Sideways*, people have been coming to this region in search of the perfect pinot. The film may have put the area on the wine map, but Santa Barbara has been producing great wines for decades, and not just pinot noir—although that volatile varietal wine is undoubtedly king (thanks to the marine air and cool climate). We recommend staying in Santa Barbara and making the 50-minute drive to the area's wineries along the Foxen and Santa Rita Hills wine trails, and around the tiny town of Los Olivos. It's a bit of a hike, but the trip is scenic, and more important, you'll fi nd luxe accommodations, great restaurants and lots of shopping along State Street in Santa Barbara to round out your trip. Solvang is a quirky Danish town with authentic bakeries and lots of shops, while Paso Robles is the wine area that everyone was hoping would stay a secret (too late).

Charming towns like Ojai provide a quiet escape with luxurious accommodations, spa treatments, and a lovely downtown area full of art galleries just outside Santa Barbara. The towns of San Luis Obispo and Cambria are frequent stops when visiting Hearst Castle, either for lunch or an overnight visit. The best way to explore the area is by driving along Highway 1. The 101 is faster but not nearly as scenic.

OJAI

Located 15 miles inland from the Pacific Coast, Ojai is a small, tranquil community surrounded by 500,000 acres of picturesque mountains, green valleys and streams, which have been the backdrop for many Hollywood productions. It's also known for its adorable downtown, which has world-class art galleries, boutiques, cafés, restaurants, bookstores, a small park and a movie theater, and a handful of luxury spas.

WHAT TO SEE

LAKE CASITAS RECREATION AREA

11311 Santa Ana Road, Ojai, 805-649-2233; www.lakecasitas.info

At this recreation area, you can do some fishing, boating, picnicking and camping (*for reservations, call 805-649-1122*). Beaches, golf courses and tennis

HIGHLIGHT

WHAT ARE THE TOP THINGS TO DO IN THE CENTRAL COAST?

BOOK SOME SPA TIME IN OJAI
The quaint little town of Ojai is home to the Ojai Valley Inn and Spa, a Spanish Colonia-style resort surrounding by rolling green hills. The recently renovated hotel includes Spa Ojai, where treatments take place in cozy rooms with murals and fireplaces. In addition to all the standard treatments, the Native American-inspired spa offers a group treatment involving clay mud and heat, and also features an artist's cottage and apothecary.

GO WINE TASTING
Santa Barbara is a great base for wine tasting in the area. It is under an hour from Los Olivos, a picture perfect town with wine tasting rooms and wonderful little restaurants. Surrounding Los Olivos you'll find dozens of wineries, including Babcock Winery and Firestone Vineyards.

VISIT HEARST CASTLE
The spectacular home of newspaper magnet William Randolph Hearst is open to the public and a tour is a must. Buses take guests up a windy road to the top of a hill where the lavish home is located. The best part: the breathtaking Roman indoor pool featuring floor-to-ceiling mosaic tiles mainly in shades of blue and orange.

STROLL THROUGH DOWNTOWN SANTA BARBARA
Downtown Santa Barbara is a lovely area filled with shops, including Saks Fifth Avenue and Betsey Johnson, and wonderful restaurants, such as Bouchon Santa Barbara, which features wine country cuisine. Visitors will also find art galleries, theaters, cafes and lounges.

MAKE A STOP IN SOLVANG
This quirky Danish town has a variety of galleries, wine tasting room and bakeries selling Danish pastries. Much of the film *Sideways* was filmed here.

courts are all nearby. Pets must be on a leash.
Daily.

OJAI CENTER FOR THE ARTS
113 S. Montgomery, Ojai, 805-646-0117; www.ojaiact.org

The center hosts rotating exhibitions of local artists and live theater productions. Check website for performance information.

OJAI VALLEY MUSEUM
130 W. Ojai Ave., Ojai, 805-640-1390; www.ojaivalleymuseum.org

Permanent and changing exhibits at this museum explore environmental, cultural and historical factors that shaped the Ojai Valley. There's also a research library.

Admission: adults $4, children 6-18 $1, children under 6 free. Thursday-Friday 1-4 p.m., Saturday 10 a.m.-4 p.m., Sunday noon-4 p.m. Guided tours Wednesday.

WHERE TO STAY

★★★OJAI VALLEY INN & SPA
905 Country Club Road, Ojai, 805-646-1111; www.ojairesort.com

Tucked in a peaceful mountain valley, Ojai Valley Inn & Spa looks just like the kind of California ranch at which presidents have been photographed riding their horses. The Spanish Colonial classic recently underwent a major renovation. There's a new lobby, 100 additional guest rooms and a revamped spa. Rooms feature luxury linens, comfortable furnishings and spacious bathrooms with Mexican titles—many rooms also have fireplaces and patios. But the amenities are the real draw: The resort sits on 220 acres and includes championship golf and tennis, and a spectacular spa that includes luxurious treatments, apothecary and artist's workshop. Guests are shuttled around the grounds on golf carts by the friendly and attentive staff, and the restaurants serve fresh California cuisine.

308 rooms. Restaurant, bar. Business center. Spa. Pets accepted. Golf. $251-350

WHERE TO EAT

★★★L'AUBERGE
314 El Paseo Road, Ojai, 805-646-2288

Nestled among oak trees and situated in a rustic cabin built in 1905, chef Christian Shaffer serves up fresh French/American country cuisine while you watch incredible sunsets over the Topa Topa Mountains. The monthly changing menu includes entrées such as oysters, clams, lamb, oxtail and venison.

Continental, French. Dinner, Sunday brunch. Closed Monday-Tuesday. Reservations recommended. Outdoor seating. $16-35

★★★THE RANCH HOUSE
102 Besant Road, Ojai, 805-646-2360; www.theranchhouse.com

One of the forerunners of California cuisine, The Ranch House made a name for itself many decades ago by offering simple, made-from-scratch dishes—many of them vegetarian—that burst with fresh flavors. The years have seen some changes, but many things remain the same here. Fresh herbs from the garden are still used in all the recipes, and the loaves of bread that are served to patrons (and sold to locals) are still made fresh daily. Dishes like wild mushroom strudel and grilled diver scallops with sweet corn sauce have been keeping guests coming back, and its garden setting with quiet streams and lush foliage make it a perfect spot for a relaxing lunch.

American. Dinner, Sunday brunch. Closed Monday. $36-85

RECOMMENDED

SUZANNE'S CUISINE
502 W. Ojai Ave., Ojai, 805-640-1961;
www.suzannescuisine.com

This cozy restaurant, run by a mother/daughter duo, serves comfort food infused with Asian, Indian, French and Mexican spices. For lunch, there is a large selection of fresh salads and sandwiches (the juicy chicken sandwich tasted like it had just come off the grill), while dinner focuses on pasta and seafood dishes. Seating is available on a flower-laden patio.

Continental. Lunch, dinner. Closed Tuesday. Bar. Reservations recommended. Outdoor seating. $16-35

SPA

★★★★SPA OJAI
905 Country Club Road, Ojai, 805-646-1111, 888-697-8780; www.ojairesort.com

Golfers, hikers and couples on romantic getaways all come to this sophisticated 31,000-square-foot sanctuary of health and well-being for a spa experience like no other. Spa Ojai features signature services such as Kuyam—a treatment that combines the therapeutic effects of cleansing mud, dry heat, inhalation therapy and guided meditation. This communal experience (kuyam means "a place to rest together") accommodates up to eight men or women. There's also an extensive array of facial, skin and body treatments, as well as a variety of art classes and an apothecary where you can mix your own potions and lotions.

SANTA BARBARA

Santa Barbara is only two hours from Los Angeles, but it might as well be a world away. Often called the "American Riviera," the historic city, an old Spanish mission town, is sandwiched between the Pacific Coast and the mountains of the Santa Ynez Valley. The sky is so blue it's almost purple. The beach is lined with palm trees, and the lush, green foothills are dotted with beautiful, Spanish-style homes.

Tourists have flocked to Santa Barbara for it's beautiful Mediterranean weather, downtown beaches and Spanish-influenced architecture. Nicknamed the "South Coast" due to its south-facing coastline, Santa Barbara boasts views from sunrise to sunset and is home to countless celebrity estates and palatial properties. With a Mission revival style of architecture adopted throughout the city, there is a distinct aura in Santa Barbara. The ordinances passed against billboards and outdoor advertising add to its unique clutter-free atmosphere. Explore the famed Santa Barbara mission and other national historic landmarks, or plan your trip for late June and attend the Summer Solstice Parade, drawing more than 100,000 for the city's most festive event. State Street brings you into the center of town, essentially an impeccably clean outdoor mall with high-end shops, world-renowned art galleries and open-air

SPECIAL EVENTS

OJAI MUSIC FESTIVAL

Libbe Bowl, 201 S. Signal St., Ojai, 805-646-2094; www.ojaifestival.org
For four days in June, the Libby Bowl hosts talented classical musicians performing pieces from composers such as Mozart, Stravinsky and Beethoven.
Early June.

OJAI SHAKESPEARE FESTIVAL

Matilija JHS Auditorium, 703 El Paseo St., Ojai, 805-646-9455; www.ojaishakespeare.org
See outdoor evening and matinee performances of Shakespeare plays.
July-August.

OJAI STUDIO ARTISTS TOUR

Ojai Art Center, 113 S. Montgomery St., Ojai, 805-646-8126; www.ojaistudioartists.com
Recognized artists open their studios to the public.
Mid-October.

OJAI VALLEY TENNIS TOURNAMENT

Ojai, 805-646-7241; www.ojaitourney.org
Held since 1895, this is the oldest amateur tennis tournament in the nation. Games take place at a variety of venues, including Libby Park, the Ojai Valley Athletic Club and area high schools and colleges.
Late April.

restaurants, cafes and bars. The city's historic buildings and Mission District are also located nearby.

Adventure junkies can take advantage of beach and mountain sports like surfing, horseback riding and fishing. Foodies have their pick of the finest restaurants, authentic Mexican taquerias and fresh fish and farmer's markets. And intellectual folk can shop for arts and antiques and go wine tasting in the valley. The weather is also spectacular, with temperatures during the day averaging between 65 and 80 degrees, making it the perfect getaway anytime of year.

WHAT TO SEE

EAST BEACH

Sun worshippers will love this picturesque stretch of sand located on East Cabrillo Boulevard. Amenities include a full beach house, snack bar, volleyball

HIGHLIGHT

RONALD REAGAN PRESIDENTIAL LIBRARY

40 Presidential Drive, Simi Valley, 800-410-8354; www.reaganfoundation.org
Ronald Reagan owned a ranch high in the Santa Barbara Mountains. Stop by his comprehensive library, located just eight miles off the 101 (take CA-23 North toward Fillmore and follow signs). Perched on a mountaintop with views of the mountains, valleys and Pacific Ocean, this 100-acre site has exhibits that follow Reagan from childhood to the glamorous world of Hollywood stardom, to his inauguration as the 40th President of the United States. Key events of his two terms are revealed through documents, photographs and artifacts.
Daily 10 a.m.-5 p.m.

courts, play area for children and bike/rollerblading paths. It also hosts the Santa Barbara Art Show on Sundays.

EL PASEO
900 State St., Santa Barbara
Pick up a few stylin' souvenirs while you're away. Built between 1921 and 1924, this block of galleries, restaurants, and clothing and gift shops is considered the oldest shopping center in California, and a Santa Barbara landmark.

MISSION SANTA BARBARA
2201 Laguna St., Santa Barbara, 805-682-4713; www.sbmission.org
This unofficial city landmark was built in 1786 as the tenth of the California missions to be founded by the Spanish Franciscans. A climb to the top of the mission's two towers provides a breathtaking view of Santa Barbara. Secular and non-secular activities take place in the mission daily.
Self-guided tours: Daily 9 a.m.-4:30 p.m.

SANTA BARBARA BOTANIC GARDEN
1212 Mission Canyon Road, Santa Barbara, 805-682-4726; www.sbbg.org
Set on 40 acres in Santa Barbara, this decades-old botanic garden allows visitors to traverse its 5.5 miles of walking paths through its 1,000-plus plant types as well as its vast herbarium including roughly 143,000 preserved species. While the botanic garden is best visited in warmer months, it is open year round and demonstrates the variety of plant life in southern California during all months.
Admission: adults $8, seniors and children 13-17 $6, children 2-12 $4, children under 1 and under free. March-October, daily 9 a.m.-6 p.m.; November-February, daily 9 a.m.-5 p.m.

SANTA BARBARA CERTIFIED FARMERS MARKET
805-962-5354; www.sbfarmersmarket.org
Each Saturday, local farmers head to the main marketplace in Santa Barbara's downtown to display a colorful bounty of agricultural products grown right in the city's backyard. (The market moves to different locations in the area during

the week.) You'll find seasonal diversity year-round, rain or shine. Music and entertainment enliven the markets and enriches the ambiance.

Closed Monday. Check the website for daily locations.

SANTA BARBARA MUSEUM OF ART

1130 State St., Santa Barbara, 805-963-4364; www.sbmuseart.org

The Santa Barbara Museum of Art is a privately funded, not-for-profit institution. Here you'll find cultural and educational activities as well as internationally recognized collections and exhibitions ranging from antique ties to contemporary art and spanning the globe. Don't miss the works on paper collection, the largest collection within the museum.

Tuesday-Sunday 11 a.m.-5 p.m. Closed Monday. Free Sunday.

SANTA BARBARA ROYAL PRESIDIO

123 E. Canon Perdido St., Santa Barbara, 805-965-0093; www.sbthp.org/presidio.htm

A former military headquarters and government center, this fortress was founded on April 21, 1782. It was the Spanish's center for defense against Native American inhabitants of the area, and two corners of the Presidio's main quadrangle remain. Today they stand as part of a state park and visitors can see what the living structures for soldiers based here were like. The location was carefully chosen as a place of outlook and defense.

Admission: adults $5, seniors $4, children under 17 free. Daily 10:30 a.m.-4:30 p.m.

STEARNS WHARF AND TY WARNER SEA CENTER

State Street and the Pacific Ocean, 805-962-2526; www.sbnature.org

Once a major shipping hub for all of southern California, this pier, built in 1872, has dramatic views of Santa Barbara, and is now home to several fresh seafood restaurants, including the delicious Santa Barbara Shellfish Company and gift shops. The Ty Warner Sea Center, part of the Santa Barbara Museum of Natural History, is an interactive marine education facility where visitors have the opportunity to work like scientists, sample and test ocean water, study animal behavior and examine microscopic marine life.

Daily 10 a.m.-5 p.m.

LOS OLIVOS

Blink and you might miss it, but the single street that makes up this cute town is pretty much the center of Santa Barbara wine country. It might be small but it has several tasting rooms (including Daniel Gehrs and Longoria) and a number of good restaurants. Stop by the Los Olivos Wine Merchant & Café *(2870 Grand Ave., Los Olivos, 888-946-3748; www.losolivoscafe.com)* for pizzas, salads and the homemade tampenade to start. They also carry more than 150 wines, making it an obvious stop on your tasting tour. Craving a warm and crusty Panini? Panino *(2900 Grand Ave., 805-688-9304)* has more than 30 options. After lunch, you can peruse the art galleries and be sure to check out Jedlicka's Saddlery *(2883 Grand Avenue, Los Olivos, 805-688-2626; www.jedlicka. com)*, an authentic Western store that has catered to ranchers and trail riders—reportedly including President more than 70 years.

HIGHLIGHT

WHERE ARE THE CENTRAL COAST'S WINERIES?

ALMA ROSA WINERY

7250 Santa Rosa Road, Buellton, 805-688-9090; www.almarosawinery.com
Owner Richard Sanford, formerly a geography major at University of California at Berkeley, is a real maverick, having planted the first pinot noir vines here in 1970. In 2005, he started Alma Rosa with his wife, Thekla. Located on the Rancho Santa Rosa, the vineyards are certified organic and produce chardonnay and pinot noir, as well as pinot gris, pinot blanc and dry pinot noir rosé.
Daily 11 a.m.-4:30 p.m.

BABCOCK WINERY

5175 E. Highway 246, Lompoc, 805-736-1455; www.babcockwinery.com
Brian Babcock is a wine rock star, anointed one of the top ten small production wine makers in the world—the only one in the U.S.—by the James Beard Foundation. The winery produces chardonnay, pinot noir, pinot grigio, sauvignon blanc, syrah and cabernet sauvignon. Babcock also has been experimenting with Italian and Spanish varietals, which he believes will be the next big thing in California winemaking.
Daily 10:30 a.m.-4 p.m.

FIRESTONE VINEYARD

5000 Zaca Station Road, Los Olivos, 805-688-3940; www.firestonewine.com
Firestone has been around since 1972, making it one of the original wineries in Santa Barbara. It sits on a hilltop like the grande dame it is and merits a visit just to admire the pretty location and tasting room. It's also the place to take a tour if you'd like to see the workings of at least one area vineyard (you also learn how the Firestone family went from tires to grapes). The winery, now owned by Bill Foley, produces chardonnay, cabernet sauvignon, merlot, sauvignon blanc and syrah.
Daily 10 a.m.-5 p.m. Tours start at 11:15 a.m., 1:15 p.m. and 3:15 p.m.

FOLEY ESTATES VINEYARD & WINERY

6121 E. Highway 246, Lompoc, 805-737-6222; www.foleywines.com
In 1998, Bill Foley purchased land on the Rancho Santa Rosa because of its south-facing hillside and limestone soil, key for producing pinot. Since then, he's built something of a wine empire, acquiring Las Hermanas Vineyard (formerly Ashley's Vineyard) and Firestone, and starting Merus in the Napa Valley to make cabernets. (In his other life, Foley is the chairman of the board of Fidelity.) The large tasting room is located next to the winery building.
Daily 10 a.m.-5 p.m.

WHERE TO STAY

★★★★BACARA RESORT & SPA

8301 Hollister Ave., Santa Barbara, 805-968-0100, 877-422-4245; www.bacararesort.com

With the Pacific Ocean on one side and the Santa Ynez Mountains on the other, Bacara is all about location. A fitness center, a saline-filled pool and secluded nooks for sunbathing flank more than 30 treatment rooms and indoor and outdoor massage stations. The spa offers an intriguing selection of global healing regimens, and an Eastern Origin menu, which features options such as reiki and shiatsu massages. The rugged terrain of the Santa Ynez Mountains is the perfect place for a rigorous walk, run or hike. Clay tennis courts, pools almost too pretty to swim in and yoga on the beach are just a few of the other fitness options.

360 rooms. Restaurant, bar. Business center. Pool. Spa. Pets accepted. $351 and up

★★★CANARY HOTEL

31 W. Carrllio St., Santa Barbara, 805-884-0300; www.andaluciasb.com

This delightful hotel is what you might imagine your perfect seaside cottage to look like: tall, four-poster beds with crisp, white sheets in front of a huge plasma TV, dark-stained wood floors, beautiful Spanish tile in the bath, and lots of homey touches strewn about—a pair of binoculars casually resting on a stack of books, pretty silver dishes, white candles in large glass hurricanes, a yoga mat in the closet. You may return home and decorate your own bedroom the same way. Restaurants and shopping are within walking distance, and the rooftop deck is the place to catch a cocktail before you crash in your relaxing digs.

97 rooms. Restaurant, bar. Fitness center. Pool. $251-350

★★★FESS PARKER'S DOUBLETREE RESORT

633 E. Cabrillo Blvd., Santa Barbara, 805-564-4333, 800-879-2929; www.fpdtr.com

This grand oceanfront resort surrounded by gardens offers friendly service, from the complimentary airport transportation to the fresh baked cookies offered upon arrival. The guest rooms are elegant, and the sprawling white-washed property, with red-tile roofs and arched walkways, offers plenty of recreation.

338 rooms. Restaurant, bar. $251-350

★★★★FOUR SEASONS RESORT THE BILTMORE SANTA BARBARA

1260 Channel Drive, Santa Barbara, 805-969-2261; www.fourseasons.com

Recently renovated by Beanie Babies owner Ty Warner, this super-luxurious property on 20 lush acres on the Pacific Ocean pays tribute to the region's Spanish colonial history with its red-tiled roof, arches and hacienda-style main building. The guest rooms, located both in the main building and in separate cottages, feature a relaxed Spanish-colonial décor and include down pillows and plush bathrobes. Crisp, white cabanas line the sparkling pool. Besides offering a full menu of massages, facials and body wraps, the spa incorporates botanicals from the gardens into its treatments. After a day on back roads squinting to find wineries, an evening at the oceanfront Bella Vista restaurant is just the ticket, particularly if you get a table close to one of the outdoor firepits.

219 rooms. Restaurant, bar. Business center. Spa. Pets accepted. $351 and up

★★★HARBOR VIEW INN

28 W. Cabrillo Blvd., Santa Barbara, 800-755-0222;
www.harborviewinnsb.com

It would be hard to beat the location of this upscale
motor inn—it's right where the city meets the shore
near Stearn's Wharf, and it's just steps from the ocean.
The comfortable rooms have private patios, and the
complex includes a pool, an adults-only fitness center
and beautiful gardens.

115 rooms. Restaurant, bar. Fitness center. Pool. $251-350

★★★★SAN YSIDRO RANCH, A ROSEWOOD HOTEL

900 San Ysidro Lane, Montecito, 805-565-1700;
www.sanysidroranch.com

Settle in at this 550-acre paradise and you'll see
why John and Jackie Kennedy spent part of their
honeymoon here, at this resort tucked away in the
foothills of Montecito. Lushly planted acres are filled
with fragrant flowers and plants, and stunning vistas of
the Pacific Ocean and the Channel Islands can be seen
in the distance. The bungalows, with their cozy blend of
overstuffed chintz armchairs, oriental rugs and vaulted,
wood-clad ceilings, provide luxuries like wood-burning
fireplaces and specialty linens. Exceptional cuisine is a
hallmark of the property, and the two restaurants here
provide charming settings for the imaginative food.

41 rooms. Restaurant, bar. Fitness center. Pool. Pets accepted.
$351 and up

★★★SANTA YNEZ VALLEY MARRIOTT

555 McMurray Road, Buellton, 805-688-1000, 800-638-8882;
www.santaynezhotels.com

This Spanish-style hotel, located in the Santa Ynez Valley
at the gateway to the Santa Barbara Wine Country, is
near more than 60 vineyards and wineries. The spacious
guest rooms are stocked with Starbucks coffee and other
amenities. Enjoy the heated outdoor pool or lap pool or
hit the spa or steam room. The casual buffet breakfast in
the hotel's restaurant is the perfect beginning to a busy
day, and a friendly game of billiards in the Winner's
Circle Pub is the perfect ending.

149 rooms. Restaurant, bar. Business center. Fitness center. Pool.
Spa. Pets accepted. $151-250

WHERE TO EAT

★★★BELLA VISTA

Four Seasons Santa Barbara,1260 Channel Drive, Santa Barbara,
805-969-2261; www.fourseasons.com

Besides incredible views of the Pacific from the
open-air patio or the window-lined dining room,
this restaurant inside the Four Seasons Santa Barbara
offers expertly prepared, locally sourced fresh and
organic food. Chef Martin Frost's specialties include
free-range chicken breast filled with goat cheese,
truffles, potato, eggplant and red pepper, or honey-
cilantro glazed sea bass. The outdoor patio has several
open-air fireplaces, perfect for cozying up to for
dessert and after-dinner drinks.

American. Breakfast, lunch, dinner. $86 and up

★★★BOUCHON

9 W. Victoria St., Santa Barbara, 805-730-1160;
www.bouchonsantabarbara.com

This French-Californian restaurant prides itself
on using the freshest local ingredients available,
including fish from the Santa Barbara Channel,
produce from the surrounding countryside, meats
and poultry from local micro-ranches and wine from
the Santa Ynez Valley. Order the pan-seared scallops
with herb risotto, or try bourbon and maple-glazed
duck. The "Molten Lava" chocolate cake is a sweet
ending to any meal.

American, French. Dinner. $36-85

★★★DOWNEY'S

1305 State St., Santa Barbara, 805-966-5006;
www.downeyssb.com

The menu at Downey's, which changes constantly,
offers appetizers such as the Santa Barbara
mussels with sweet corn and a chili vinaigrette,
or homemade duck sausage with lentils. Signature
entrées include grilled lamb loin or local sea bass
with a ragout of prawns and spring vegetables.
The relaxed setting combines to make the place
a local favorite.

*American. Dinner. Closed Monday. Reservations recom-
mended. $36-85*

★★★★MIRÓ AT BACARA RESORT

Bacara Resort & Spa, 8301 Hollister Ave., Santa Barbara,
805-9681800, 877-422-4245; www.bacararesort.com

Santa Barbara's luxurious Bacara Resort is home to
the swank Miró Restaurant. Joan Miró-style artwork,

WHAT'S THE BEST BOUTIQUE HOTEL?

Canary Hotel:
This delightful hotel is
what you might imagine
your perfect seaside
cottage to look like: tall,
four-poster beds with
crisp, white sheets in front
of a huge plasma TV,
dark-stained wood floors,
beautiful Spanish tile in
the bath, and plenty of
homey touches.

SOLVANG

A detour into the village of Solvang—the Danish Capital of America—and the Santa Ynez Valley's thousands of acres of award-winning vineyards (which were highlighted in the Oscar-nominated movie *Sideways*) is a must. If you're in Santa Barbara, hop in the car and drive northwest on the 101 for about 32 miles until you reach Highway 246, which will bring you east to Solvang. This authentic Danish community offers quaint inns, Scandinavian restaurants that serve delicacies like aebleskiver and smorgaasbord, The Hans Christian Anderson museum and dozens of shops that sell everything from Old World antiques to homemade candy. After you've had your fill of Danish delicacies, take Highway 246 to Alamo-Pintado Road, which will lead you north to Los Olivos and the Santa Ynez Wine Loop. This three-mile triangle features about 10 vineyards.

deep red dining chairs, a contemporary carpet and fantastic views of the Pacific Ocean set the scene, while the chef creates masterful renditions of traditional Spanish cooking such as oak-grilled lamb chops with aged sherry and pan roasted lobster with oven-roasted tomatoes. The 12,000-bottle wine cellar has something to match every meal. For a more casual alternative, the Miró Bar and Lounge features homemade sangria and tasty tapas.

Basque, Catalonian. Dinner. Closed Monday. Outdoor seating. Bar. $86 and up

RECOMMENDED

D'ANGELO BREAD

25 W. Gutierrez St., 805-962-5466

D'Angelo's is the place to go in town for breakfast. Wonderful breads and pastries are available, as well as a wide variety of breakfast dishes made with these delectable products, such as the Eggs Rose (poached eggs on kalamata olive bread with an artichoke spread) and Bananas Foster French Toast. What more could you ask for? Except, perhaps, a foamy latte on the side.

Bakery. Breakfast, lunch. $15 and under

ELEMENTS

129 E. Anapamu St., Santa Barbara, 805-884-9218; www.elementsrestaurantandbar.com

The inventive cuisine at Elements is best enjoyed in the fresh air; you can have lunch, brunch and dinner on the patio here while viewing a national landmark, the Santa Barbara Courthouse and Sunken Gardens. Specialties include the grilled Ahi tuna wrap with wasabi mayo and cinnamon spiced duck confit risotto.

Pacific. Lunch, dinner, Sunday brunch. Reservations recommended. Outdoor seating. $16-35

HUNGRY CAT

1134 Chapala St., Santa Barbara, 805-884-4701; www.thehungrycat.com

It's small, it's cramped and they don't take reservations, but that doesn't stop locals from coming to this restaurant once, twice, or even three times a week. After a glance at the seafood menu (peel n' eat shrimp, Maine lobster, oysters), you might think the place belongs on the East Coast, but it's actually the Santa Barbara outpost of a popular Hollywood restaurant. Don't care for seafood? The Pug Burger, with bacon, avocado, blue cheese and onion rings, will make you happy to go along. There's also a tasty noodle dish with pancetta and morels. For seafood lovers, the huge platters are the ticket. They serve an "afternoon snack" between 3 p.m. and 5 p.m. on weekends, as well as brunch.

American. Brunch, late lunch, dinner. No reservations. $36-85

LA SUPER-RICA TAQUERIA

622 N. Milpas St., Santa Barbara, 805-963-4940

Don't let the funky, rundown shacklike exterior deter you from sampling Santa Barbara's most famous authentic Mexican food, a one-time favorite of gourmet Julia Child. The lines are endless but the fresh tamales and cheap tacos—handmade corn tortillas filled with carne asada, marinated pork, chicken, occasionally Dover sole and more—are beyond delicious and well worth the wait.

Mexican. Lunch, dinner. Closed Wenesday. Cash only. $15 and under

OLIO E LIMONE

11 West Victoria St., Santa Barbara, 805-899-2699; www.olioelimone.com

Another favorite of once-local Julia Child, this upscale yet low-key restaurant is the place where both locals and out-of-towners go for the best Italian in the area. Signature dishes include the spaghetti alla bottarga, duck breast, panna cotta and pear carpaccio.

Italian. Lunch, dinner. Reservations recommended. $16-35

SAMBO'S

216 W. Cabrillo Blvd., Santa Barbara, 805-965-3269; www.sambosrestaurant.com

For the best breakfast on the beach, sit on the outdoor patio at Sambo's and order up a plate of fluffy pancakes, a delicious omelet or a breakfast burrito, made with fresh local avocado.

American. Breakfast, lunch. Outdoor seating. $15 and under

SANTA BARBARA SHELLFISH COMPANY

230 Stearns Wharf, Santa Barbara, 805-966-6676; www.sbfishhouse.com

If you head to historic Stearns Wharf, be sure to walk all the way to the very end of the pier or you'll miss this great fish shack. Grab a stool at the small bar inside and order up the best of Santa Barbara clam chowder, fresh oysters and mussels, or the whole shebang in the Cioppino: mussels, clams, shrimp, crab and scallops all steaming in a giant bread bowl.

Seafood. Lunch, dinner. Outdoor seating. $15 and under

TUPELO JUNCTION CAFE

1218 State St., Santa Barbara, 805-899-3100; www.tupelojunction.com

For a hearty, homestyle breakfast, try the southern style-meets eclectic home cooking at Tupelo Junction. Don't-miss menu items include the cinnamon apple beignets, old-fashioned buttermilk biscuits slathered in gravy, and poached eggs on crispy crab cakes with fresh avocado.

American. Breakfast, lunch, dinner. Reservations recommended. $15 and under

SPAS

★★★★BACARA SPA

Bacara Resort & Spa, 8301 Hollister Ave., Santa Barbara, 805-968-1800, 877-422-4245; www.bacararesort.com

A saline-filled pool and secluded nooks for sunbathing flank more than 30 treatment rooms and indoor and outdoor massage stations at this heavenly spa. You'll find a variety of traditional treatments here, as well as an Eastern menu that offers Thai massage, reflexology and shiatsu. Ayurvedic treatments include the Shirodhara with Tibetan foot treatment, in which a technician pours warm oil on your forehead (or "third eye"), gives you a scalp massage and applies a warm thermal foot wrap. You'll feel more Zen from head to toe. The rugged terrain of the Santa Ynez Mountains is the perfect place for a rigorous walk, run or hike. Clay tennis courts, pools almost too pretty to swim in and yoga on the beach are just a few of the other fitness options.

★★★★SPA AT FOUR SEASONS RESORT THE BILTMORE SANTA BARBARA

1260 Channel Drive, Santa Barbara, 805-969-2261, 800-819-5053; www.fourseasons.com

Pure luxury sums up the look and feel of this oceanfront spa, whose design echoes the Spanish colonial style of the Four Seasons Resort in which it's located. Treatment rooms are more residential than spa-like, with kiva fireplaces, plush treatment tables and mission-style furniture. Since you're in wine country, you must try one of the vino-centric treatments. The Vineyard Harvest has you soaking in grapeseed, jasmine, rose and red wine—all of which are full of antioxidants that supposedly help your skin (it can't hurt). A chardonnay clay wrap is then used to remove toxins, followed by a massage. And why not drink the stuff at the same time? A cheese plate and a glass of local wine come along with the treatment. Now that's what we call super-relaxing.

PISMO BEACH

Pismo Beach is famous for its 23 miles of scenic beaches. Ocean fishing, dunes, swimming, surfing, diving, golf, horseback riding and camping make the area popular with vacationers. Pismo Beach is also in a growing wine region. It is the last Pacific oceanfront community where autos can still be driven on the beach (access ramps are at two locations along the sand). A more dramatic and rugged coastline is found at Shell Beach to the north, which has been incorporated into Pismo Beach.

WHERE TO STAY

★★★THE CLIFFS RESORT

2757 Shell Beach Road, Pismo Beach, 805-773-5000, 800-826-7827; www.cliffsresort.com

The cliff-top location overlooking the Pacific, inn-style hospitality and proximity to the local airport make this resort a good choice. Guest rooms feature work desks, Italian marble baths, and private balconies or patios with coastal or mountain views. Activities such as surfing, kayaking, hiking and golf are available onsite or nearby, and dozens of wineries are within driving distance.

160 rooms. Restaurant, bar. Business center. Pool. Pets accepted. $151-250

WHERE TO EAT

F. MCLINTOCK'S
750 Mattie Road, Pismo Beach, 805-773-1892; www.mclintocks.com

F. McLintock's is a Pismo Beach favorite, so be prepared to wait. And definitely come hungry. Steaks and ribs are cooked over an oat-pit barbeque, and dinners come with so many sides (onion rings, beans, garlic bread, sherbet for dessert), you'll be stuffed for days.

Steak. Dinner. $16-35

SAN LUIS OBISPO

San Luis Obispo (Spanish for St. Louis, the Bishop) is about halfway between San Francisco and Los Angeles on the Central Coast. The city, referred to locally as SLO or "San Luis," is one of California's oldest communities. It was built around the Mission San Luis Obispo de Tolosa, which was founded by Father Fray Junipero Serra in 1772. After the thatched mission roofs burned several times, a tile-making technique was developed that soon set the style for all California missions. The bustling downtown is full of shops, restaurants and students from California Polytechnic University, making it a pleasant stopover; it's also a good place to stop while touring the Edna Valley wine country.

WHAT TO SEE

MISSION SAN LUIS OBISPO DE TOLOSA
751 Palm St., San Luis Obispo, 805-781-8214; www.missionsanluisobispo.org

The fifth of the California missions founded in 1772 still serves as the parish church. An eight-room museum also contains an extensive Chumash collection and artifacts from early settlers. The first olive orchard in California was planted here, and two original trees still stand.

Daily 9 a.m.-5 p.m.

SAN LUIS OBISPO COUNTY MUSEUM AND HISTORY CENTER
696 Monterey St., San Luis Obispo, 805-543-0638; www.slochs.org

Across the street from the mission, this museum showcases local history exhibits and decorative arts reflecting Native American life and farm life.

Wednesday-Sunday 10 a.m.-4 p.m.

WHERE TO STAY

★★★APPLE FARM TRELLIS COURT
2015 Monterey St., San Luis Obispo, 805-544-2040, 800-255-2040; www.applefarm.com

This quaint hotel combines the charm of a Victorian inn with the conveniences of a luxury hotel. Rooms feature four-poster beds, fireplaces and high-speed Internet access. There are free treats, including an evening wine reception and a welcome basket.

104 rooms. Restaurant. Pool. $151-250

SPECIAL EVENTS

MADONNARI ITALIAN STREET PAINTING FESTIVAL

Mission Plaza, Monterey and 1039 Chorro streets, San Luis Obispo, 805-781-2777; www.slochamber.org
Local artists decorate the streets around the mission with chalk drawings. Music, Italian cuisine and an open-air market also set a festive mood.
Mid-September.

MOZART FESTIVAL

3165 Broad St., San Luis Obispo, 805-781-3008; www.mozartfestival.com
For this festival, recitals, chamber music, orchestra concerts and choral music held at various locations throughout the county, including Mission San Luis Obispo de Tolosa and California Polytechnic State University campus.
Mid-July-early August.

RENAISSANCE FESTIVAL

1087 Santa Rosa St., San Luis Obispo
Celebrate the Renaissance with period costumes, food booths, entertainment, arts and crafts.
July.

SLO INTERNATIONAL FILM FESTIVAL

San Luis Obispo, 805-546-3456; www.slofilmfest.org
This festival showcases the history and art of filmmaking with screenings of new releases, classics, short films and documentaries. Additional events include seminars, a film competition and the annual sing-along, where moviegoers dress as characters from the featured musical and channel their inner Julie Andrews.
Early-mid-March.

WHERE TO EAT

RECOMMENDED
APPLE FARM RESTAURANT AND BAKERY
2015 Monterey St., San Luis Obispo, 805-544-2040, 800-255-2040; www.applefarm.com
The Apple Farm Restaurant and Bakery has long been a favorite in San Luis Obispo. Fresh, comfort food dishes like turkey pot pie and chicken and dumplings are on the menu here. Enjoy lunch out on the patio—and be sure to save room for the famous hot apple dumpling dessert.
American. Breakfast, lunch, dinner. $16-35

CAFE ROMA

1020 Railroad Way, San Luis Obispo, 805-541-6800; www.caferomaslo.com

For fresh Italian food such as burschetta with fresh tomato, crispy calamari and spagetti carbonara, Café Roma is just the spot. The menu features an array of starters, fresh salads, pizzas, pastas and meat and fish dishes. The wine list includes varietals from nearby Paso Robles and features a new wine each month.

Italian. Lunch (Monday-Friday), dinner. Closed Sunday. $16-35

MORRO BAY

Located halfway between Los Angeles and San Francisco, Morro Bay is a peaceful, slow-paced waterfront retreat. Its most striking feature is a 576-foot volcanic dome discovered by Juan Rodriguez Cabrillo in 1542 at the entrance to the harbor. A number of attractions are found here, including beaches, gardens and whale-and seal-watching. Enjoy water sports, golfing and winery tours nearby.

WHAT TO SEE

MONTANA DE ORO STATE PARK

350 Pecho Valley Road, Los Osos, 805-528-0513, 800-772-7434; www.parks.ca.gov

There's spectacular scenery along seven miles of shoreline with tide pools, beaches and camping. Hikers enjoy trails up the 1,347-foot Valencia Peak. The park is also popular for whale-watching and viewing harbor seals and sea otters along the shore.

MORRO BAY STATE PARK

Morro Bay, 805-772-2560; www.parks.ca.gov

Approximately 2,400 acres on Morro Bay make up this park. Fishing, boating, an 18-hole golf course, picnicking, hiking, and tent and trailer camping are available.

Daily 10 a.m.-5 p.m.

MORRO ROCK

845 Embarcadero Road and Coleman Drive, Morro Bay, 805-772-4467;
www.morrobay.org

This 576-foot-high volcanic boulder is often called "the Gibraltar of the Pacific," or simply "the Rock." Drive to the base of the rock for optimum viewing.

Daily.

WHERE TO STAY

★★★THE INN AT MORRO BAY HOTEL

60 State Park Road, Morro Bay, 805-772-5651, 800-321-9566; www.innatmorrobay.com

Located in Morro Bay State Park, this coastal hideaway made up of Cape Cod-style buildings is a destination itself. After a day of sightseeing, golf or bike riding, return to a gourmet meal before sinking into a feather bed. The inn also offers a full range of body treatments in the spa.

98 rooms. Restaurant, bar. Pool. Spa. $151-250

WHERE TO EAT

RECOMMENDED
HOFBRAU
901 Embarcadero Road, Morro Bay, 805-772-5166; www.hofbraurestaurant.com

If you're going to eat one meal in Morro Bay, make it one of the French dip sandwiches at Hofbrau, with the hot German potato salad on the side. The restaurant has been selling hand-carved beef for more than 35 years. You'll also find burgers, fish sandwiches, soups and salads. Beers are on tap.

American. Lunch, dinner. $15 and under

CAMBRIA

Centrally located between San Francisco and Los Angeles, this laid-back coastal community is a frequent stop between L.A. and Big Sur, and is just six miles from San Simeon where Hearst Castle is located (if you're driving up to Big Sur from L.A. and plan to tour Hearst Castle, it's best to stay overnight in Cambria rather than attempt the mountainous drive after dark). Cambria's peaceful and somewhat remote setting attracted many artists back in the 1970s. Today, the downtown area is packed with charming art galleries and gift and antique shops.

WHAT TO SEE

MOONSTONE BEACH
This pretty stretch of beach with waves crashing on the rocks is perfect for a walk along the coastline. A boardwalk winds along the beach and the large rocks are a refuge for sea lions.

WHERE TO STAY

RECOMMENDED
EL COLIBRI HOTEL AND SPA
5620 Moonstone Beach Drive, Cambria, 805-924-3003 www.elcolibrihotel.com

If you need a place to stay while driving up the coast (especially if you just killed half your day at Hearst Castle—it happens), this new hotel in Cambria is a good place to rest (and wait for sunlight) before setting off on the curvy road to Big Sur. Rooms have fireplaces, sleigh beds with pillow-top mattresses, deep-soaking tubs and flat-screen televisions. Colibri Wine Bar is a nice option to unwind before retreating to your room. Before you hit the road, enjoy a complimentary breakfast.

34 rooms. Bar. Spa. $251-350

WHERE TO EAT

ROBIN'S
4095 Burton Drive, Cambria, 805-927-5007; www.robinsrestaurant.com

Located in an old home in the historic east village, Robin's focuses on fresh, made-from-scratch meals with an eclectic menu. Start off with the salmon bisque and a hunk of sourdough garlic bread or the meze platter with taboulleh, roasted red pepper hummus, tzaziki, Greek olives, feta and whole wheat chips. Dinners range from pork osso bucco to lobster enchiladas to a number of

---

HIGHLIGHT

HEARST CASTLE

Crowning La Cuesta Encantada—the Enchanted Hill—is the former home of William Randolph Hearst. William Randolph Hearst, the media entrepreneur who built a publishing empire on newspapers and magazines, grew up camping on his father's ranch in Big Sur. With Hearst Castle, he attempted to build the most opulent castle and grounds in the coastal U.S. Construction began in 1919 under the direction of noted architect Julia Morgan and took 28 years to finish. Hearst spared no expense, hauling parts of ancient European buildings and the treasures within to adorn his compound. For years, Hearst Castle could only be glimpsed through a telescope at the nearby village of San Simeon, but today it's open to the public.

The estate includes 165 rooms and three guest houses. Features of the castle include the Refectory, a long room with a hand-carved ceiling and life-size statues of saints, silk banners from Siena and 15th-century choir stalls from a Spanish cathedral; the Assembly Room, with priceless tapestries; and the lavish theater where the latest motion pictures were shown.

The grounds include the Neptune Pool, with a colonnade leading to an ancient Roman temple façade and an array of marble statuary, an indoor pool and magnificent gardens with fountains and walkways. Hearst entertained some of the great figures of his time here, including Winston Churchill, Charlie Chaplin and Cary Grant. The place is completely over-the-top but yet down to earth (witness the ketchup bottles on the dining room table).

After Hearst's death in 1951, the estate was given to California as a memorial to the late publisher's mother, Phoebe Anderson Hearst. This landmark is so expansive, and its history so rich, there are five separate tours to guide you through it all. But if you want to marvel in this one-of-a-kind castle, reserve tickets well in advance. Day tours take approximately one hour and 45 minutes; evening tours take approximately 2 hours and 15 minutes. Reservations are recommended and are available up to eight weeks in advance by calling 800-444-4445. Tickets are also available at the ticket office in the visitor center. *Daily. Information: 750 Hearst Castle Road, San Simeon, 805-927-2020; www.hearstcastle.com*

---

curries. The Angus burger with vine ripe tomatoes, grilled sweet onions, white cheddar, house pickles and garlic herb fries is a crowd-pleaser at lunch.
International. Lunch, dinner. $16-35

PASO ROBLES

Paso Robles is booming with vineyards—nearly 100 wineries dot the countryside. The downtown area has a small town charm, full of antique stores, eateries and tasting rooms.

WHERE TO STAY

RECOMMENDED
HOTEL CHEVAL
1021 Pine Street, Paso Robles, 866-522-6999; www.hotelcheval.com
This boutique hotel located in downtown Paso Robles is a great choice while

wine tasting in the area. Comforting touches include warm chocolate chip cookies when you arrive, complimentary breakfast when you arise, organic chocolate upon turndown, outdoor stone wood-burning fireplaces and a cozy library. Rooms are a soothing mix of neutrals with subtle pops of color, comfortable beds and wooden shutters on the windows. Some rooms feature window seats, bathtubs, fireplaces and outdoor patios with teak furniture. The hotel offers tours of the wine country in a luxury SUV and will plan your day for you. On Fridays and Saturdays, there's a complimentary horse-drawn carriage to take you to a nearby restaurant. The Pony Club bar is a great spot for a refreshment at the horseshoe-shaped zinc bar.

16 rooms. Bar. $351 and up

WHERE TO EAT

ARTISAN

This delightful American bistro features locally grown produce and foods, and a wine list which encompasses the best of the region. Starters might include a smoked gouda and porter fondue and herbed roasted meatballs with ricotta gnocchi. Comforting main dishes might include farm raised chicken with a new crop potato salad or a grass fed beef flatiron with french fries and a cabernet butter. Side dishes might feature summer succotash or jalapeño cornbread with honey butter. It all depends on what's in season. Order one of the featured flights from the wine menu or allow the server to point you to just the right bottle (or, if you picked up your own on your day of wine tasting, there's a $15 corkage fee with a two bottle limit). If you'd rather take a break from wine, there's also a nice beer list. Dessert is the same sort of local/sustainable/organic affair—think: blueberry buckle wtih Meyer lemon ice cream or strawberry semifreddo with hibiscus rhubarb, vanilla-anise and burnt honey.

$36-85. Lunch, dinner, Sunday brunch.

BISTRO LAURENT

This wine shop and bistro serves up country French cuisine which includes crispy tarts and entrees such as crab risotto with sautéed shrimp and herbs beurre blanc, and roasted free range chicken with garlic, rosemary and puree of potatoes. You'll also find a variety of French Artisian cheeses. Four and five-course tasting menus are available and are a real bargain. The four-course menu is $48 ($59 with wine pairings) and may include a salad of smoked salmon with arugula and crispy fried beets or a warm salad of lobster with orange vinaigrette; a crispy tart with ratatouille, goat cheese and prociutto; local white sea bass; and braised veal cheeks in red wine with fingerling potatoes. The restaurant aims to be welcoming with its reasonable prices and the wine shop features a nice selection of local wines.

$36-85. Lunch, dinner.

INDEX

Numbers

20-Mule-Team Canyon
  Lone Pine, **61**

A

Addison
  San Diego, **33**
Aerospace Museum and Hall
    of Fame
  San Diego, **15**
Ago, **107**, **113**
Alma Rosa Winery
  Buelton, **178**
Alpine Slide at Magic
    Mountain
  Big Bear Lake, **166**
American Rag
  Midtown, **116**
Anaheim, **63**
Anaheim White House
  Anaheim, **66**
Andaz Hotel
  San Diego, **26**
Andaz West Hollywood
  West Hollywood, **99**
Andrea
  Newport Coast, **76**
Angelini Osteria, **114**
  Midtown, **114**

Animal, **107**
  West Hollywood, **107**
Anisette Brasserie
  Santa Monica, **156**
Anza-Borrego Desert State
    Park
  Borrego Springs, **39**
AOC
  Midtown, **114**
Apartment 3, **117**
Apple Farm Restaurant and
    Bakery
  San Luis Obispo, **186**
Apple Farm Trellis Court
  San Luis Obispo, **185**
Aquarium of the Pacific
  Long Beach, **161**
Aqua Star Spa at the Beverly
    Hilton
  Beverly Hills, **133**
Arcadia, **160**
Arrowhead Queen & Leroy's
    Sports
  Lake Arrowhead, **167**
Artisan, **190**
Artist's Palette, **61**
A.R. Valentien
  La Jolla, **46**

Autry National Center
  Los Feliz, 158
Avalon Hotel Beverly Hills
  Beverly Hills, 121

B

Babcock Winery
  Lompoc, 178
Bacara Resort & Spa
  Santa Barbara, 179
Bacara Spa
  Santa Barbara, 184
Baci
  San Diego, 33
Baily's
  Temecula, 81
Balboa Bay Club & Resort
  Newport Beach, 73
Balboa Fun Zone
  Newport Beach, 71
Balboa Island
  Newport Beach, 70
Balboa Park
  San Diego, 16, 18
Balboa Park December
    Nights-The Annual
    Celebration of Christ-
    mas on the Prado
  San Diego, 25

Balloon and Wine Festival
  Temecula, 81
Barnsdall Art Park
  Hollywood, 92
The Bazaar
  Beverly Hills, 126
Bella Vista
  Santa Barbara, 181
Belmont Park
  San Diego, 16
The Belvedere
  Beverly Hills, 126
Bertrand at Mister A's
  San Diego, 33
The Beverly Hills Hotel and
    Bungalows
  Beverly Hills, 121
The Beverly Hills Hotel Spa
    by La Prairie, 134
  Beverly Hills, 133
The Beverly Hilton
  Beverly Hills, 122
Beverly Hills/Bel Air, 120
Beverly Wilshire, a Four
    Seasons Hotel
  Beverly Hills, 122
Big Bear Lake, 166
Big Bear Marina
  Big Bear Lake, 166
Big Bear Mountain Resorts
  Big Bear Lake, 166

Birch Aquarium at Scripps
  La Jolla, **44**
Bistro 45
  Pasadena, **170**
Bistro Laurent
  Paso Robles, **190**
BLD, **107**
BLT Steak
  West Hollywood, **108**
Blue Point Coastal Cuisine
  San Diego, **33**
BOA Steakhouse
  West Hollywood, **108**
Bob Hope Classic
  Rancho Mirage, **52**
Bondst
  Beverly Hills, **126**
Borrego Springs, **39**
Bouchon
  Santa Barbara, **181**
Bouchon Beverly Hills
  Beverly Hills, **127**
Bristol Hotel
  San Diego, **26**
Buffalo Safari
  Avalon, **68**
Busalacchi's on Fifth
  San Diego, **33**
Butterfield Room
  Borrego Springs, **39**

C

Cabrillo National
    Monument
  San Diego, **16**
Cafe Champagne
  Temecula, **82**
Café La Boheme
  West Hollywood, **109**
Café Pinot
  Downtown, **91**
Cafe Roma
  San Luis Obispo, **187**
California Cuisine
  San Diego, **34**
California Dreamin'
  Temecula, **80**
California Science Center
  South Central, **82**
Callaway Vineyard and
    Winery
  Temecula, **80**
Cambria, **188**
Campanile
  Midtown, **109**
Canary Hotel
  Santa Barbara, **179**
Capo
  Santa Monica, **152**
Carlsbad, **40**
Catalina Express
  San Pedro, **161**

Catalina Island, 67

Catalina Tours and Trips
  Avalon, 68

Catch Restaurant & Sushi
    Bar
  Santa Monica, 152

The Cellar
  Fullerton, 67

Center Theatre Group
  Culver City, 83

Central Coast, 3, 171

Central Coast Wineries, 10

Century City/Westwood/
    Culver City, 137

Chamberlain West
    Hollywood
  West Hollywood, 100

Chateau Marmont Hotel and
    Bungalows
  West Hollywood, 100

Chaya Brasserie
  Beverly Hills, 131

Chez Melange
  Redondo Beach, 164

The New Children's Museum
  San Diego, 20

Chinois on Main
  Santa Monica, 152

Christmas Boat Parade
  Newport Beach, 72

Church and State
  Downtown, 91

Classic Club
  Palm Desert, 51

The Cliffs Resort
  Pismo Beach, 184

Colony Palms Hotel
  Palm Springs, 54

Comme Ça
  West Hollywood, 109

Corona del Mar
  Newport Beach, 71

Coronado, 41

Coronado Island
  San Diego, 16

Corpus Christi Fiesta
  San Diego, 25

The Crescent
  Beverly Hills, 123

Crowne Plaza
  Redondo Beach, 164

Crustacean
  Beverly Hills, 127

Crystal Cove State Park, 71

Cucina Urbana
  Downtown, 36

CUT
  Beverly Hills, 128

D

Dakota
  Hollywood, 110
Dana Point, 72, 75, 79
D'Angelo Bread, 182
Dante's View, 61
Death Valley National Park, 61
Decades, 117
Del Mar, 43
Desert Springs JW Marriott Resort & Spa
  Palm Desert, 54
Desert Willow Golf Resort
  Palm Desert, 51
Devil's Golf Course, 61
Diavolina
  West Hollywood, 116
The Dining Room
  Pasadena, 171
Disneyland
  Anaheim, 63
Disney's California Adventure
  Anaheim, 65
Disney's Grand Californian
  Anaheim, 65
Doheny State Beach
  Dana Point, 72
Doral Desert Princess Resort
  Cathedral City, 54

Downey's
  Santa Barbara, 181
Downtown/Chinatown
  Downtown, 85
Downtown Los Angeles Art Walk
  Downtown, 83
Drago Centro
  Downtown, 153

E

East Beach, 175
Edendale Grill, 159
  Silver Lake, 159
El Bizcocho
  San Diego, 34
El Chavo
  Los Feliz, 159
El Colibri Hotel and Spa
  Cambria, 188
Elements
  Santa Barbara, 182
El Paseo
  Santa Barbara, 176
The Embarcadero
  San Diego, 16
Ethnic Food Fair
  San Diego, 25

F

The Fairmont Miramar
Hotel & Bungalows
Santa Monica, **145**
Fairmont Newport Beach
Newport Beach, **73**
Farmers Market
Midtown, **93**
Fashion Island
Corona Del Mar, **80**
Fashion Valley
San Diego, **37**
Fess Parker's Doubletree
Resort
Santa Barbara, **179**
Festival of Arts and Pageant
of the Masters
Laguna Beach, **72**
Festival of Bells
San Diego, **25**
Figaro Bistro
Loz Feliz, **160**
Filsinger Winery
Temecula, **80**
Firestone Vineyard
Los Olivos, **178**
Fisherman's Village
Marina del Rey, **141**
Fleming's Prime Steakhouse
& Wine Bar
La Jolla, **47**

F. McLintock's
Pismo Beach, **185**
Foley Estates Vineyard &
Winery
Lompoc, **178**
Four Seasons Hotel Los
Angeles at Beverly
Hills
Beverly Hills, **123**
Four Seasons Hotel Westlake
Village
Westlake Village, **165**
Four Seasons Resort the
Biltmore Santa
Barbara
Santa Barbara, **179**
Fred62
Los Feliz, **160**
Furnace Creek Resorts, **62**

G

Galleria at South Bay
Redondo Beach, **164**
Gamble House
Pasadena, **168**
Gaslamp Quarter
San Diego, **17**
Geoffrey's Malibu
Malibu, **156**
The Georgian Hotel
Santa Monica, **145**

The Getty Center
  Brentwood, 141
The Getty Villa
  Pacific Palisades, 141
Gjelina, 156
Glorietta Bay Inn
  Coronado, 42
Golden Canyon
  *Death Valley National
    Park,* 62
Gordon Ramsay at the
    London
  West Hollywood, 110
Grace
  Hollywood, 110
The Grafton on Sunset
  West Hollywood, 100
The Grand Del Mar
  San Diego, 27
Grauman's Chinese Theatre
  Hollywood, 93
Griffith Observatory
  Los Feliz, 158
Griffith Park
  Los Feliz, 158
Grill on the Alley
  Beverly Hills, 128
The Groundlings
  West Hollywood, 94

G-Star Raw
  San Diego, 37

H

Hammer Museum
  Westwood, 137
Harbor View Inn
  Santa Barbara, 180
Hatfield's
  Hollywood, 111
Hearst Castle, 189
Hidden Valley Nature Trail,
    60
Hillary Rush
  West Hollywood, 117
Hillcrest
  San Diego, 37
Hilton Airport/Harbor
    Island
  San Diego, 27
Hilton Checkers Los
    Angeles, 88
  Downtown Los Angeles,
    88
Hilton La Jolla Torrey Pines
  La Jolla, 46
Hilton Long Beach
  Long Beach, 163
Hilton Palm Springs Resort
  Palm Springs, 55

Hilton Pasadena
  Pasadena, 170
Hilton San Diego/Del Mar
  Del Mar, 43
Hilton San Diego Gaslamp
  Quarter
  San Diego, 27
Hilton San Diego Mission
  Valley
  San Diego, 28
Hilton San Diego Resort
  San Diego, 28
Hilton Suites Anaheim/
  Orange
  Orange, 66
Hofbrau
  Morro Bay, 188
Holiday Inn Santa Monica
  Beach – At the Pier
  Santa Monica, 151
Hollywood Forever
  Memorial Park
  Hollywood, 94
Hollywood Museum, 94
Hollywood Roosevelt Hotel
  Hollywood, 100
Hollywood Sign
  Hollywood, 94
Hollywood Walk of Fame
  Hollywood, 95

Hollywood Wax Museum
  Hollywood, 95
Hollywood/West
  Hollywood/
  Midtown, 92
Horton Plaza
  San Diego, 17, 38
Hotel Bel-Air
  Bel Air, 123
Hotel Casa Del Mar
  Santa Monica, 146
Hotel Cheval
  Paso Robles, 189
Hotel Del Coronado
  Coronado, 41
Hotel Metropole
  Avalon, 69
Hotel Oceana Santa Monica
  Santa Monica, 146
Hotel Palomar Los
  Angeles-Westwood
  Westwood, 138
Hotel Parisi
  La Jolla, 46
Humphrey's Concerts by the
  Bay
  San Diego, 17
Hungry Cat
  Santa Barbara, 182

Huntington Library and
    Gardens
  San Marino, 168
The Huntley
  Santa Monica, 146
Hyatt Grand Champions
    Resort and Spa
  Indian Wells, 57
Hyatt Regency
  Irvine, 70
Hyatt Regency Century
    Plaza
  Century City, 138
Hyatt Regency La Jolla at
    Avertine
  San Diego, 46
Hyatt Regency Long Beach
  Long Beach, 163
Hyatt Regency Mission Bay
    Spa and Marina
  San Diego, 28
Hyatt Regency Newport
    Beach
  Newport Beach, 73
Hyatt Regency Orange
    County
  Garden Grove, 66
Hyatt Regency Suites Palm
    Springs
  Palm Springs, 55

Hyatt Westlake Plaza
  Westlake Village, 165

I

Il Cielo
  Beverly Hills, 128
Il Pastaio
  Beverly Hills, 131
Indian Canyons
  Palm Springs, 52
Indian Wells, 57
Indian Wells Resort Hotel
  Indian Wells, 57
Ingleside Inn
  Palm Springs, 55
The Inn at Morro Bay Hotel
  Morro Bay, 187
The Inn at Mt. Ada
  Avalon (Catalina Island),
    69
Inn at Rancho Santa Fe
  Rancho Sante Fe, 49
Inn of the Seventh Ray
  Topanga, 153
InterContinental Los Ange-
    les Century City
  Century City, 139
Irvine, 69
The Island Hotel, Newport
    Beach
  Newport Beach, 74

The Ivy, 132
  Beverly Hills, 132

J

Jar
  West Hollywood, 111
Jenni Kayne
  West Hollywood, 119
Jillian's
  Palm Desert, 58
Joshua Tree National Park,
    60
Joshua Tree's Uprising
      Adventure Guides, 60
Josie
  Santa Monica, 153
Jw Marriott
  Downtown, 90

K

Katana
  West Hollywood, 111
The Keating
  San Diego, 28
Ken Cinema
  San Diego, 17
Keys View, 60
Kidspace Children's Museum
  Pasadena, 169
Kitson
  West Hollywood, 117

Knott's Soak City Water Park
    Palm Springs
    Palm Springs, 52
Kobey's Swap Meet
  San Diego, 17
Kodak Theatre
  Hollywood, 96
Koi, 111
Kona Kai Hotel & Spa
  San Diego, 29

L

La Cachette Bistro
  Santa Monica, 157
La Casa Del Zorro
  Borrego Springs, 39
La Costa Resort and Spa
  Carlsbad, 40
Laguna Art Museum
  Laguna Beach, 71
Laguna Beach, 71, 75, 77, 79
Laguna Cliffs Resort & Spa
    by Marriott
    Dana Point, 75
Laguna Playhouse
  Laguna Beach, 71
La Jolla, 43
La Jolla Cove
  La Jolla, 44
La Jolla Playhouse
  La Jolla, 44

La Jolla Shores
La Jolla, 44
Lake Arrowhead, 167
Lake Arrowhead Resort and Spa
Lake Arrowhead, 167
Lake Casitas Recreation Area
Ojai, 171
The Langham, Huntington Hotel & Spa, Pasadena
Pasadena, 170
LA Opera
Downtown, 86
La Paella, 132
Beverly Hills, 132
La Poubelle
Hollywood, 114
La Super-Rica Taqueria
Santa Barbara, 183
L'Auberge
Ojai, 173
L'Auberge Del Mar Resort and Spa
Del Mar, 43
The Laugh Factory
Hollywood, 96
Legoland
Carlsbad, 40

Le Merigot
Santa Monica, 147
Le Montrose Suite Hotel
West Hollywood, 101
Le Parc Suite Hotel, 101
L'Ermitage Beverly Hills
Beverly Hills, 124
Le Saint Germain
Indian Wells, 57
Le Vallauris
Palm Springs, 59
L'Hirondelle
San Jose Capistrano, 70
Lisa Kline
West Hollywood, 118
Living Desert
Palm Desert, 52
Lodge at Torrey Pines
La Jolla, 46
Loews Coronado Bay Resort
Coronado, 42
Loews Santa Monica Beach Hotel
Santa Monica, 147
The London West Hollywood
West Hollywood, 102
Long Beach, 161
Long Beach Jazz Festival
Long Beach, 162

Long Beach Museum of Art
   Long Beach, 162
L'Opera Ristorante
   Long Beach, 163
Los Angeles, 3, 10, 82
Los Angeles Ballet
   Downtown, 83
Los Angeles County
      Arboretum & Botanic
      Garden
   Arcadia, 160
Los Angeles County
      Museum of Art/
Broad Contemporary Art
      Museum
   Midtown, 96
Los Angeles Fashion District
   Downtown Los Angeles,
   86
Los Angeles Marriott
      Downtown
   Downtown, 88
Los Angeles Zoo
   Los feliz, 159
Los Feliz/Silver Lake/Echo
   Park, 158
Lost Palms Canyon, 60
Lucques
   West Hollywood, 112
Luna Park, 114
   Midtown, 115

M

Madonnari Italian Street
      Painting Festival
   San Luis Obispo, 186
Maison 140 Beverly Hills
   Beverly Hills, 124
Mako, 132
Malibu Beach Inn - Carbon
      Beach
   Malibu, 148
Malibu Country Inn
   Malibu, 148
Manchester Grand Hyatt San
      Diego
   San Diego, 29
Marina Del Rey Marriott
   Marina Del Rey, 149
Marine Room
   La Jolla, 47
Maritime Museum San
      Diego
   San Diego, 18
Marriott Coronado Island
      Resort
   Coronado, 42
Marriott San Diego Hotel &
      Marina
   San Diego, 29
Marriott San Diego Mission
      Valley
   San Diego, 29

Mastro's Steakhouse
  Beverly Hills, 129
Maxfield
  West Hollywood, 119
Mélisse
  Santa Monica, 153
Melvyn's
  Palm Springs, 59
Michael's
  Santa Monica, 154
Mildred E. Mathias
    Botanical Garden
  Westwood, 137
Milk
  West Hollywood, 119
Mille Fleurs
  Rancho Sante Fe, 50
Millennium Biltmore Hotel
    Los Angeles
  Downtown, 89
Mingei International
    Museum of World
    Folk Art
  San Diego, 18
Miramonte Resort and Spa
  Indian Wells, 57
Miró at Bacara Resort
  Santa Barbara, 181
Mission Bay Park
  San Diego, 18

Mission Federal Artwalk
  San Diego, 25
Mission San Diego de Alcala
  San Diego, 18
Mission San Luis Obispo de
    Tolosa
  San Luis Obispo, 185
Mission Santa Barbara
  Santa Barbara, 176
Mistral at Loews Coronado
    Bay Reorts
  Coronado, 42
Mondrian
  West Hollywood, 102
Montage Beverly Hills
  Beverly Hills, 124
Montage Laguna Beach
  Laguna Beach, 75
Montana de Oro State Park
  Los Osos, 187
Moonshadows
  Malibu, 157
Moonstone Beach, 188
Moorten's Botanical Garden
  Palm Springs, 52
Morgan Run Resort & Club
  Rancho Sante Fe, 49
Morro Bay, 187
Morro Bay State Park
  Morro Bay, 187

Morro Rock
  Morro Bay, 187
Mount Woodson Rock
      Climbing, 19
Mozart Festival
  San Luis Obispo, 186
Mr. Chow, 133
  Beverly Hills, 133
Museum of
      Contemporary Art
  La Jolla, 45
Museum of Contemporary
      Art (MOCA)
  Downtown, 86
Museum of Contemporary
      Art San Diego
  San Diego, 19
Museum of Man
  San Diego, 19
Museum of
      Photographic Arts
  San Diego, 19
Museum of Tolerance
  Beverly Hills, 120
Musso and Frank Grill
  Hollywood, 115

N

Naples Christmas Boat
      Parade
  Long Beach, 162

Nate 'n Al Delicatessen
      Restaurant
  Beverly Hills, 133
Natural History Museum of
      Los Angeles County
  South Central, 87
Newport Beach, 70, 73, 76,
      78
Newport Beach Marriott
      Bayview
  Newport Beach, 74
Newport Beach Marriott
      Hotel and Spa
  Newport Beach, 74
Nickel Diner
  Downtown, 92
Nobu
  Malibu, 154
Northwoods Resort and
      Conference Center
  Big Bear Lake, 167
Norton Simon Museum
  Pasadena, 169

O

Oasis Visitor Center, 60
The Oceanaire Seafood
      Room
  San Diego, 34

Ocean Beach Farmers' Market
San Diego, 20

Ojai, 171

Ojai Center for the Arts
Ojai, 173

Ojai Music Festival
Ojai, 175

Ojai Shakespeare Festival
Ojai, 175

Ojai Studio Artists Tour
Ojai, 175

Ojai Valley Inn & Spa
Ojai, 173

Ojai Valley Museum
Ojai, 173

Ojai Valley Tennis Tournament
Ojai, 175

Old Globe
San Diego, 20

Old Town, 20

Olio e Limone
Santa Barbara, 183

Olvera Street
Downtown, 87

Omni Los Angeles Hotel at California Plaza
Downtown, 89

One Pico
Santa Monica, 154

Opening Ceremony
West Hollywood, 119

Orange County, 63

Orange County Coastal Towns, 10, 70

Orange County Museum of Arts
Newport Beach, 71

The Orlando
West Hollywood, 103

Ortolan, 129
Beverly Hills, 129

Osteria Mozza, 112, 130

P

Pacific Asia Museum
Pasadena, 169

Pacific Terrace Hotel
San Diego, 30

Page Museum at the La Brea Tar Pits
Midtown, 97

The Paley Center for Media
Beverly Hills, 120

Palihouse Holloway
West Hollywood, 103

Palm Desert, 51, 58

The Palms at Indian Head
Borrego Springs, 39

Palm Springs, 10, 50, 52, 59

Palm Springs Aerial
     Tramway
  Palm Springs, 52
Palm Springs Air Museum
  Palm Springs, 53
Palm Springs Desert
     Museum
  Palm Springs, 53
Palm Springs Historical
     Society on Village
     Green
  Palm Springs, 53
Pantages Theater
  Hollywood, 98
Paradise Point Resort & Spa
  San Diego, 30
Paramount Film and
     Television Studios
  Hollywood, 98
Park Hyatt Aviara Resort
  Carlsbad, 41
Parq
  Beverly Hills, 133
Pasadena, 167
Pasadena Museum of
     History
  Pasadena, 169
Paso Robles, 189
Paso Robles Wine Festival
  Paso Robles, 190

Patina, **91**, **107**, **130**
  Downtown, 91
Pechanga Resort & Casino
  Temecula, 81
Pecorino, 157
  Brentwood, 157
The Peninsula Beverly Hills
  Beverly Hills, 125
The Peninsula Spa
  Beverly Hills, 134
The Penthouse
  Santa Monica, 155
Petersen Automotive
     Museum
  Midtown, 98
Piatti Ristorante
  La Jolla, 47
Pismo Beach, 184
Pizzeria Mozza
  Hollywood, 115
Polkadots and Moonbeams,
     117
Polo Lounge, 129
  Beverly Hills, 129
The Prado at Balboa Park
  San Diego, 34
Prego
  San Diego, 34
Providence
  Hollywood, 112

Q

Queen Mary Seaport
Long Beach, 162

R

Rainwater's
San Diego, 35
The Ranch House
Ojai, 173
Rancho Bernardo Inn
San Diego, 30
Rancho Las Palmas Resort
and Spa
Rancho Mirage, 55
Rancho Valencia Resort &
Spa
Rancho Sante Fe, 49
Sante Fe, 49
Redfern Gallery At Montage
Resort
Laguna Beach, 72
Redondo Beach, 164
Redondo Beach Pier
Redondo Beach, 164
Renaissance Esmeralda
Resort
Indian Wells, 57
Renaissance Festival
San Luis Obispo, 186

Renaissance Hollywood
Hotel & Spa
Hollywood, 104
Renaissance Long Beach
Hotel
Long Beach, 163
Renaissance Montura Hotel
Los Angeles Airport
Playa Del Rey, 149
The Resort at Pelican Hill
Newport Coast, 74
The Restaurant at the Hotel
Bel-Air
Bel Air, 129
The Restaurant Rancho
Valencia
Rancho Sante Fe, 50
Restaurant 162'
Dana Point, 77
Restaurant Nishimura
West Hollywood, 113
Reuben H. Fleet Science
Center
San Diego, 21
Rhyolite Ghost Town
*Death Valley National
Park*, 62
Richard Nixon Library and
Birthplace
Yorba Linda, 67

Ristorante Mamma Gina
  Palm Desert, **58**
The Ritz
  Newport Beach, **77**
The Ritz-Carlton, Laguna
    Niguel
  Dana Point, **76**
The Ritz-Carlton, Marina
    Del Rey
  Marina Del Rey, **149**
The Ritz-Carlton Spa,
    Laguna Niguel
  Dana Point, **79**
Ritz Carlton Los Angeles
  Downtown, **90**
Robin's
  Cambria, **188**
Rodeo Drive
  Beverly Hills, **121**
Ronald Reagan Presidential
    Library
  Simi Valley, **176**
Roppongi
  La Jolla, **47**
Rose Bowl
  Pasadena, **169**
Runyon Canyon
  Hollywood, **99**
Ruth's Chris Steak House
  Irvine, **70**
  Palm Desert, **58**

San Diego, **35**

S

Sally's
  San Diego, **35**
Salvatore's
  San Diego, **35**
Sambo's
  Santa Barbara, **183**
Sammy G's Tuscan Grill
  Palm Springs, **59**
San Diego, 3
San Diego, 15
San Diego Bay Parade of
    Lights
  San Diego, **25**
San Diego Early Music
    Society
  San Diego, **21**
San Diego Hall of Champi-
    ons Sports Museum
  San Diego, **21**
San Diego Harbor Excursion
  San Diego, **21**
San Diego Junior Theatre at
    the Casa Del Prado
    Theater
  San Diego, **18, 22**
San Diego Museum of Art
  San Diego, **22**

San Diego Natural History
Museum
San Diego, 22
San Diego Opera
San Diego, 22
San Diego Scenic Tours
San Diego, 22
San Diego Trolley
San Diego, 22
San Diego Zoo
San Diego, 23
San Luis Obispo, 185
San Luis Obispo County
Museum and History
Center
San Luis Obispo, 185
Santa Anita Park
Arcadia, 161
Santa Barbara, 174
Santa Barbara Botanic
Garden
Santa Barbara, 176
Santa Barbara Certified
Farmers Market
Santa Barbara, 176
Santa Barbara Museum of
Art
Santa Barbara, 177
Santa Barbara Royal Presidio
Santa Barbara, 177

Santa Barbara Shellfish
Company
Santa Barbara, 183
Santa Monica/Brentwood/
Beach Towns, 140
Santa Monica Mountains
National Recreation
Area
Ventura County, 143
Santa Monica Pier
Santa Monica, 143
Santa Monica Pier Aquarium
Santa Monica, 143
Santa Ynez Valley Marriott
Buelton, 180
Sante Ristorante
La Jolla, 48
San Ysidro Ranch, A
Rosewood Hotel
Montecito, 180
Satine
West Hollywood, 120
Sawdust Fine Arts and Crafts
Festival
Laguna Beach, 72
Scotty's Castle
*Death Valley National
Park,* 62
Seaport Village
San Diego, 23, 38

SeaWorld San Diego
  San Diego, 18, 23
Serra Museum
  San Diego, 23
Se San Diego
  San Diego, 30
Shade Hotel
  Manhattan Beach, 149
Shareen's Vintage
  Downtown, 117
Sheraton Anaheim Hotel
  Anaheim, 66
Sheraton Cerritos Hotel
  Cerritos, 66
Sheraton Gateway Hotel Los
    Angeles
  Playa Del Rey, 150
Sheraton Los Angeles
    Downtown Hotel, 90
  Downtown, 90
Sheraton Pasadena Hotel
  Pasadena, 170
Sheraton San Diego Hotel
    and Marina
  San Diego, 31
Sheraton Suites San Diego at
    Symphony Hall
  San Diego, 31
Shoreline Village
  Long Beach, 163

Shutters Hotel on the Beach
  Santa Monica, 150
Sielian's Vintage Apparel,
  West Hollywood, 117
SLO International Film
    Festival
  San Luis Obispo, 186
SLS Hotel at Beverly Hills
  Midtown, 104
Sofitel Los Angeles
  Midtown, 105
Sona, 109
Sony Pictures Studio Tour
  Culver City, 138
South Bay Bicycle Trail
  Pacific Palisades, 144
The Spa at Beverly Wilshire
  Beverly Hills, 135
The Spa at Equinox Century
    City
  Century City, 140
The Spa at Four Seasons
    Hotel, Beverly Hills
  Beverly Hills, 135
The Spa at Four Seasons
    Westlake Village
  Westlake Village, 165
The Spa at Rancho Valencia
  Rancho Sante Fe, 50

The Spa at The Grand Del Mar
  San Diego, 43
The Spa at the Island Hotel
  Newport Beach, 78
The Spa at The Resort at Pelican Hill
  Newport Coast, 78
The Spa at Torrey Pines
  La Jolla, 48
Spa at Four Seasons Resort Santa Barbara
  Santa Barbara, 184
Spa Gaucin
  Dana Point, 79
Spago Beverly Hills, 130, 131
Spa Montage
  Beverly Hills, 135
Spa Montage, Laguna Beach
  Laguna Beach, 79
Spanish Village Arts Center
  San Diego, 38
Spa Ojai
  Ojai, 174
Spa Resort Casino
  Palm Springs, 55
Spa Se
  San Diego, 37
Spreckels Organ Concerts
  San Diego, 23

Staples Center
  Downtown, 87
Starlight Bowl/Starlight Theatre
  San Diego, 24
Starline Tours, 97
The Steakhouse at Azul La Jolla
  La Jolla, 48
Stearns Wharf and Ty Warner Sea Center
  Pacific Ocean, 177
Stonehill Tavern
  Dana Point, 78
Street, 153, 156
  Hollywood, 115
St. Regis Resort, Monarch Beach
  Dana Point, 76
Stuart Cellars
  Temecula, 81
Studio
  Laguna Beach, 78
Summit House Restaurant
  Fullerton, 67
Sunset Marquis Hotel & Villas
  West Hollywood, 105
Sunset Ranch
  Hollywood, 99

Sunset Tower Hotel, **105**
  West Hollywood, **106**
Surf & Sand Resort
  Laguna Beach, **75**
Suzanne's Cuisine
  Ojai, **174**

T

Tahquitz Creek Golf Resort
  Palm Springs, **53**
Taka
  San Diego, **35**
Tapenade
  La Jolla, **48**
Taste of Newport
  Newport Beach, **72**
Tavern
  Brentwood, **155**
Telescope Peak
  *Death Valley National
  Park,* **62**
Temecula, **80**
Temecula Creek Inn
  Temecula, **81**
Tengu
  Westwood, **139**
Thee Bungalow
  San Diego, **36**
Third Street Promenade
  Santa Monica, **144**

Thompson Beverly Hills
  Beverly Hills, **125**
Timken Museum of Art
  San Diego, **24**
Top of the Market
  San Diego, **36**
Torrey Pines Gliderport
  La Jolla, **45**
Torrey Pines State Reserve
  La Jolla, **45**
Tower 23
  San Diego, **31**
Toyota Grand Prix
  Long Beach, **162**
Tradition by Pascal
  Newport Beach, **77**
Travel Town
  Los Feliz, **159**
Tupelo Junction Cafe
  Santa Barbara, **183**
Tuscany
  Palm Desert, **58**

U

Ubehebe Crater
  *Death Valley National
  Park,* **62**
University Town Center
  San Diego, **38**
Upright Citizens Brigade
  Hollywood, **99**

Urth Caffé, 116
  West Hollywood, 116
U.S. Grant Hotel
  San Diego, 27, 31

V

Valentino, 155
Venice Beach and Boardwalk
  Venice, 144
Versailles
  Culver City, 140
Veterans Memorial Center
    Museum
  San Diego, 24
Viceroy Palm Springs
  Palm Springs, 56
Viceroy Santa Monica
  Santa Monica, 151
The Villa Royale Inn
  Palm Springs, 56
Vivace
  Carlsbad, 41

W

Walt Disney Concert Hall
  Downtown Los Angeles,
    88
Water Grill, 91
  Downtown, 91
Watts Towers
  Watts, 88

The Well Spa at Miramonte
    Resort
  Indian Wells, 59
Westgate Hotel
  San Diego, 32
The Westin Mission Hills
    Resort and Spa
  Rancho Mirage, 56
Westin Horton Plaza
  San Diego, 32
Westin Pasadena
  Pasadena, 170
Westin San Diego
  San Diego, 32
Westlake Village, 165
Westlake Village Inn
  Westlake Village, 165
Whale-Watching Trips
  San Diego, 24
Whist
  Santa Monica, 155
W Hollywood
  Hollywood, 106
Wild Animal Park
  Escondido, 26
Wild Rivers Waterpark
  Irvine, 69
William Heath Davis Home
  San Diego, 26

Will Rogers State Historic
        Park
  Pacific Palisades, **145**
Windansea Beach
  La Jolla, **45**
Winesellar and Brasserie
  San Diego, **36**
W Los Angeles - Westwood
  Westwood, **139**
Wrigley Memorial and
        Botanical Garden
  Avalon, **68**
W San Diego
  San Diego, **32**

X

XIV
  West Hollywood, **106**

Z

Zabriskie Point
  *Death Valley National
        Park,* **62**
Zocalo Grill
  San Diego, **36**

SOUTHERN CALIFORNIA OVERVIEW

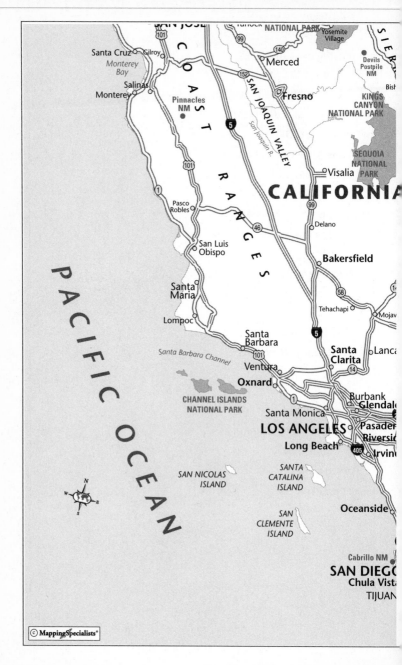

© MappingSpecialists®

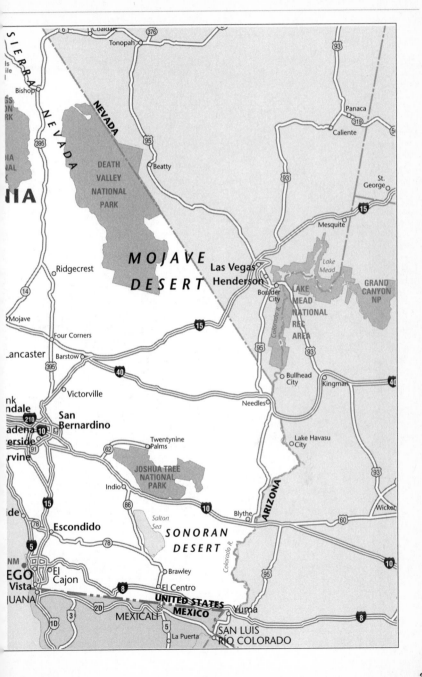

LOS ANGELES OVERVIEW

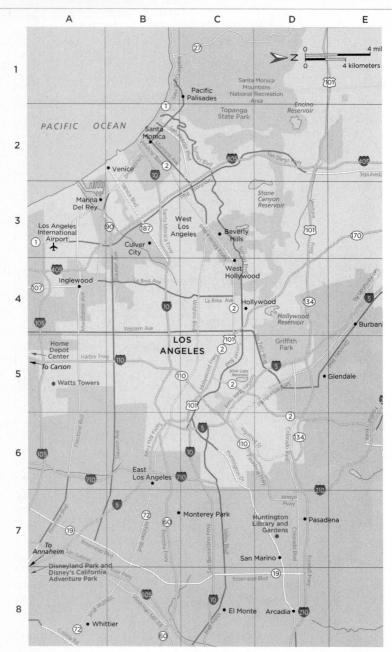

DOWNTOWN AND EAST LOS ANGELES

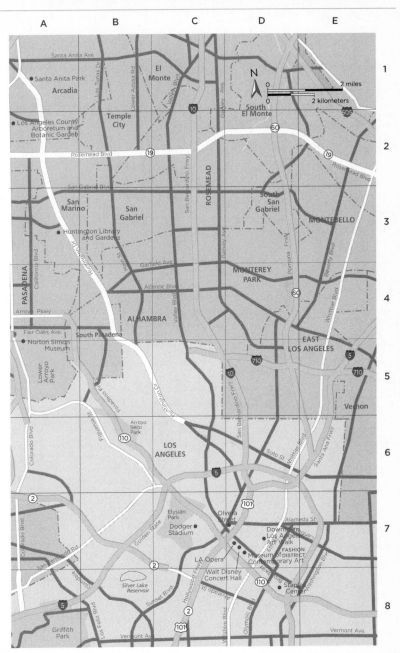

BEVERLY HILLS, HOLLYWOOD AND WEST HOLLYWOOD

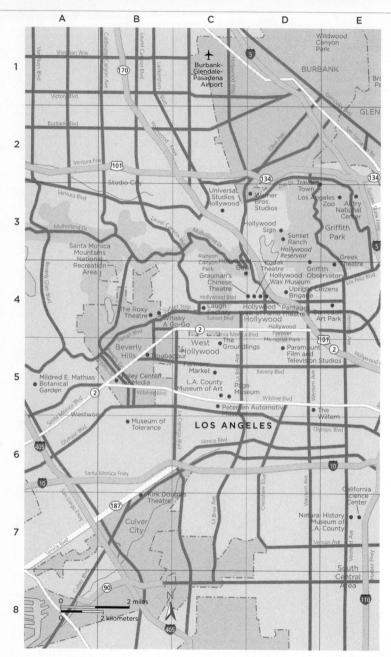

SANTA MONICA AND THE COAST

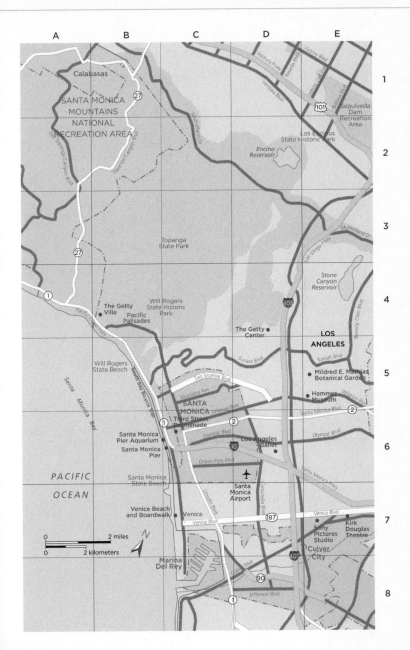

NOTES